Mirabile mysterium declaratur hodie, innovantur naturae:
Deus homo factus est, id, quod fuit, permansit, et quod non
era, assumpsit, non commixtionem passus neque divisionem.

(A wondrous mystery is proclaimed today; all natures are
renewed: God has become human: he remained what he was,
and what he was not he became, suffering neither confusion
nor division.)

Jacob Handl (1550–91), Mirabile mysterium

The Scandal
of the
Evangelical Mind

Mark A. Noll

WILLIAM B. EERDMANS PUBLISHING COMPANY
GRAND RAPIDS, MICHIGAN

INTER-VARSITY PRESS
LEICESTER, ENGLAND

First published jointly 1994 in the United States by Wm. Eerdmans Publishing Co.
and in the U. K. by Inter-Varsity Press
38 De Montfort Street, Leicester LE1 7GP, England

Printed in the United States of America

00 99 98 97 96 95 94   7 6 5 4 3 2 1

Library of Congress Cataloging-in-Publication Data

Noll, Mark A., 1946-
The scandal of the evangelical mind / Mark A. Noll.
p.   cm.
Includes bibliographical references and index.
ISBN 0-8028-3715-8
1. Evangelicalism — United States. 2. Christianity — United States — Forecasting.
3. Christianity and culture. I. Title.
BR1642.U5N65 1994
280'.4'0973 — dc20   94-18843
                                                    CIP

British Library Cataloguing in Publication Data

A catalogue record for this book is available from the British Library

Inter-Varsity Press ISBN 0-85111-148-3

Unless otherwise indicated, all biblical quotations in this work are taken from the HOLY
BIBLE: NEW INTERNATIONAL VERSION. Copyright © 1973, 1978, 1984 by the
International Bible Society. Used by permission of Zondervan Bible Publishers.

*Inter-Varsity Press is the book-publishing division of the Universities and Colleges Christian
Fellowship (formerly the Inter-Varsity Fellowship), a student movement linking Christian Unions
in universities and colleges throughout the United Kingdom and the Republic of Ireland, and
a member movement of the International Fellowship of Evangelical Students. For information
about local and national activities write to UCCF, 38 de Montfort Street, Leicester LE1 7GP.*

To
the faculty and trustees of Wheaton College

Contents

vii

PART 4
HOPE?

Preface

This book is an epistle from a wounded lover. As one who is in love with the life of the mind but who has also been drawn to faith in Christ through the love of evangelical Protestants, I find myself in a situation where wounding is commonplace. Although the thought has occurred to me regularly over the past two decades that, at least in the United States, it is simply impossible to be, with integrity, both evangelical and intellectual, this epistle is not a letter of resignation from the evangelical movement. It intends rather to be a cri du coeur on behalf of the intellectual life by one who, for very personal reasons, still embraces the Christian faith in an evangelical form.

As one might expect from an evangelical on such a subject, this is not a thoroughly intellectual volume. It is rather a historical meditation in which sermonizing and the making of hypotheses vie with more ordinary exposition. It is meant to incite more than it is meant to inform. The notes are here to show where fuller academic treatments, a few of them by myself, may be found. Several of the chapters were first given as talks or lectures, although everything has been rewritten for this volume.

The book is dedicated with gratitude and respect to my colleagues at Wheaton College, where we together fight the fights and inflict, sometimes on each other, the wounds that are the subject of this book.

PART 1

THE SCANDAL

CHAPTER 1

The Contemporary Scandal

The scandal of the evangelical mind is that there is not much of an evangelical mind. An extraordinary range of virtues is found among the sprawling throngs of evangelical Protestants in North America, including great sacrifice in spreading the message of salvation in Jesus Christ, open-hearted generosity to the needy, heroic personal exertion on behalf of troubled individuals, and the unheralded sustenance of countless church and parachurch communities. Notwithstanding all their other virtues, however, American evangelicals are not exemplary for their thinking, and they have not been so for several generations.

Despite dynamic success at a popular level, modern American evangelicals have failed notably in sustaining serious intellectual life. They have nourished millions of believers in the simple verities of the gospel but have largely abandoned the universities, the arts, and other realms of "high" culture. Even in its more progressive and culturally upscale subgroups, evangelicalism has little intellectual muscle. Feeding the hungry, living simply, and banning the bomb are tasks at which different sorts of evangelicals willingly expend great energy, but these tasks do not by themselves assist intellectual vitality. Evangelicals sponsor dozens of theological seminaries, scores of colleges, hundreds of radio stations, and thousands of unbelievably diverse parachurch agencies — but not a single research university or a single periodical devoted to in-depth interaction with modern culture.[1]

Evangelical inattention to intellectual life is a curiosity for several reasons. One of the self-defining convictions of modern evangelicalism has been its adherence to the Bible as the revealed Word of God. Most evangelicals also acknowledge that in the Scriptures God stands revealed plainly as the author of nature, as the sustainer of human institutions (family, work, and government), and as the source of harmony, creativity, and beauty. Yet it has been precisely these Bible-believers par excellence who have neglected sober analysis of nature, human society, and the arts.

The historical situation is similarly curious. Modern evangelicals are the spiritual descendants of leaders and movements distinguished by probing, creative, fruitful attention to the mind. Most of the original Protestant traditions (Lutheran, Reformed, Anglican) either developed a vigorous intellectual life or worked out theological principles that could (and often did) sustain penetrating, and penetratingly Christian, intellectual endeavor. Closer to the American situation, the Puritans, the leaders of the eighteenth-century evangelical awakenings like John Wesley and Jonathan Edwards, and a worthy line of North American stalwarts in the nineteenth century — like the Methodist Francis Asbury, the Presbyterian Charles Hodge, the Congregationalist Moses Stuart, and the Canadian Presbyterian George Monro Grant, to mention only a few — all held that diligent, rigorous mental activity was a way to glorify God. None of them believed that intellectual activity was the only way to glorify God, or even the highest way, but they all believed in the life of the mind, and they believed in it *because* they were evangelical Christians. Unlike their spiritual ancestors, modern evangelicals have not pursued comprehensive thinking under God or sought a mind shaped to its furthest reaches by Christian perspectives.

We evangelicals are, rather, in the position once described by Henry Blamires for theological conservatives in Great Britain:

1. The assessment of modern evangelical culture in this book depends heavily on the work of Nathan O. Hatch, especially "Strengthening American Protestant Evangelical Scholarship" (unpublished memorandum, ca. 1989) and (with Michael Hamilton) "Can Evangelicalism Survive Its Success?" *Christianity Today,* Oct. 5, 1992, pp. 20–31.

In contradistinction to the secular mind, no vital Christian mind plays fruitfully, as a coherent and recognizable influence, upon our social, political, or cultural life. . . . Except over a very narrow field of thinking, chiefly touching questions of strictly personal conduct, we Christians in the modern world accept, for the purpose of mental activity, a frame of reference constructed by the secular mind and a set of criteria reflecting secular evaluations. There is no Christian mind; there is no shared field of discourse in which we can move at ease as thinking Christians by trodden ways and past established landmarks. . . . Without denying the impact of important isolated utterances, one must admit that there is no packed contemporary field of discourse in which writers are reflecting christianly on the modern world and modern man.[2]

Blamire's picture describes American evangelicals even better than it does traditional Christians in Britain. To be sure, something of a revival of intellectual activity has been taking place among evangelical Protestants since World War II. Yet it would be a delusion to conclude that evangelical thinking has progressed very far. Recent gains have been modest. The general impact of Christian thinking on the evangelicals of North America, much less on learned culture as a whole, is slight. Evangelicals of several types may be taking the first steps in doing what needs to be done to develop a Christian mind, or at least we have begun to talk about what would need to be done for such a mind to develop. But there is a long, long way to go.

Definitions

But now it is necessary to define more carefully the critical terms of the book, including "America," "the (life of the) mind," "evangelical," and "anti-intellectual."

2. Henry Blamires, *The Christian Mind: How Should a Christian Think?* (London: SPCK, 1963), 4, 7.

"America"

Throughout the book, "America" will mostly mean the United States, even though the inclusion of Canada in the study of Christian developments in North America is an immensely rewarding effort. Occasional efforts will be made to include Canada in the pages that follow.[3] But the structures and habits of evangelical thinking in Canada are just different enough from those in the United States to prohibit extensive treatment, even though that treatment would reveal helpful ways in which Canadian evangelicals have escaped some of the intellectual perils found in the United States and perhaps some ways in which Canadian evangelicals have had more difficulty than their counterparts in the United States at sustaining the life of the mind.[4]

"The Life of the Mind"

By "the mind" or "the life of the mind," I am not thinking primarily of theology as such. As I will suggest below, I do feel that contemporary evangelical theologians labor under several unusual difficulties that greatly reduce the importance their work should have in the evangelical community. But the effort to articulate a theology that is faithful both

3. I have tried to suggest the virtues of that kind of comparative study in *A History of Christianity in the United States and Canada* (Grand Rapids: Eerdmans, 1992).

4. As guides to comparative analysis, see, for the critically important nineteenth century, Michael Gauvreau, *The Evangelical Century: College and Creed in English Canada from the Great Revival to the Great Depression* (Montreal and Kingston: McGill-Queen's University Press, 1991), and Marguerite Van Die, *An Evangelical Mind: Nathanael Burwash and the Methodist Tradition in Canada* (Montreal and Kingston: McGill-Queen's University Press, 1989); for the era of transition to the modern university that was also critical in the United States, George A. Rawlyk, ed., *Canadian Baptists and Christian Higher Education* (Montreal and Kingston: McGill-Queen's University Press, 1988); and for institutional differences among institutions of higher learning, D. C. Masters, *Protestant Church Colleges in Canada* (Toronto: University of Toronto Press, 1966), and John G. Stackhouse, Jr., "Respectfully Submitted for American Consideration: Canadian Options in Christian Higher Education," *Faculty Dialogue* 17 (Spring 1992): 51–71.

to the evangelical tradition and to modern standards of academic discourse is not in itself the primary problem for the evangelical mind. In fact, with the contemporary work of evangelical theologians from several different subtraditions — including William Abraham, Donald Bloesch, Gabriel Fackre, Richard Mouw, Thomas Oden, J. I. Packer, Clark Pinnock, Ronald Sider, David Wells, and William Willimon — North American evangelicals enjoy a rich theological harvest. Much the same could be said about advanced work in biblical scholarship, although, as a general rule, evangelical Bible scholars do not extend their insights into wider areas of thought as regularly or as fruitfully as do the best evangelical theologians.[5]

By an evangelical "life of the mind" I mean more the effort to think like a Christian — to think within a specifically Christian framework — across the whole spectrum of modern learning, including economics and political science, literary criticism and imaginative writing, historical inquiry and philosophical studies, linguistics and the history of science, social theory and the arts. Academic disciplines provide modern categories for the life of the mind, but the point is not simply whether evangelicals can learn how to succeed in the modern academy. The much more important matter is what it means to think like a Christian about the nature and workings of the physical world, the character of human social structures like government and the economy, the meaning of the past, the nature of artistic creation, and the circumstances attending our perception of the world outside ourselves. Failure to exercise the mind for Christ in these areas has become acute in the twentieth century. That failure is the scandal of the evangelical mind.

"Evangelical"

But what is an "evangelical," and how might recent efforts to ascertain the scope of the North American evangelical constituency add to the urgency of this book?

5. For a fuller assessment of the picture with biblical scholars, see Mark A. Noll, *Between Faith and Criticism: Evangelicals, Scholarship, and the Bible,* 2d ed. (Grand Rapids: Baker, 1991).

"Evangelicalism" is not, and never has been, an "-ism" like other Christian isms — for example, Catholicism, Orthodoxy, Presbyterianism, Anglicanism, or even Pentecostalism (where, despite many internal differences, the practice of sign gifts like tongues speaking provides a well-defined boundary). Rather, "evangelicalism" has always been made up of shifting movements, temporary alliances, and the lengthened shadows of individuals. All discussions of evangelicalism, therefore, are always both descriptions of the way things really are as well as efforts within our own minds to provide some order for a multifaceted, complex set of impulses and organizations.

The basic evangelical impulses, however, have been quite clear from the mid-eighteenth century, when leaders like George Whitefield, John Wesley, Jonathan Edwards, and Nicholas von Zinzendorf worked to revive churches in northern Europe and North America and so brought "evangelicalism" into existence. In one of the most useful general definitions of the phenomenon, the British historian David Bebbington has identified the key ingredients of evangelicalism as conversionism (an emphasis on the "new birth" as a life-changing religious experience), biblicism (a reliance on the Bible as ultimate religious authority), activism (a concern for sharing the faith), and crucicentrism (a focus on Christ's redeeming work on the cross).[6] But these evangelical impulses have never by themselves yielded cohesive, institutionally compact, easily definable, well-coordinated, or clearly demarcated groups of Christians. Rather, the history of these evangelical impulses has always been marked by shifts in which groups, leaders, institutions, goals, concerns, opponents, and aspirations become more or less visible and more or less influential over time. Institutions that may emphasize evangelical distinctives at one point in time may not do so at another. Yet there have always been denominations, local congregations, and voluntary bodies that served as institutional manifestations of these impulses.[7]

6. David Bebbington, *Evangelicalism in Modern Britain: A History from the 1730s to the 1980s* (London: Unwin Hyman, 1989), 2–19.

7. The best efforts to work through the knotty issues surrounding the definition of "evangelicals" for the United States are George M. Marsden, "The Evangelical Denomination," in *Evangelicalism and Modern America,* ed. Marsden (Grand Rapids:

One thing seems clear from several surveys by social scientists that are now being carried out with a sophistication unknown as recently as five years ago. For both the United States and Canada, evangelicals now constitute the largest and most active component of religious life in North America. For the United States, a recent national survey showed that over 30 percent of 4,001 respondents were attached to evangelical denominations, that is, to denominations that stress the need for a supernatural new birth, profess faith in the Bible as a revelation from God, encourage spreading the gospel through missions and personal evangelism, and emphasize the saving character of Jesus' death and resurrection.[8] Adherents to largely white, evangelical Protestant denominations by themselves make up a proportion of the population roughly the same size as the Roman Catholic constituency, but quite a bit larger than the total number of adherents to mainline Protestant denominations.

The same survey showed, moreover, that a much higher proportion of adherents to evangelical denominations practice their faith actively than do either Catholics or mainline Protestants. Based on queries concerning personal religious commitment, church attendance, prayer, belief in life after death, and other matters of faith and practice, the survey shows over 61 percent of the "white evangelicals" and over 63 percent of the "black Protestants" rank in the highest categories of religious activity, percentages far higher than for mainline Protestants, Roman Catholics, the Orthodox, Jews, or nontraditional religions. Thus, not only is a very large proportion of the American population

---

Eerdmans, 1984); Douglas A. Sweeney, "The Essential Evangelicalism Dialectic: The Historiography of the Early Neo-Evangelical Movement and the Observer-Participant Dilemma," *Church History* 60 (March 1991): 70–84; the material by Donald W. Dayton and Robert K. Johnston in *The Variety of American Evangelicalism,* ed. Dayton and Johnston (Knoxville: University of Tennessee Press; Downers Grove, IL: InterVarsity Press, 1991); and several of the essays in David Dockery, ed., *Are Southern Baptists Evangelicals?* (Nashville: Broadman, 1993).

8. From the "Akron Survey of Religion and Politics in America" (1992), by investigators John Green (University of Akron), James Guth (Furman University), Lyman Kellstedt (Wheaton College), and Corwin Smidt (Calvin College). The survey identified 25.7 percent of the population as "white evangelicals" and another 7.8 percent as "black Protestants," most of whom could be classified as evangelicals.

definably evangelical, but that proportion of the population is the nation's most actively involved set of believers.

For Canada, a recent in-depth survey showed that individuals holding evangelical beliefs made up a larger proportion of the Canadian population than most pundits had thought. In an interesting variation on most surveys in the United States, this Canadian study enumerated Catholics and Protestants together. It found that 13 percent of the national population was active, committed, self-identified evangelicals (one-fourth of that number Catholics), while another 11 percent of the population (one-half of that number Catholics) held evangelical beliefs about the Bible, the person and work of Christ, the necessity for personal salvation, and the like but were only occasional participants in formal church life.[9]

The most intriguing result of such surveys for this book is that, on any given Sunday in the United States and Canada, a majority of those who attend church hold evangelical beliefs and follow norms of evangelical practice, yet in neither country do these great numbers of practicing evangelicals appear to play significant roles in either nation's intellectual life. What a British Roman Catholic said at midcentury after looking back over more than one hundred years of rapid Catholic growth in Britain may be said equally about evangelicals in North America: "On the one hand there is the enormous growth of the Church, and on the other its almost complete lack of influence."[10]

"Anti-Intellectual"

Is it simply that evangelicals are "anti-intellectual"? Maybe so, but the term itself is a problem. The temptation has been great in historical

9. A preliminary report from the survey is presented as "God Is Alive: Canada Is a Nation of Believers," *Maclean's*, Apr. 12, 1993, pp. 32–50. Principal investigators are Andrew Grenville (Angus Reid Group) and George A. Rawlyk (Queen's University, Kingston, Ontario).

10. Ronald Chapman, "The Optimism of the 1840s," *Tablet*, Dec. 18, 1954, as quoted in John Tracy Ellis, *American Catholics and the Intellectual Life* (Chicago: Heritage Foundation, 1956), 36.

analyses of evangelical, pentecostal, fundamentalist, or pietistic movements simply to label adherents "anti-intellectual" and then move on to other considerations. Some classic books have come close to adopting this procedure. Ronald Knox's scintillating study *Enthusiasm,* for example, contrasted traditional Roman Catholic thinking (where grace perfects nature) with the approach of "enthusiasm" (where grace destroys nature and replaces it). Of the "Enthusiast" (a category that for him included most evangelicals), Knox concluded as follows: "That God speaks to us through the intellect is a notion which he may accept on paper, but fears, in practice, to apply."[11]

Closer to the American situation, Richard Hofstadter's Pulitzer-prize-winning book *Anti-Intellectualism in American Life* identified "the evangelical spirit" as one of the prime sources of American anti-intellectualism. For Hofstadter, there was a common reasoning process by which evangelicals had chosen to evacuate the mind:

> One begins with the hardly contestable proposition that religious faith is not, in the main, propagated by logic or learning. One moves on from this to the idea that it is best propagated (in the judgment of Christ and on historical evidence) by men who have been unlearned and ignorant. It seems to follow from this that the kind of wisdom and truth possessed by such men is superior to what learned and cultivated minds have. In fact, learning and cultivation appear to be handicaps in the propagation of faith. And since the propagation of faith is the most important task before man, those who are as "ignorant as babes" have, in the most fundamental virtue, greater strength than men who have addicted themselves to logic and learning. Accordingly, though one shrinks from a bald statement of the conclusion, humble ignorance is far better as a human quality than a cultivated mind. At bottom, this proposition, despite all the difficulties that attend it, has been eminently congenial both to American evangelicalism and to American democracy.[12]

11. R. A. Knox, *Enthusiasm: A Chapter in the History of Religion, with Special Reference to the Seventeenth and Eighteenth Centuries* (New York: Oxford University Press, 1950), 3.

12. Richard Hofstadter, *Anti-Intellectualism in American Life* (New York: Vintage, 1962), quotation, 48–49n.8; "The Evangelical Spirit," 55–80.

The anti-intellectual attitude described by Knox and Hofstadter has not been absent from the history of American evangelicals, but its description may be too simple. True, evangelicals have often contrasted the intuitions of the Spirit with the mechanics of worldly learning. There may exist, however, a genuinely Christian justification for this contrast that need not lead as directly to intellectually disastrous consequences as Hofstadter and Knox suggest. In any event, the question for American evangelicals is not just the presence of an anti-intellectual bias but the sometimes vigorous prosecution of the wrong sort of intellectual life. That is, various modes of intellectual activity may fit better or worse with the shape of Christianity itself. As I will try to show in the chapters that follow, the scandal of evangelical thinking in America has just as often resulted from a way of pursuing knowledge that does not accord with Christianity as it has been an "anti-intellectual" desire to play the fool for Christ.

Aspects of the Scandal

The scandal of the evangelical mind has at least three dimensions — cultural, institutional, and theological — each of which deserves brief mention here before receiving more extensive treatment in the chapters that follow.

Cultural

To put it most simply, the evangelical ethos is activistic, populist, pragmatic, and utilitarian. It allows little space for broader or deeper intellectual effort because it is dominated by the urgencies of the moment. In addition, habits of mind that in previous generations may have stood evangelicals in good stead have in the twentieth century run amock. As the Canadian scholar N. K. Clifford once aptly summarized the matter: "The Evangelical Protestant mind has never relished complexity. Indeed its crusading genius, whether in religion or politics, has always tended toward an over-simplification of issues and the substitution of inspiration and zeal for critical analysis and serious reflection.

The limitations of such a mind-set were less apparent in the relative simplicity of a rural frontier society."[13]

Recently two very good, but also very disquieting, books have illustrated the weaknesses of evangelical intellectual life. Both are from historians who teach at the University of Wisconsin. Ronald Numbers's book *The Creationists* (Knopf, 1992) explains how a popular belief known as "creationism" — a theory that the earth is ten thousand or less years old — has spread like wildfire in our century from its humble beginnings in the writings of Ellen White, the founder of Seventh-day Adventism, to its current status as a gospel truth embraced by tens of millions of Bible-believing evangelicals and fundamentalists around the world. Paul Boyer's *When Time Shall Be No More: Prophecy Belief in Modern American Culture* (Harvard University Press, 1992) documents the remarkable popularity among American Bible-believing Christians — again mostly evangelicals and fundamentalists — of radical apocalyptic speculation. Boyer concludes that Christian fascination with the end of the world has existed for a very long time, but also that recent evangelical fixation on such matters — where contemporary events are labeled with great self-confidence as the fulfillment of biblical prophecies heralding the End of Time — has been particularly intense.

For those who doubt the continuing domination of this way of thinking among evangelicals, it is worth remembering the Gulf War of 1991. Within weeks of the outbreak of this conflict, evangelical publishers provided a spate of books featuring efforts to read this latest Middle East crisis as a direct fulfillment of biblical prophecy heralding the end of the world.[14] The books came to various conclusions, but they all shared the disconcerting conviction that the best way of providing moral judgment about what was happening in the Middle East was *not* to study carefully what was going on in the Middle East. Rather, they featured a kind of Bible study that drew attention away from

13. N. K. Clifford, "His Dominion: A Vision in Crisis," *Sciences Religieuses/Studies in Religion* 2 (1973): 323.

14. The titles that ended up as runaway best-sellers were John F. Walvoord, *Armageddon, Oil, and the Middle East Crisis* (1974; revised Grand Rapids: Zondervan, 1990); and Charles Dyer, *The Rise of Babylon: Sign of the End Times* (Carol Stream, IL: Tyndale House, 1991).

careful analysis of the complexities of Middle Eastern culture or the tangled twentieth-century history of the region toward speculation about some of the most esoteric and widely debated passages of the Bible. Moreover, that speculation was carried on with only slight attention to the central themes of the Bible (like the divine standard of justice applied in all human situations), which are crystal clear and about which there is wide agreement among evangelicals and other theologically conservative Christians. How did the evangelical public respond to these books? It responded by immediately vaulting several of these titles to the top of religious best-seller lists.[15]

Both Numbers and Boyer are first-rate scholars who write with sympathy for their subjects. Neither is an antireligious zealot. But their books tell a sad tale: Numbers describes how a fatally flawed interpretive scheme of the sort that no responsible Christian teacher in the history of the church ever endorsed before this century came to dominate the minds of American evangelicals on scientific questions; Boyer discusses how an equally unsound hermeneutic has been used with wanton abandon to dominate twentieth-century evangelical thinking about world affairs.

These are exhaustively researched books by truly professional historians who have few bones to pick with basic Christian teachings. They share in common the picture of an evangelical world almost completely adrift in using the mind for careful thought about the world. As the authors describe them, evangelicals — bereft of self-criticism, intellectual subtlety, or an awareness of complexity — are blown about by every wind of apocalyptic speculation and enslaved to the cruder spirits of populist science. In reality, Numbers and Boyer show even more — they show millions of evangelicals thinking they are honoring the Scriptures, yet interpreting the Scriptures on questions of science and world affairs in ways that fundamentally contradict the deeper, broader, and historically well-established meanings of the Bible itself.

The culture Numbers and Boyer describe is one in which careful thinking about the world has never loomed large. To be sure, it is also a culture where intense, detailed, and precise efforts have been made to understand the Bible. But it is not a culture where the same effort

15. *Publishers Weekly,* Feb. 1, 1991, p. 61; Feb. 15, 1991, p. 96; Mar. 1, 1991, p. 30; Mar. 15, 1991, p. 64; and Apr. 19, 1991, p. 72.

has been expended to understand the world or, even more important, the processes by which wisdom from Scripture should be brought into relation with knowledge about the world. The problem is intellectual, but it grows out of the historical development of America's distinctly evangelical culture. Most of this book is an effort to describe the formation of that culture.

Institutional

Institutional dimensions to the scandal of the evangelical mind are most obvious for colleges and seminaries, but they are also a feature of other intellectual efforts. Evangelicals, for example, have always been astute at using the periodical press for propagation, networking, edification, self-promotion, and debate. Throughout the nineteenth century and into the early years of the twentieth, noteworthy intellectual endeavor maintained a solid, if always minority, place in the evangelical press.[16] Throughout this century, however, the intellectual component in the evangelical press has shriveled nearly to the vanishing point. A contrast with other religious traditions is in order. Over the last twenty years, a number of new journals have been formed, either out of specific religious communities or with specific religious intentions, in order to address selected features of modern culture with deadly (though sometimes also comic) seriousness. Examples of these journals include the *Lutheran Forum,* the Catholic-related *New Oxford Review* and *The Crisis,* the theological journal *Pro Ecclesia,* and the journal of political affairs *First Things.* By contrast, over the same period, evangelical periodicals that once gave at least some of their pages to intellectual considerations of nature, modern culture, and the arts — like the *Reformed Journal, HIS,* and *Eternity* — have gone out of business. *Christianity Today,* which, for a decade or so after its founding in 1956, aspired to intellectual leadership, has been transformed into a journal of news and middle-brow religious commentary in order simply to stay in business. The result is that, at the current time, there is not a single

16. For references, consult Mark A. Noll, "The Princeton Theological Review," *Westminster Theological Journal* 50 (Fall 1988): 283–304.

evangelical periodical in the United States or Canada that exists for the purpose of seriously considering the worlds of nature, society, politics, or the arts in the way that the *Atlantic,* the *New York Review of Books,* the *New York Times Sunday Magazine,* or the *Washington Post's National Weekly Edition* do for the general public.[17]

Difficulties for Christian thinking in the world of evangelical higher education may be even more profound than those found in the evangelical press. These difficulties, however, are complex, for the myriad Bible schools, liberal arts colleges, and theological seminaries that make up evangelical higher education present a landscape of great diversity. These institutions were created for specifically religious purposes; many are successful, some remarkably so, in promoting those goals. Virtually without exception, however, they were not designed to promote thorough Christian reflection on the nature of the world, society, and the arts. It is little wonder they miss so badly that for which they do not aim.

Diffused educational energies. Part of the problem is the diffused structure of evangelical culture, which promotes a rich breadth, but also an appalling thinness, in educational institutions.[18] Evangelicals spend enormous sums on higher education, but the diffusion of resources among hundreds of colleges and seminaries means that almost none can begin to afford a research faculty, theological or otherwise. The problem is compounded by the syndrome of the reinvented wheel. Popular authority figures like Bill Bright, Oral Roberts, Jerry Falwell,

17. Evangelicals do sponsor several quarterlies that include serious intellectual analysis of the world more generally, such as *Christian Scholar's Review* or *Crucible* (from the graduate students division of InterVarsity Christian Fellowship), and a few of the many quarterlies sponsored by evangelical seminaries, especially *Crux* from Regent College in Vancouver, contain some cultural analysis.

18. An outstanding analysis of the situation for evangelical colleges is Nathan O. Hatch, "Evangelical Colleges and the Challenge of Christian Thinking," *Reformed Journal,* Sept. 1985, pp. 10–18, reprinted in Joel A. Carpenter and Kenneth W. Shipps, eds., *Making Higher Education Christian: The History and Mission of Evangelical Colleges in America* (Grand Rapids: Eerdmans, 1987); this entire book has important insights for the institutional problems of evangelical higher education. The concerns of the book are well updated by Kenneth W. Shipps, "Church-Related Colleges and Academics," *New Directions for Higher Education* 79 (Fall 1992): 29–42.

and Pat Robertson all assume that no previously existing educational enterprise is capable of meeting the demands of the hour. Despite the absence of formal educational credentials, each man presumes to establish a Christian university. Small wonder that evangelical thinking so often appears naïve, inept, or tendentious.

Colleges have a different goal from the research universities. Most important, they function under entirely different reward structures. At evangelical colleges, professors teach broadly to undergraduates and try to do so in ways that are generally Christian. The entire point of such institutions is to provide general guidance, general orientation, and general introduction. They are not designed to do the work that sets intellectual agendas, but to synthesize the work of intellectual leaders elsewhere. Associations such as the Christian College Coalition and the Christian College Consortium do some tasks very well, but they are not very helpful in bridging the gap between general learning and first-order scholarship because they represent the interests of only the collegiate side. Their goals are not scholarship per se but the support of their constituent institutions, strong and weak.

To be sure, a few evangelical colleges — among others, Calvin, Messiah, Redeemer, Samford, Steubenville, and Wheaton — have made some progress in the postwar years at promoting scholarship alongside the more general goals of broad learning and basic Christian orientation. But the distance remaining before such places become first-rate reservoirs of thought is still very great. A recent essay by the Princeton sociologist Robert Wuthnow, himself sympathetic to evangelical convictions, highlights some of the problems of the evangelical colleges. Wuthnow pointed out that the deep structures of modern intellectual life are shaped largely by the works of non- or anti-Christians. Nineteenth-century theorists like Marx, Weber, Durkheim, and Freud established the intellectual conventions of the modern university. Their legacy, for good and for ill, provides the framework in which Christians do their advanced studies.[19] The same is true for the principal theorists of the twentieth century — Milton Friedman, Ferdinand Saussure, Ferdinand Braudel, E. P. Thompson, Thomas Kuhn, Jacques Derrida — none of whom is

19. Robert Wuthnow, "The Costs of Marginality," in *The Struggle for America's Soul: Evangelicals, Liberals, and Secularism* (Grand Rapids: Eerdmans, 1989), 158–76.

concerned about the Christian implications of his work; yet they have set the agenda for what goes on throughout the academy.

Inadequate resources. More than just the framework of modern intellectual life keeps evangelical colleges from promoting first-order learning. The widely varying distribution of academic resources also is crucial. A handful of national research universities act as gatekeepers, intellectual and otherwise, for most of the learned professions. If evangelicals are to be academically certified, they must pass through those gates. But then, if they would mount convincing efforts to reassess the academic landscape from a specifically Christian perspective, they must do so with resources that cannot begin to compare with those enjoyed by the major research universities. As Wuthnow puts it, "Those who would wish to see a distinctively evangelical scholarly orientation advanced are at a tremendous competitive disadvantage. To pit even the strong intellectual aspirations of a Wheaton College or a Calvin College, or the massive fund-raising network of a Liberty University, against the multibillion dollar endowments of a Princeton or a Harvard reveals the vast extent of this deficit in resources."[20]

Small institutions with modest budgets can still exert a life-changing influence on their students. But by their nature they are not designed for the kinds of patient, creative study that alters the way we think about the world and ourselves.

Seminaries versus colleges. Another part of the institutional problem in evangelical higher education concerns the division of labor between seminaries and colleges. Evangelical seminaries, of which there are at least a dozen with substantial resources and large student bodies and several score of more modest size, are the institutional descendents of the theological schools founded in the first third of the nineteenth century. Andover (1808), Princeton (1812), and Yale (1822) led the way in training ministers for the rapidly expanding national population.[21] But by the Civil War almost all major denominational families

20. Ibid., 164.
21. Glenn T. Miller, *Piety and Intellect: The Aims and Purposes of Ante-Bellum Theological Education* (Atlanta: Scholars Press, 1990); and Mark A. Noll, introduction to *The Christian College: A History of Protestant Higher Education in America,* by William C. Ringenberg (Grand Rapids: Eerdmans, 1984), 20–24.

in the United States had founded seminaries for the training of ministers. Before the Civil War these institutions provided the most advanced training of any schools in the United States. After the Civil War the rise of the modern university pushed the seminaries toward the intellectual backwater. By 1900, advanced study at universities had developed far beyond that done at seminaries.

The seminaries — then and now — have done their job well. They have served as effective training grounds for Christian workers and were one of the reasons why Canadian and American missionary efforts possessed the personnel to accomplish their great tasks. The autonomous seminary, separate from college or university and often under the direct control of a denomination, was a singularly American creation. It has exerted a profound influence on the shape of Christianity in North America.

Its existence, however, has also created problems for more general intellectual life. If seminaries specialized in theology and encouraged systematic reflection on Christian interaction with the world, what religious role remained for the colleges? Should colleges become miniature seminaries in focusing their curriculum on biblical and theological subjects? Was theological reflection, and consideration of how revelation affects other areas of thought, to be left to the seminaries? To this day, professors at evangelical seminaries enjoy the most thorough technical training of all professional academics identified with evangelical institutions, and their work is read far more widely in evangelical circles than work from professors in the evangelical colleges.

The problem for Christian thinking does not rise from the academic quality of seminary faculties, which has been steadily rising since the Second World War. The problem concerns rather the connections between theology and other forms of learning. The American pattern of seminary formation led to a situation where experts in Scripture and theology worked in different institutions from those trained in the wider range of academic subjects. Nothing exists for evangelicals in the United States like the universities of Britain and the Continent, where the most serious work in Bible and theology goes on next to serious work in the other academic disciplines.[22] In the United States, the fourfold insti-

22. Canadian casualness about the separation of church and state, as well as a

tutional division between Bible schools, Christian liberal arts colleges, evangelical seminaries, and secular research universities has preserved important values. Independent Bible schools, colleges, and seminaries, for example, are institutionally insulated from at least some of the secularizing pressures that prevail in the modern research university. But a price has been paid for such religious security.

The price is a loss of first-level cross-fertilization between theological reflection and reflection in the arts and sciences. Evangelical seminaries have often enjoyed brilliant biblical scholars, but these scholars are isolated from comparably brilliant Christians in the evangelical colleges (whose mandate is broad and general) and in the research universities (whose mandate is narrow and deep). All teachers in the evangelical institutions suffer under a further problem created by the absence of non-Christian scholars, or Christian scholars who are not evangelical Protestants. Despite good intentions, it is almost always easier to misconstrue the arguments of others if they are not present.

The existence of separate institutional structures preserves autonomy and may be safe socially. What is lost, however, is an ideal of Christian intellectual life in which theologians, biblical scholars, and scholars from other disciplines work in constant connection with each other. In such an ideal, scholars in Scripture would provide the others with fruits of their labor in biblical study and theology. The others would offer biblical scholars interpretations of modern learning and creative ventures in applying the results of their labors to Christian teaching. Both together would reflect on the foundational commitments and philosophical presuppositions that shape inquiry in every field of thought. And, at least in theory, such work could be done with the specific aim of promoting first-order reflection about the whole world under the lordship of the one true God.

Hints of this ideal have been realized in evangelical life, but only as scholars from various institutions have pooled their work and reached

---

rich set of precedents where confessionally identified colleges have formed a part of Canadian universities, means that Christian learning that integrates theology and other study is possible in ways largely unknown in the United States. Whether Canadian believers have been able to exploit this structural opportunity is a question requiring separate study.

SAVIOR — SOUL — THE SPIRITUAL
LORD — BODY — THE PHYSICAL

out across institutional barriers to others (evangelicals of their own sort, other sorts of evangelicals, other sorts of Christians, and non-Christians). More generally, however, the divided structures of evangelical learning have nurtured a divided evangelical mentality. Attempts to think — both profoundly and as Christians — about history, nature, the arts, and society have been frustrated by the very success of an institutional arrangement that maintains several mutually distinct forms of academic endeavor.

A shortage of scholars. Institutional dimensions of the intellectual scandal do not exhaust the difficulties for evangelical higher education. A further problem is created by the generations-long failure of the evangelical community to nurture the life of the mind. That failure has created what William Hull, provost of Samford University, has called "the tragic imbalance which now exists according to which the dominant religion in America is almost destitute of intellectual firepower." As Hull describes it, the desire to carry "the Christian dimension to the heart of the learning process" must advance realistically. College administrators and intellectuals in the churches must face the sober realities that Hull encountered when he sought to define such a goal at his own university:

> Long experience in academic personnel recruitment convinces me that a sufficiently large pool of qualified candidates to staff [an] entire University faculty with Christian scholars . . . is just not out there. . . . Suffice it to say that the church has failed to define its intellectual responsibilities in compelling terms, to call out from among its own those gifted to discharge this neglected stewardship, and to provide such budding scholars with support for the kind of advanced training that will equip them to do credible work on so exacting a frontier. The very few who decide to make the integration of Christianity and scholarship a lifelong calling usually do so at their own initiative, with precious little encouragement either from the church or from the academy. Ironically, the handful who do express an early interest in the vocation of Christian scholar are usually shunted into seminary for graduate theological study, producing a surplus of those qualified to teach religion but a paucity of those trained to teach the other ninety-five percent of the academic disciplines as they relate to the Christian faith. . . . We must not deceive ourselves into supposing that there is a large guild of seasoned

Christian scholars somewhere on which we can draw in staffing our University faculty.[23]

Graduate school. The problem of recruiting faculty who are able to do their work both with rigor as scholars and with savvy as Christians relates directly to yet another difficulty for institutions of evangelical higher learning. The graduate programs that qualify individuals to teach in colleges and seminaries are almost uniformly uninterested in the questions of Christian perspective that are prerequisite for first-order evangelical thinking. With the exception of a few theologians who may have finished their most advanced work in evangelical seminaries, the professors at evangelical (or Catholic) institutions have done their most advanced study at places little concerned about what, at evangelical colleges and seminaries, should be the most important matters. Nowhere in the Western world is it possible to find an institution for graduate training — that is, for the training required to teach at evangelical institutions of higher learning — that exists for the primary purpose of promoting Christian scholarship defined in a Protestant, evangelical way. Thankfully, there are a few Roman Catholic and Jewish institutions where Catholic or Jewish understandings of God and the world receive careful attention, and evangelical scholars have sometimes made use of such institutions. But for most of the faculty members at most evangelical institutions of higher learning, to ask in the course of their most advanced training the deepest and highest questions about the relationship between God and the world would be irrelevant, or it would create prejudice against them. Yet, once called to evangelical institutions, part of the task of these same scholars is to guide students and publish research that asks precisely those questions.

In sum, the scandal of the evangelical mind arises from the specific institutional arrangements of evangelical higher learning in North America. Even if an evangelical were convinced that deep, probing study of the world should be undertaken as a specifically Christian task, it is by no means self-evident where that task could be pursued.

23. William E. Hull, "Toward Samford as a Christian University — Occasional Papers of the Provost," Samford University, Birmingham, AL, July 15, 1990, pp. 2–5

Theological

Finally, there is a theological dimension to the scandal of the evangelical mind. For an entire Christian community to neglect, generation after generation, serious attention to the mind, nature, society, the arts — all spheres created by God and sustained for his own glory — may be, in fact, sinful. Os Guinness has recently called attention to this dimension in a memorable passage worth quoting at length:

> Evangelicals have been deeply sinful in being anti-intellectual ever since the 1820s and 1830s. For the longest time we didn't pay the cultural price for that because we had the numbers, the social zeal, and the spiritual passion for the gospel. But today we are beginning to pay the cultural price. And you can see that most evangelicals simply don't think. For example, there has been no serious evangelical public philosophy in this century. . . . It has always been a sin not to love the Lord our God with our minds as well as our hearts and souls. . . . We have excused this with a degree of pietism and pretend[ing] that this is something other than what it is — that is, sin. . . . Evangelicals need to repent of their refusal to think Christianly and to develop the mind of Christ.[24]

The scandal of the evangelical mind is a scandal from whichever direction it is viewed. It is a scandal arising from the historical experience of an entire subculture. It is a scandal to which the shape of evangelical institutions have contributed. Most of all, it is a scandal because it scorns the good gifts of a loving God. The rest of this book is an effort to show why this scandal emerged as it did in North America and how it might be possible to minimize its pernicious effects.

Arguments

The chapters that follow makes several arguments about why, in the late twentieth century, American evangelicals experience relative intel-

---

24. "Persuasion for the New World: An Interview with Dr. Os Guinness," *Crucible* 4, 2 (Summer 1992): 15.

lectual poverty. The most general of these arguments suggests that from at least the mid-eighteenth century, American evangelicalism has existed primarily as an affectional and organizational movement. The very character of the revival that made evangelical religion into a potent force in North America weakened its intellectual power. The career of Jonathan Edwards — the greatest evangelical mind in American history and one of the truly seminal thinkers in Christian history of the last few centuries — supports this argument, for despite his own remarkable efforts as an evangelical thinker, Edwards had no intellectual successors.

Yet because of its location in American history, evangelicalism in the last part of the eighteenth century and the early years of the nineteenth did develop an elaborate intellectual system. That system added selected elements from the Revolutionary and democratic movements of the late eighteenth century to historic Protestant emphases. The result was a distinctly evangelical approach to the life of the mind that featured the philosophy of common sense, the moral instincts of republicanism, the science of Francis Bacon, and a disposition toward evidential reasoning in theology. This system had significant intellectual shortcomings, but these shortcomings were not noticed (and may not have been too important) so long as Americans were preoccupied with constructing a stable society. The flaws in the system became more apparent when evangelicals responded to the new social and intellectual conditions of the mid to late nineteenth century. Fundamentalism, dispensational premillennialism, the Higher Life movement, and Pentecostalism were all evangelical strategies of survival in response to the religious crises of the late nineteenth century. In different ways each preserved something essential of the Christian faith. But together they were a disaster for the life of the mind. This disaster could be explored from several different angles, but I have chosen to address it in separate chapters on evangelical political reflection and evangelical attitudes toward science, two intellectual areas that have suffered among evangelicals in the twentieth century, not so much for evangelical anti-intellectualism as for the wrong kind of intellectual attention. It has taken two full generations to begin to recover from the intellectual disaster of the late nineteenth century. In the meantime, new cultural and intellectual problems have arisen for which evangelical intellectual traditions offer only scant resources.

AFFECTIONAL — THERAPEUTIC
ORGANIZATIONAL — MANAGERIAL
INTELLECTUAL — COGNITIVE

Summarized like this, the arguments of this book paint a bleak picture. Along the way, however, a brighter light will appear, for it is a minor paradox worthy of the larger paradoxes of Christianity itself that the historical circumstances resulting in the decline of evangelical thinking were the very conditions that sustained the possibility of its renewal. Those possibilities are the subject of the last two chapters, which examine, first, recent efforts by evangelicals to overcome the neglect of the mind and, second, the resources from within the evangelical tradition itself that may counteract the baleful influences of the scandal. Of those resources, the most potent is yet another scandal, though one with an entirely different consequence for those who willingly embrace it. It is, in short, the scandal of the Cross, which may yet overcome the scandal of the evangelical mind.

The most thoroughly Christian analysis of the intellectual situation for modern American evangelicals comes from an unexpected source. Charles Malik, a Lebanese diplomat, scholar, and Eastern Orthodox Christian, was invited in 1980 to open the Billy Graham Center at Wheaton College with an address. Few of those assembled on that day were prepared for the acute wisdom of Malik's remarks. I was there but hardly realized at the time how much a decade or more of study would move me to reinforce, with halting historical argumentation, what he put so succinctly as the manifesto of a Christian intellectual to his friends in the faith. Malik's address was powerful because it focused on the question of ends more directly than the question of means. With great gentleness and magnanimity of soul, but also with great courage, Malik took us evangelicals straight to the woodshed. First he defined what was at stake in the modern university: "At the heart of all the problems facing Western civilization — the general nervousness and restlessness, the dearth of grace and beauty and quiet and peace of soul, the manifold blemishes and perversions of personal character; problems of the family and of social relations in general, problems of economics and politics, problems of the media, problems affecting the school itself and the church itself, problems in the international order — at the heart of the crisis in Western civilization lies the state of the mind and the spirit of the universities." Malik went on to suggest that since the dilemmas of modern life were intellectual dilemmas of the sort that universities exist to explore, it was important for Christians to realize the magnitude of their intellectual task — "The problem is not only to win souls but to save minds. If you win the whole world and lose the mind of the world, you will soon discover you have not won the world. Indeed it may turn out that you have actually lost the world."

But then Malik turned to look at the contribution of evangelicals. He was not unappreciative of the intellectual exertions some evangelicals had been making, but his words described the nature of the intellectual challenge with uncommon force:

> The greatest danger besetting American Evangelical Christianity is the danger of anti-intellectualism. The mind as to its greatest and deepest reaches is not cared for enough. This cannot take place apart from profound immersion for a period of years in the history of thought and the spirit. People are in a hurry to get out of the university and start earning money or serving the church or preaching the Gospel. They have no idea of the infinite value of spending years of leisure in conversing with the greatest minds and souls of the past, and thereby ripening and sharpening and enlarging their powers of thinking. The result is that the arena of creative thinking is abdicated and vacated to the enemy. Who among the evangelicals can stand up to the great secular or naturalistic or atheistic scholars on their own terms of scholarship and research? Who among the evangelical scholars is quoted as a normative source by the greatest secular authorities on history or philosophy or psychology or sociology or politics? Does your mode of thinking have the slightest chance of becoming the dominant mode of thinking in the great universities of Europe and America which stamp your entire civilization with their own spirit and ideas?
>
> It will take a different spirit altogether to overcome this great danger of anti-intellectualism. . . . Even if you start now on a crash program in this and other domains, it will be a century at least before you catch up with the Harvards and Tuebingens and the Sorbonnes, and think of where these universities will be then! For the sake of greater effectiveness in witnessing to Jesus Christ Himself, as well as for their own sakes, the Evangelicals cannot afford to keep on living on the periphery of responsible intellectual existence.[25]

25. Charles Malik, *The Two Tasks* (Westchester, IL: Cornerstore, 1980), 29–34.

This book is a historical footnote in support of Malik's sage words. It is undertaken with the conviction that Malik was exactly right — fidelity to Jesus Christ demands from evangelicals a more responsible intellectual existence than we have practiced throughout much of our history.

CHAPTER 2

Why the Scandal Matters

So what? might be a characteristically evangelical response. So what if American evangelicals commit themselves much more thoroughly to creating television networks than to creating universities? So what if evangelical activism allows scant room for the cultivation of the mind? So what if evangelical populism regularly verges on anti-intellectualism? What — from the standpoint of essential Christianity — is at stake in letting the mind go to waste?

Objections to the proposition that evangelicals should repent for not cultivating the mind deserve to be taken seriously. In the first instance, the history of Christianity in North America might be read to show how useful it is for believers to neglect the life of the mind. In the United States, evangelicals have given themselves to problem solving and the accomplishments of know-how. And has not this strategy turned out well? While European churches over the last centuries have descended into lifeless formalism, and while America's mainline churches — with their aspirations to learned culture — have shrunk dramatically over the last decades, America's self-confessed evangelicals have become more numerous, more vocal, and more visible. While others were taking care of the thinking, we evangelicals have been activists in missions and reform. Would not the state of the church around the world today suggest that we have chosen the better way?

An even more substantial objection grows from a consideration of the modern academy. Surely evangelicals are better off *avoiding* the

political in-fighting, manifest secularization, power mongering, and
ideological warfare that so often characterize modern academic life and
that have been the subject of sharp public criticism in recent years.[1] If
evangelicals inhabit a brackish intellectual backwater, they are still
spared the perils of a tumultuous sea upon which ships are going
nowhere. A great modern university might keep the sort of inscription
that still adorns Kinsey Hall on the campus of the University of California at Los Angeles — "Psalm 119:18. Open thou mine eyes that I
may behold wondrous things out of thy law." But the reality of what
occurs in the research universities often mocks the pieties of earlier
generations.

When this argument is made with Christian subtlety — as it has
been made, for instance, in a recent apology for teaching-centered
higher education by Mark Schwehn of Valparaiso University — the
argument carries weight.[2] Schwehn's case for the virtues of attending
to students as people as opposed to the pursuit of research as an end
in itself, for historically anchored religious conviction over ultra-chic
ideological posturing, is compelling.

The weight of such an argument means that an appeal for intellectual effort must be precise. In appealing for Christian scholarship,
the point is not primarily academic respectability, and certainly not the
mindless pursuit of publication for its own sake that bedevils the
modern university. The point is rather that the comprehensive reality
of Christianity itself demands specifically Christian consideration of
the world we inhabit, whether that consideration is of social theory,
the history of science, other historical changes, the body, the arts,
literature, or more. Christian appeals for learning should not ask for a
downgrading of teaching, an elitist rejection of insights from ordinary
people, or an aestheticism that excludes all but the cognoscenti. They

1. For examples of that criticism, see Arthur Schlesinger, Jr., *The Disuniting of
America* (New York: Norton, 1992); Page Smith, *Killing the Spirit: Higher Education
in America* (New York: Penguin, 1991); Dinesh DiSouza, *Illiberal Education: The
Politics of Race and Sex on Campus* (New York: Free Press, 1991); and Allan Bloom,
*The Closing of the American Mind: How Higher Education Has Failed Democracy and
Impoverished the Souls of Today's Students* (New York: Simon & Schuster, 1987).
2. Mark R. Schwehn, *Exiles from Eden: Religion and the Academic Vocation in
America* (New York: Oxford University Press, 1993).

should ask rather that explorations into the broader and deeper reaches of the intellect be considered a complement to, rather than competition against, person-oriented, teaching-focused, and democratically inspired intellectual life.

The most serious objection to the promotion of Christian learning comes, however, from the Scriptures. The words of Jesus that commend a childlike spirit or that relativize the wisdom of the world provoke sober reflection. "I praise you, Father, Lord of heaven and earth," is the prayer recorded in Matthew 11:25–26, "because you have hidden these things from the wise and learned, and revealed them to little children. Yes, Father, for this was your good pleasure." An even stronger check to the unqualified pursuit of knowledge comes from the apostle Paul, who, with cutting force, told the Corinthians why they should not swarm for the wisdom of the world: "Think of what you were when you were called. Not many of you were wise by human standards; not many were influential; not many were of noble birth. But God chose the foolish things of the world to shame the wise; God chose the weak things of the world to shame the strong. He chose the lowly things of this world and the despised things — and the things that are not — to nullify the things that are . . ." (1 Cor. 1:26–28).

The force of such passages is underscored by the undeniable fact that higher learning has often been a snare to faith. In the first instance, the conclusions that intellectuals have reached about the human condition or the structures of the world have often undermined Christian beliefs. More damaging to Christianity than the things learned, however, is pride in learning itself. The kind of blunt observation that Martyn Lloyd-Jones offered to a group of college students in 1969 — "If you are out for intellectual respectability you will soon get into trouble in your faith"[3] — lacks nuance, but it also reflects hard-won wisdom. The world of learning is a treacherous place. Pride of intellectual accomplishment is a real threat to humble faith. Intellectuals are susceptible to a temptation to trust in their own wisdom as a substitute for trusting in the "foolishness" of the gospel. Appeals for learning must acknowledge the seriousness of these objections.

---

3. Quoted in Iain H. Murray, *D. Martyn Lloyd-Jones: The Fight of Faith, 1939–1981* (Edinburgh: Banner of Truth, 1990), 608.

At the same time, however, *Christian appeals* for *Christian learning* are able to show how resources of the faith itself justify an unpretentious, humble pursuit of knowledge. Paul ended his recommendation of "the foolish things of the world" by stating his main concerns: that "no one may boast before him" (v. 29), that the Corinthians would recognize that in Christ is found the ultimate "wisdom from God" (v. 30), and that they would cultivate the habit of "boast[ing] in the Lord" (v. 31).

Learning may have a greater tendency to inculcate pride than some other human activities, but only relatively so. Business executives who boast in their firms, parents who boast in their children, gardeners who boast in their tomatoes, patriots who boast in their nations — all are called, with scholars who boast in their books, to subordinate the object of their affections to the absolute glory that belongs to God alone.

A Christian appeal for Christian learning also will not presume that learning is the ultimate or only value. Instead, by following Paul's precepts in 1 Corinthians 12:14–26, the Christian who is committed to the life of the mind will regard the tasks to which other believers are called with the same respect that he or she accords to the intellectual life. Just as, in the apostle's phrase, "the eye cannot say to the hand, 'I don't need you,'" so the scholar cannot say to the illiterate believers, "I don't need you." And vice versa.

Evangelical culture in America has run to antagonistic polarities: conversion to the exclusion of gradual growth in grace, the immediate experience of the Holy Spirit instead of the contemplation of God in the created realm, the prizing of popular wisdom over against pronouncements from authorities, a fascination with heaven while slighting attention to earth, a devotion to the supernatural and a neglect of the natural. A Christian appeal for Christian learning does not ask for these polarities to be reversed — for example, to have the natural exclude the supernatural or the present exclude the future. It calls rather for the mutual interdependence of the body, a reunion of characteristics that American experience has ruthlessly divorced, and a willingness to acknowledge that the sovereign Christ can be exalted by humble activity in every legitimate sphere of human life, including the life of the mind.

The importance of cultivating the mind for Christ can also be seen more generally by realizing the practical matters at stake in such activity, by heeding the weight of two different historical arguments, and — most important — by attending to the truth concerning God, the world, and ourselves.

Utility

Two questions highlight the reasons why attention to the mind is an intensely practical matter. Apart from all concern for what is true, or what the church has done historically with respect to the intellect, believers in the modern world should recognize that the *thinking* of Christians is a matter of immensely pragmatic significance.

First is a question with great practical implications. Who will be our tutors, the ones who teach us and our children about life? The institutions of learned culture and the great engine of the American mass media are the two prime contenders for this task in our world. The universities nourish the thinkers who propose grand paradigms through which we examine the world. To mention only one of several possible examples, the related problems of medical ethics and equitable provision of health care are immensely complex issues. They also bear, directly or indirectly, on Christian values at every point. Yet evangelicals have not been in the habit of thinking long and hard about the ramifications of such matters. Thomas Harris, chair of the department of biomedical engineering at Vanderbilt University, states succinctly the problem with that inattention: "I fear evangelical and conservative Christianity is not coming to grips with these issues, particularly within higher education."[4] The same could be said about many other issues of our day — principles to guide foreign relations with the troubled nations of the formerly Communist world; insights into the complicated questions of human understanding that currently plague every sphere of academic endeavor; criteria by which to support (or dismantle) programs for providing the jobs that mean so much for human dignity (and, for the church, a way to support its many activities); and means to pacify the racial tensions that at the end of the twentieth

4. Quoted in Louis A. Moore, "CLC's 1993 Seminar on Medical Ethics," *Light: The Christian Life Commission of the Southern Baptist Convention*, May–June 1993, p. 1.

LEARNED CULTURE—UNIVERSITIES
POPULAR CULTURE — MEDIA

century constitute the most obvious threats to peaceful civilization over the whole world. These are all issues that require two things if Christians are to bring the love of Jesus into the modern world as it really is — first, profound study of the issues themselves; second, study informed by profoundly Christian convictions.

The world of popular culture looks very different from the worlds of academia and professional think tanks, yet popular culture provides as much instruction for our daily lives as do the universities. David Letterman, George Lucas, the producers of MTV, and the movers and shakers of Hollywood offer a never-ending series of flashy stimulants that have a profound intellectual effect. Each of us is developing a mind, with which we reason about all areas of life — political allegiance as well as Christian conversion, the meaning of money as well as the meaning of the Bible, the effects of democracy as well as the effects of sin. Who will teach us how to reason about these matters? Who will be our guides pointing us to truth and light? If evangelicals do not take seriously the larger world of the intellect, we say, in effect, that we want our minds to be shaped by the conventions of our modern universities and the assumptions of Madison Avenue, instead of by God and the servants of God. But if we take this action by inaction, we are saying that we want our lives to be shaped by cultural forces — including intellectual forces — that contradict the heart of our religion.

A second, related question asks how we will live in the world. This too is an intensely intellectual question. How we live in the world depends in large measure on how we think about the world. For contemporary Christians of all sorts it is a very easy matter simply to adopt the herd instincts of mass popular culture — to assume that life exists as a series of opportunities for pleasure, self-expression, and the increase of comfort. But it is also possible as Christians to take the other extreme, to think that the world through which we move is just an unreal shadow preparing the way for our home beyond the skies. Such thinking is not altogether wrong. The Christian belief in eternity is one of the most important of our convictions. At the same time, not to think about the ways in which life can be lived because of God and for God is to cheapen a whole realm of existence. In contrast, to accept life in this world as a gift from God, to live as though a deeper understanding of existence leads to a deeper understanding of God,

HOW WE THINK ABOUT THE WORLD — MIND-SET
HOW WE LIVE IN THE WORLD — LIFE-STYLE

requires dedicated and persistent thought, even as it requires dedicated and persistent spiritual vitality.

In 1912, the Presbyterian Bible scholar J. Gresham Machen stated carefully the way that thinking affects practical life. His words are as prescient today as they were for the less complicated world that he addressed: "We may preach with all the fervor of a reformer, and yet succeed only in winning a straggler here and there, if we permit the whole collective thought of the nation or of the world to be controlled by ideas which, by the resistless force of logic, prevent Christianity from being regarded as anything more than a harmless delusion. . . . What is to-day a matter of academic speculation, begins to-morrow to move armies and pull down empires."[5]

The Message of the Past

Two different historical arguments can also be made to show how important the life of the mind is for ongoing Christian vitality. The first of these concerns evangelical Protestants specifically by noting the rich heritage of fruitful intellectual labor that accompanied the rise of Protestantism. The second is more general because it involves specific lessons about the vitality of Christian movements both before and after the Reformation.

Protestant Precedent

The condition of the evangelical mind in contemporary America could not be described as a scandal unless an earlier history existed to show that serious intellectual labor had been the norm for at least many Protestants in the evangelical tradition. In fact, that is just what a history of Protestantism reveals. The intellectual history of the Protestant movement as a whole is a daunting subject of gargantuan proportions.

5. J. Gresham Machen, "Christianity and Culture," *Princeton Theological Review* 11 (1913): 7; for discussion, see George Marsden, "Understanding J. Gresham Machen," *Princeton Seminary Bulletin*, n.s., 11 (1990): 46–60.

Enough can be offered here briefly, however, to show that the twen-tieth-century evangelical neglect of the mind is an aberration in a long history of Protestant efforts to give the intellect its due.

At the start of the Reformation in the sixteenth century, many observers felt that Protestantism spelled death for the mind, not its renewal.[6] They thought that it would bring to an end the very long tradition of Christian attention to the mind that was rooted in the early church and that had survived — sometimes with overwhelming brilli-ance and sometimes by the skin of its teeth — throughout the Middle Ages.[7] By contrast, some of the Reformers' first followers called into question the entire project of the intellect because of historic connec-tions between the Catholic Church and Europe's traditional educational institutions. The new Protestant commitment to the priesthood of believers also seemed to undercut the need for intellectual experts. Protestant belief in the activity of the Holy Spirit among the entire church seemed to deny the need for special efforts in learning. Was not merely "the Bible alone" enough? If a person possessed the inner testi-mony of the Holy Spirit, what need was there for learning? So it was that the Reformation appeared at least to some as a profoundly anti-intellectual movement.

The counterargument — that mental activity was essential for valid Christian life — came from the leading Protestants themselves. They saw quickly that the cultivation of a more biblical spirituality required a more thorough attention to the mind. Martin Luther, who was never one to mince his words, promised in 1529 to write a book against parents who neglected the education of their children. In that

6. References to some of the scholarly literature on this general subject can be found in Mark A. Noll, "The Earliest Protestants and the Reformation of Education," *Westminster Theological Journal* 43 (1980): 208–30.

7. For examples from that long history, see L. Miller, ed., *Classical Statements on Faith and Reason* (New York: Random House, 1970), 3–69; for a perceptive recent application of that long history, see Robert L. Wilkin, "The Christian Intellectual Tradition," *First Things,* June/July 1991, pp. 13–18; and for two illuminating surveys by Colin Brown, whose treatments extend into the Protestant era (with much to say about the concerns of this book), see *Philosophy and the Christian Faith: A Historical Sketch from the Middle Ages to the Present Day* (Chicago: InterVarsity Press, 1969) and *Christianity and Western Thought,* vol. 1 (Downers Grove, IL: InterVarsity Press, 1990).

book, he said, "I shall really go after the shameful, despicable, damnable parents who are no parents at all but despicable hogs and venomous beasts, devouring their own young."[8] Cultivating the mind was absolutely essential, Luther held, because people needed to understand both the word of Scripture and the nature of the world in which the word would take root. Furthermore, insistence on the priesthood of believers demanded more education, not less. It demanded that education be brought to the most ordinary levels and to the most ordinary people. Protestantism, in fact, marks the start of the move to universal education in Europe because its leaders insisted that all individuals had a responsibility to understand the world in which they lived and the spiritual world held out to them by Christian teaching.

As a consequence of this defense of education, Protestants were active in establishing schools of all sorts. Inevitably, where Protestant schools were strongest, the Protestant Reformation made its greatest impact.[9]

Perhaps the most significant of the Protestant efforts to encourage Christian thinking took place in the Geneva of John Calvin.[10] From his earliest days in that city, Calvin worked to instruct the mind and inspire the heart together. Calvin's theology was not intellectualist; he believed that the Spirit must change the heart before the mind would accept the gospel. He also held that God manifested his sovereignty over every part of life, including the mind. Yet Calvin also believed that the Spirit of God had created the world so that it could be studied. He believed that the Spirit enabled nonbelievers to understand the workings of nature and human relationships in the world. These activities of the Spirit therefore deserved consistent attention in order to shape the minds of Christians to see all of life as the arena of God's activity. Calvin championed learning in the home, he broadened the scope of education for the young people of Geneva, and he founded an academy, or

8. Quoted by Robert C. Schultz, ed., "Sermon on Keeping Children in School," in *Luther's Works*, American ed., vol. 46 (Philadelphia: Fortress, 1967), 211.

9. The point is made indirectly in a fine older study, Karl Holl, *The Cultural Significance of the Reformation* (Cleveland: World, 1969).

10. An excellent recent account is Susan E. Schreiner, *The Theater of His Glory: Nature and the Natural Order in the Thought of John Calvin* (Durham, NC: Labyrinth Press, 1991).

INSTRUCT THE MIND
INSPIRE ~~CHALLENGE~~ THE HEART
CHALLENGE THE WILL

university, for advanced study, to which Protestants came from all over Europe. There they found great seriousness about the gospel message itself, but also great seriousness about the classical languages, medicine, the natural world, and what we would today call politics and sociology.

To be sure, Calvin did not glide effortlessly from his contemplation of God to the intellectual pursuit of the world. He was aware that God "chose the foolish things of the world to shame the wise." He insisted, as William Bouwsma has summarized, "on the limits of human rationality" and was open "to all the contradictory realities of human experience."[11] In his characteristic way, Calvin worked on the biblical passages that seemed to imply a rejection of human wisdom until he thought he had reached a satisfactory conclusion:

> By "being fools" we do not mean being stupid; nor do we direct those who are learned in the liberal sciences to jettison their knowledge, and those who are gifted with quickness of mind to become dull, as if a man cannot be a Christian unless he is more like a beast than a man. The profession of Christianity requires us to be immature, not in our thinking, but in malice (1 Cor. 14:20). But do not let anyone bring trust in his own mental resources or his learning into the school of Christ; do not let anyone be swollen with pride or full of distaste, and so be quick to reject what he is told, indeed even before he has sampled it.[12]

Calvin's synthesis, combining a high view of God's sovereignty with an earnestness about the mind, also characterized other parts of Protestant Europe, especially southern Germany, Holland, Scotland, and certain parts of England. In these places the faith of the Reformation became as influential for the shaping of thought as Thomas Aquinas's work had earlier been for Catholic Europe. The goal was to bring every aspect of life under the general guidance of Christian thinking, to have each question in life answered by a response from a Christian perspective, and to extract from each savant of classical or Roman

11. William J. Bouwsma, *John Calvin: A Sixteenth-Century Portrait* (New York: Oxford University Press, 1988), 161.

12. John Calvin, *Concerning Scandals,* trans. John W. Fraser (Grand Rapids: Eerdmans, 1978), 18–19.

Catholic learning what was compatible with Calvin's Protestant understanding of the Bible.[13]

In consequence, Protestants were encouraged to labor as scientists so that their scientific work could rise to the praise of God.[14] By so doing, the early Protestants expressed their belief that God had made the natural world to be explored and that the results of such exploration showed forth his glory. At least some statesmen and theologians among the early Protestants carried on the same sort of enterprise with respect to government. They not only worked to make political and social organizations reflect the norms of justice they found in Scripture but also examined the contrasting rights of individuals, kings, and parliaments, and contributed to theories about democracy and the existence of republics.[15] In general, they did what they could to make life in society reflect the goodness of God.[16]

Similarly, over its first centuries, Protestantism — sometimes in the face of contradictory ascetic tendencies — nonetheless provided an ethos in which artistic expression of unusually high quality flourished. It gave one musical genius — J. S. Bach — many of the themes for his noblest work.[17] It undergirded a whole school of visual artists, who painted natural, urban, and domestic scenes sublimely on the bases of its principles.[18]

---

13. For a recent study of how the Reformers' effort to winnow the thinking of the ancients and of their religious opponents fit into the church's general efforts in that direction, see Jacob Klapwijk, Sander Griffioen, and Gerben Groenewoud, eds., *Bringing into Captivity Every Thought: Capita Selecta in the History of Christian Evaluations of Non-Christian Philosophy* (Lanham, MD: University Press of America, 1991).

14. Nicely nuanced studies of an often controversial subject are Gary B. Deason, "Reformation Theology and the Mechanistic Conception of Nature," and Charles Webster, "Puritanism, Separatism, and Science," both in *God and Nature: Historical Essays on the Encounter between Christianity and Science,* ed. David C. Lindberg and Ronald L. Numbers (Berkeley: University of California Press, 1986).

15. Quentin Skinner, *The Foundations of Modern Political Thought,* vol. 2: *The Reformation* (Cambridge: Cambridge University Press, 1978).

16. W. Fred Graham, *The Constructive Revolutionary: John Calvin and His Socio-Economic Impact* (Atlanta: John Knox, 1971).

17. See Jaroslav Pelikan, *Bach among the Theologians* (Philadelphia: Fortress, 1986).

18. For an outstanding account of how Protestant theories inspired such art, see E. John Walford, *Jacob van Ruisdael and the Perception of Landscape* (New Haven: Yale University Press, 1992).

And it developed a poetics that, in the words of Barbara Lewalski, powerfully stimulated the poetic imagination "by promoting a profound creative response to the written word of scripture and inviting a searching scrutiny of the human heart."[19] In science, public life, the arts, and still other spheres, these early Protestants were attempting, in other words, to develop a Christian mind.

The immediate ancestors of American evangelicals — those British Protestants who settled North America — were of this sort too. We know them as the Puritans because they attempted to purify England's state church, purify the nation, and purify themselves as individuals. The English Puritans who migrated to Plymouth, Boston, New Haven, and other North American sites did so in order to continue the efforts to purify self, church, and society that were being frustrated in the mother country. Of many striking features of the Puritans, one of the most remarkable was their zeal in developing a Christian mind.[20]

In some respects, Puritans remained fundamentally ambiguous about the mind. They retained all of the earlier Protestants' commitment to the supernatural character of God's grace and the freedom of God in the operation of that grace in the world. In the last analysis, they did not worship a predictable deity. At the same time, the Puritans viewed the whole of life as a gift from the God of grace. They did not separate social, ecclesiastical, and theological concerns into artificially separated categories. The Puritan point of view was comprehensive; it saw religious significance in public acts and public significance in religious acts. Since they felt that good and evil could be readily identified in human affairs, the Puritans could not tolerate barriers between theological judgment and the events of daily life. Since they held that the battle between good and

THEOLOGICAL JUDGMENTS
EVENTS OF DAILY

19. Barbara Kiefer Lewalski, *Protestant Poetics and the Seventeenth-Century Religious Lyric* (Princeton: Princeton University Press, 1979), 426. The poets Lewalski described were John Donne, George Herbert, Henry Vaughan, Thomas Traherne, and Edward Taylor.

20. From a vast body of literature, helpful works illuminating the Puritan attention to the mind are Patrick Collinson, *The Elizabethan Puritan Movement* (London: Jonathan Cape, 1967); Christopher Hill, *Society and Puritanism in Pre-Revolutionary England* (New York: Schocken, 1967); Edmund S. Morgan, *The Puritan Dilemma: The Story of John Winthrop* (Boston: Little, Brown, 1958); and Leland Ryken, *Worldly Saints: The Puritans As They Really Were* (Grand Rapids: Zondervan, 1986).

evil, between God and Satan, extended into every aspect of life, decisions in the communal life of the wider society had a moral significance equal to those enacted within the narrow confines of the church. Puritans, in sum, refused to compartmentalize life or exempt nonecclesiastical matters from religious scrutiny. Puritans did not minimize the theological conundrums involved in trying to understand the world within a Christian framework. But they persevered in the attempt. As the best recent student of the subject, John Morgan, has written, Puritans did not oppose Scripture and inspiration, on the one hand, against learning and traditional knowledge, on the other, but rather "attempted the more difficult task of scrupulously maintaining a delicate balance of spirit and philosophy"; they pursued "the dialectic of enthusiasm and learning." In the apostle Paul's own efforts to reason like a true follower of Christ, "they found the perfect historical parallel for their own existential quest for a way to balance, if not fully blend, enthusiasm and humane learning."[21]

Undergirding the comprehensive scope of Puritan concern were deeply held convictions about God's character and the revelation of himself to humankind. Puritans were strenuous moral athletes because of their vision of God, "a Spirit, infinite, eternal, and unchangeable, in his being, wisdom, power, holiness, justice, goodness, and truth."[22] Such a being deserved all the love, dedication, energy, and devotion that the creature, by God's grace, could give back to him. Puritans, furthermore, believed that the Bible was God's authoritative revelation to humanity and that its pages contained necessary and sufficient guidelines for the proper ordering of personal, ecclesiastical, and social life. Puritans developed an elaborate system of covenants, with intricate interweaving of personal salvation, church structure, and political organization. These covenants, Puritans felt, were merely the faithful exposition of the divine plan laid out in Scripture. Because God had graciously revealed his will in Scripture, Puritans proceeded with the confidence that every aspect of life could be ordered to the glory of God.

21. John Morgan, *Godly Learning: Puritan Attitudes towards Reason, Learning, and Education, 1560–1640* (New York: Cambridge University Press, 1986), 77, 292, 306.

22. *Westminster Shorter Catechism* (1647), question 4.

The distinguishing characteristic of Puritanism was its effort to unite the theology of the Reformation with a comprehensive view of the world. From the testimony of the Continental Reformers and their own study of Scripture, the Puritans were convinced that a vital personal religion was the wellspring of all earthly good. They were equally convinced that all aspects of life — whether political, social, cultural, economic, artistic, or ecclesiastical — needed to be brought into subjection to God. This Puritan synthesis of heart religion and comprehensive concern for all areas of life drew upon the Continental heritage of Protestantism, but it was, in its fullest expression, the unique contribution of the English-speaking Reformation to the development of American civilization.

The key contribution of the Puritans to the intellectual life of later evangelicals is their gift of a mind as well as a theological position, a set of principles concerning society as well as a stance toward the church, a worldview as well as a spirituality. The Puritans may have been wrong on particular questions involving the intellect. For example, I think they were altogether too confident that their specific interpretations of the Bible could be equated with the message of Scripture itself. They were just as blameworthy when they resorted to coercion to force these particular interpretations upon Quakers, Catholics, Baptists, and Native Americans who questioned their wisdom. Without making light of such failures, it is still possible to say that the glory of the Puritans was to believe what they believed and do what they did as parts of a self-consciously comprehensive intellectual effort. As a result, with Puritans like John Milton, John Bunyan, Anne Bradstreet, and Edward Taylor we can observe an identifiably Puritan aesthetic;[23] with rulers like John Winthrop, William Bradford, and Oliver Cromwell we find the rudiments of an identifiably Puritan politics;[24] and from many ministers and magistrates we discover a well-articulated Puritan social theory. In addition, the Puritans also worked out particular views on

23. Perry Miller and Thomas H. Johnson, eds., "Poetry" and "Literary Theory," in *The Puritans: A Sourcebook of Their Writings,* 2 vols., rev. ed. (New York: Harper & Row, 1963), 2:545–684.

24. Robert S. Paul, *The Lord Protector: Religion and Politics in the Life of Oliver Cromwell* (Grand Rapids: Eerdmans, 1964); and Timothy H. Breen, *The Character of the Good Ruler: Puritan Political Ideas in New England, 1630–1730* (New Haven: Yale University Press, 1970).

work, business ethics, recreation, sexual love, and many other spheres of what we now often call secular life.[25]

These manifestations of Christian thinking were rooted in the Puritans' theology, ecclesiology, and piety, but they went well beyond these more explicitly "religious" concerns. What we see among the Puritans, in other words, are the fruits of a Christian mind.

Modern evangelicals are descendants of the Puritans. And yet, for some reason, the Puritan kind of comprehensive thinking under God, the sort of mind shaped to its furthest reaches by Christian influences, we modern evangelicals do not enjoy. Other sorts of historical arguments show why that neglect touches the character of the faith itself.

More General Historical Lessons

Hard intellectual labor has never by itself led to a healthy church.[26] Sometimes, in fact, the pursuit of learning has been a means to escape the claims of the gospel or the requirements of God's law. It is also true that vital Christianity has existed, at least for brief periods, without a noticeable increase in seriousness about the intellect. Yet, generally, the picture over the long term is different. Where Christian faith is securely rooted, where it penetrates deeply into a culture to change individual lives and redirect institutions, where it continues for more than a generation as a living testimony to the grace of God — in these situations, we almost invariably find Christians ardently cultivating the intellect for the glory of God.

The links between deep Christian life, long-lasting Christian influence, and dedicated Christian thought characterize virtually all of the high moments in the history of the church. On the other side of the picture, the history of the church contains a number of sobering examples of what happens when a spirituality develops with no place for self-conscious thought. The path to danger is not always the same,

25. Ryken, *Worldly Saints*, is especially helpful on such matters.
26. The "lessons" considered in this section are explored at greater length in Mark A. Noll, "Christian World Views and Some Lessons of History," in *The Making of a Christian Mind: A Christian World View and the Academic Enterprise*, ed. Arthur Holmes (Downers Grove, IL: InterVarsity Press, 1985).

but the results of neglecting the mind are uniform: Christian faith degenerates, lapses into gross error, or simply passes out of existence.

In the history of the church, Christian movements of long-lasting significance regularly have involved thinking at the most serious and most comprehensive levels. To be sure, such movements almost never arise because of intellectual efforts as such. Much more often they come into existence out of deep inner responses to God's grace. Yet as such movements develop, they show great concern for the way in which Christians view the world at large. They are vitally interested in the Christian mind.

We have seen that this was the case in the Reformation. It was also true for the monastic movements of the Middle Ages, which were (it is only a slight exaggeration to say) responsible for almost everything of lasting Christian value from roughly A.D. 350 to 1400.[27] The great pulses of monastic reform — whether Benedict in the sixth century, the monks at Cluny in the tenth century, or the Dominicans and Franciscans in the thirteenth century — all had certain things in common. They all encouraged serious contemplation of God, acknowledged the desperateness of the human condition apart from God, and turned people inward to meditate on Scripture and to ponder the mercies of Christ. They all encouraged heroic missionary efforts and practical aid for the downtrodden. And they all promoted serious learning as an offering to the Lord.

The intellectual activity of the monks during the so-called Dark Ages is justly famous. When the light of learning flickered low in Europe, monks preserved the precious texts of Scripture and other Christian writings. Monks kept alive an interest in the languages. Monks and friars founded schools that eventually became the great universities of Europe. Monks, in short, preserved the life of the mind when almost no one else was giving it a thought. By so doing, by God's grace, they preserved the church.

The culmination of intellectual activity among the monks was the work of Thomas Aquinas (ca. 1225–74).[28] Aquinas was a Dominican

---

27. For orientation, see Christopher Dawson, *The Formation of Christendom* (New York: Sheed & Ward, 1967), chap. 11, "The Foundation of Europe: The Monks of the West"; and David Knowles, *The Evolution of Medieval Thought* (New York: Random House, 1962).

28. See Ralph M. McInerny, *St. Thomas Aquinas* (Boston: G. K. Hall, 1977);

friar who composed hymns, wrote biblical commentaries, preached, prepared manuals for missionary work among the Muslims, spent long hours in contemplating the work of Christ, and almost single-handedly reconstructed systematic Christian thinking. His most notable achievement was to adopt for Christian faith the teaching of Aristotle, newly rediscovered in Europe and widely considered to be the best possible guide for understanding the world. In all this, Thomas devoted rigorous intellectual efforts, as G. K. Chesterton once put it, to "the praise of Life, the praise of Being, the praise of God as the Creator of the World."[29]

The work of Aquinas and like-minded friars left an extremely important legacy. He provided a model for reconciling the knowledge we gain through the senses with the truths we discover in Scripture. He proposed a theoretical explanation for some of the mysteries of the faith like the Lord's Supper. And he offered a model for apologetics that respected both the intellect of non-Christians and the missionary mandate for believers. In an age where the thought forms of Aristotle had come to dominate learned discourse, Aquinas taught Aristotle to "speak like a Christian" and so preserved the conceptual power of Christian faith.

Thomas Aquinas did not provide the last word on any of these matters. Luther and Calvin, for example, felt that he had overemphasized what we learn about God from nature at the expense of what we learn from Scripture. Yet what Thomas did provide was a formulation of the faith that has encouraged generations of believers to labor with their minds for the glory of God. In so doing, he left an intellectual perspective that has helped sustain the wider Christian church to this very day.

Medieval monasticism along with the Protestant Reformation has been among the most influential movements in the history of the church. One of the reasons is that each cultivated the life of the mind. Each sought to develop specifically Christian thinking on the whole

---

and Etienne Gilson, *The Christian Philosophy of St. Thomas Aquinas* (New York: Random House, 1956).

29. G. K. Chesterton, *Saint Thomas Aquinas* (Garden City, NY: Doubleday, 1956), 105.

range of human experience. It is possible to make legitimate criticisms of both monasticism and the Reformation. Yet the positive lessons they teach are more important. These lessons concern Christian faithfulness, immersion in Scripture, zeal in spreading the gospel, and commitment to holistic Christian service. But perhaps the most important lesson concerns the Christianization of thinking, the elaboration of a Christian mind. That is one of the major reasons why both movements still speak powerfully to believers today who pray for the renewal of their minds in Christ.

If the history of Christianity shows how fruitful it can be to cultivate the mind for Christ, it also indicates how dangerous it can be to neglect such activity. A word or caution is in order at this point. To follow either intellectuals who criticize simple piety or advocates of Christian experience who attack the life of the mind leads to difficulty. The gospel properly calls the whole person. In keeping with the Bible's teaching concerning the various tasks given to different parts of the body, we may naturally expect Christians in different times and places to stress some things rather than others. The danger comes when the parts of the body, which are to complement each other — in this case, piety and the life of the mind — fall upon each other.

One of the more interesting protest movements of the Middle Ages was mounted by the Albigenses. Their history illustrates how easy it is for Christian groups that undervalue the mind to lapse into the employment of non-Christian thinking. The Albigenses are named for the region in southern France where they flourished in the twelfth and thirteenth centuries. They were a variation of the Cathari, or "Pure Ones," who in the Middle Ages attempted to keep themselves unspotted from the pollutions of the flesh.[30]

Beyond doubt, the Albigenses possessed exemplary traits. In contrast to much official Catholicism, Albigensianism took morality and pastoral care with great seriousness. Albigenses knew the value of following God's law. Their ascetic conduct often shamed less scrupulous church members, and so they were respected by the common people

30. Steven Runciman, *The Medieval Manichee* (Cambridge: Cambridge University Press, 1947).

of southern France for nearly two hundred years. In the thirteenth century, internal crusades and an inquisition destroyed the movement.

For our purposes the Albigenses are significant because they made it a principle to slight formal intellectual labor. Above all else they were moralists. The one thing that mattered was to live without fault. From the perspective of the late twentieth century, this aspiration seems entirely admirable, until we realize how thoroughly the Albigensian commitment to morality excluded cultivation of the mind. There was no interest in formal thought, even if there had been time. To devote attention to formal learning was to waste effort that was required for cultivating the ascetic life.

This abandonment of the mind, however, encouraged a slide toward the ancient heresy of Manichaeism. This set of convictions, which had existed in various forms since the classical period, was dualistic; it made a sharp distinction between the life of the spirit and the life of the body. To the Albigenses matter itself was suspect. Redemption meant freeing the spirit from the body. With these beliefs the Albigenses were forced to interpret Scripture allegorically. Old Testament prophets could not have meant it literally when they urged the faithful to establish justice in Israel; Christ could never have taken on an actual body of flesh; the kingdom of God must be an utterly ethereal thing, not something that begins in the day-to-day life of each believer during this age. Given the precommitments of the Manichaean worldview, Albigenses found it necessary to twist the Scriptures. For the words and concepts of the Bible they retained a great affection. But because they had adopted a worldview opposed to that of the prophets, apostles, and Jesus himself, they were forced to reinterpret biblical words and ideas in order to harmonize them with their underlying worldview. The result was a group that did teach the church some valuable lessons about ethical seriousness. But it was also a group that, because it rejected in principle the cultivation of the mind, found itself trapped by a worldview alien to the gospel.

The pietistic movements of the seventeenth and eighteenth centuries also illustrate the perils involved in not treating the mind as a Christian resource. In general, Pietism was a very good thing, for it breathed a badly needed vitality into several parts of the church, including Protestants in Germany, Holland, England, and America, as well as their Catholic counterparts in France and other parts of southern Europe.[31] But Pietism could also be carried to a dangerous extreme.

The thrust of Pietism was to draw believers back from formal, dogmatic rigidity toward living Christian experience. This was a timely appeal, for much calcification had taken place in the churches since the cleansing experiences of the Reformation and Counter-Reformation. Many valuable things came from the Pietists, especially from the remarkably energetic work of Philipp Jakob Spener, August Hermann Francke, and the numerous institutions they established at Halle near Berlin. German Pietists inaugurated the first widespread missionary efforts among Protestants. Pietists generally encouraged renewed seriousness about the priesthood of believers, they turned laypeople back to eager study of the Bible, and they encouraged many acts of social compassion.

The intellectual problem of Pietism lay in its excesses. Pietists had rediscovered the truth that Christianity is a life as well as a set of beliefs. The difficulty arose when some Pietists began to view Christian faith as only a life, without a concern for beliefs at all. This led to fascination with practice, deep involvement in spiritual experience, and absorption in the psychological dimensions of the faith. Objective realities of revelation were sometimes almost totally eclipsed. In the late eighteenth century, Immanuel Kant, who had been trained by Pietists, gave weighty support to the idea that God could not act in the world in ways unknown to human experience.[32] In the early nineteenth century, certain Christian teachers trained by Pietists, of whom Friedrich Schleiermacher was the most famous, began to urge that "a feeling of dependence" was the foundation of Christianity. Always the church had had a place for Christian experience, but in living communion

---

31. For excellent studies, see F. Ernest Stoeffler, *The Rise of Evangelical Pietism* (Leiden: E. J. Brill, 1965); Stoeffler, *German Pietism during the Eighteenth Century* (Leiden: E. J. Brill, 1973); Stoeffler, ed., *Continental Pietism and Early American Christianity* (Grand Rapids: Eerdmans, 1976); and W. R. Ward, *The Protestant Evangelical Awakening* (Cambridge: Cambridge University Press, 1992).

32. See Franklin L. Baumer, *Modern European Thought: Continuity and Change in Ideas, 1600–1950* (New York: Macmillan, 1977), with special attention to sections on Romanticism and the general discussion of Immanuel Kant and F. E. D. Schleiermacher.

with the objective character of the gospel. Pietists quite properly protested when this objectivity came to be regarded as the sum and substance of the faith. But some overreacted by picturing the *experience* of the faith as the new totality.

At its extreme, the Pietist emphasis on religious life gave very little attention to self-conscious Christian thought. To be consumed by feeling was to have no time for thinking through the relationship between God and his creation. Once this point had been reached, it soon became difficult to distinguish between those forms of feeling that remained within the Christian orbit and those that had spun off as meteorites with no fixed center. Pietism played an important role in the revitalization of the church in the seventeenth and eighteenth centuries. Unchecked Pietism, however, played a role in the development of theological liberalism with liberalism's fascination for the forms of religious experience. It played a part in developing the humanistic romanticism of the nineteenth and twentieth centuries, where a vague nature mysticism replaced a more orthodox understanding of God and the world. And for more orthodox believers, Pietism sometimes led to a morbid fixation upon the Christian's personal state at the expense of evangelism, study, or social outreach.

The Pietism that degenerated to these extremes teaches modern believers a complex lesson. Pietism contributes something essential to Christianity. A problem arises, however, when a necessary means of renewal becomes the sum of the faith, when a part of more general Christian life dominates the whole. The Pietist attack on self-conscious Christian thinking was the cause of special difficulty. It meant the weakening of the faith toward sentimentality, its captivity by alien philosophies, or its decline to dangerous modernisms. The proper response to such an episode in church history is not to deny the need for piety but to draw the Pietists' corrective into a larger framework shaped by a fuller Christian appreciation for the life of the mind.

Truth and Intellectual Heresy

As much as practical considerations or the bearing of historical arguments might justify Christian support of the intellectual life, in the

YELLOW — NATURE MYSTICISM

RED — NATURE MECHANISM

end the study of nature, society, and humanity is justified primarily for nonutilitarian reasons. It is the nature of God and his loving work, not primarily the practical benefits, that requires cultivation of the mind.

For a Christian, the most important consideration is not pragmatic results, or even the weight of history, but the truth. Learning matters because the world matters — the world both as material object and as the accumulated network of human institutions. For a Christian, the most important reason for exercising the life of the mind is the implicit acknowledgment that things do not exist on their own. This acknowledgment is a specifically Christian presupposition; its denial characterizes much of the scholarship that shapes our lives so decisively. When we study something, we are of course learning about that thing. But even more, we are learning about the One who made that thing.

Ironically, some the clearest expressions of this reality came from an American evangelical, Jonathan Edwards, whose intellectual legacy, as we will see in the next chapter, was abandoned by later American evangelicals. When he was still in his teens, the young Jonathan Edwards wrote down an extensive description of the shape, construction, and purpose of a spider's web. There are many true things we can say about the physical character of the web, but according to Edwards, the ultimate thing shown by the spider in its spinning is "the exuberant goodness of the Creator, who hath not only provided for all the necessities, but also for the pleasure and recreation of all sorts of creatures, even the insects."[33] When he was older, Edwards put the matter more formally. True knowledge was not, in the last analysis, an abstract correspondence of our thinking with reality. True knowledge was rather "the consistency and agreement of our ideas with the ideas of God."[34] The implications of this conviction for studying the world were equally clear. Because it is God who created the things that people studied and who made it possible for humans to understand something of the world, Edwards held that "all the arts and sciences, the more they are perfected, the more they issue in divinity, and coincide with it, and appear to be

33. Jonathan Edwards, "Of Insects" (ca. 1723), in *The Works of Jonathan Edwards: Scientific and Philosophical Writings,* ed. Wallace E. Anderson (New Haven: Yale University Press, 1980), 158.

34. Jonathan Edwards, "Notes on the Mind," in ibid., 341–42.

as parts of it."[35] In a word, Edwards understood that the final reason for exercising our intelligence is to know more of God and his loving ways with the world.

For a Christian, the mind is important because God is important. Who, after all, made the world of nature, and then made possible the development of sciences through which we find out more about nature? Who formed the universe of human interactions, and so provided the raw material of politics, economics, sociology, and history? Who is the source of harmony, form, and narrative pattern, and so lies behind all artistic and literary possibilities? Who created the human mind in such a way that it could grasp the realities of nature, of human interactions, of beauty, and so made possible the theories on such matters by philosophers and psychologists? Who, moment by moment, sustains the natural world, the world of human interactions, and the harmonies of existence? Who, moment by moment, maintains the connections between what is in our minds and what is in the world beyond our minds? The answer in every case is the same. God did it, and God does it.

It is of small consequence — or none — that evangelicals have no research university, or that they have no Nobel laureates. It is of immense significance that evangelicals are not doing the kind of work for which research universities exist and which is recognized by Nobel Prizes. Why? Because the great institutions of higher learning in Western culture function as the *mind* of Western culture. They define what is important, they specify procedures to be respected, they set agendas for analyzing the practical problems of the world, they provide vocabulary for dealing with the perennial Great Issues, they produce the books that get read and that over decades continue to influence thinking around the world — and they do these tasks not only for the people who are aware of their existence but for us all.

Evangelicals who think that the basic intellectual operations performed by the modern research universities can be conceded to "the world" without doing fundamental damage to the cause of Christ may think of themselves as orthodox Christians. In reality, however, they are modern-day Manichaeans, gnostics, or docetists.

---

35. Jonathan Edwards, "Outline of 'A Rational Account,'" in ibid., 397.

Manichaeism

As we have seen, Manichaeans divided the world into two radically disjointed sections — the children of light and the children of darkness. Evangelicals have often promoted a Manichaean attitude by assuming that we, and only we, have the truth, while nonbelievers, or Christian believers who are not evangelicals, practice only error. The Bible, however, shows the fallacy of such assumptions. The children of Israel readily put to use such human enterprises as music, husbandry, and the crafting of precious metals, even though Genesis 4 records that these enterprises were first developed by the descendants of Cain. In the New Testament, the apostle Paul showed the same willingness to employ the wisdom of the world when, as recorded in Acts 17, he quoted selectively from Greek philosophers in order to present Christianity to the Athenians. These biblical precedents suggest to modern evangelicals that heeding instruction from broader intellectual worlds would pay great rewards, as long as that attention is critical, selective, and discerning.

Gnosticism

Gnosticism refers to a whole range of mystical religions that were practiced widely in the Mediterranean world shortly after the time of Christ. Gnostics differed dramatically among themselves in their beliefs and practices, but they held in common a fear of matter as inherently evil and a tendency toward ethical extremism (either ardent asceticism or wanton licentiousness). They were called Gnostics (= people of special knowledge) because they practiced secret rituals where the supposedly most important knowledge about God and the world was passed along in esoteric formulas from adept to initiate. Evangelicals display a gnostic strand when we treat the Bible as if it were an esoteric code to be deciphered as a way of obtaining privileged information about the creation of the natural world, the disposition of historical events, or the unfolding of the future. This tendency, unfortunately, leads evangelicals to shortchange the Bible, as well as the serious study of nature, history, or the more general world of human affairs.

The Bible points to a better way by repeating without equivoca-

tion that followers of the one true God are to find out about the world
that God has made by looking at the world, and not by prying specific
information from the Scriptures. The psalmist declared that the heavens
and the skies "day after day . . . pour forth speech; night after night
they display knowledge. . . . Their voice goes out into all the earth,
their words to the ends of the world" (Ps. 19:2, 4). But this is a speech
that must be listened to if it is to be heard. Against the tendency present
in the New Testament church to "follow deceiving spirits and things
taught by demons," which led mistaken teachers to prohibit marriage
and the eating of certain foods, the apostle reminded the church that
God had made marriage and eating (and, by implication, the whole
realm of nature) "to be received with thanksgiving by those who believe
and who know the truth." He went on with an even more expansive
observation: "For everything God created is good, and nothing is to be
rejected if it is received with thanksgiving, because it is consecrated
by the word of God and prayer" (1 Tim. 4:1–5).[36]

The Bible will always provide the deepest and most far-reaching
orientation for carrying on the life of the mind. But proper examination
of the world is required in conjunction with proper use of the Bible in
order to understand the world as God ordained that it should be
understood. Nowhere has the potential harmony of that conjunction
been better described than in the Belgic Confession (1561), one of the
early formulations of Christian belief for European Protestants, in
which the older idea of God's "two books" is adapted for a Protestant
audience:

> We know [God] by two means: first, by the creation, preservation,
> and government of the universe, which is before our eyes as a most
> elegant book, wherein all creatures, great and small, are as so many
> characters, leading us to contemplate the invisible things of God,
> namely, his eternal power and Godhead, as the Apostle Paul saith

36. Among other intriguing passages suggesting the importance of the natural
realm are Genesis 2:4–25 (where God provides unfallen humanity with intellectual
tasks such as naming the animals as well as with responsibilities in agricultural,
domestic, economic, and religious spheres) and Exodus 31:1–11 (where the men
charged with building and equipping the Tent of Meeting receive God's Spirit to carry
out these tasks).

(Rom. 1:20). All which things are sufficient to convince men, and leave them without excuse. Secondly, he makes himself more clearly and fully known to us by his holy and divine Word; that is to say, as far as is necessary for us to know in this life, to his glory and our salvation.[37]

In order to understand what is in the "second book" that comes so graciously to us from God, we must open it up, and we must read it.

Docetism

Docetism was an ancient heresy that carried Gnostic themes into the Christian church. The specific error of Docetists was to believe that, since the material world by its nature was hopelessly polluted, Jesus only "seemed" (= *dokeō* in Greek) to have a real body, to suffer hunger and thirst, to touch the sick, and to suffer as a human being on the cross. Evangelicals indulge a docetic tendency when we think, without qualification, that since "this world is not my home," it is of no importance to learn about the world, the structures of human society, and the potential of human creativity. It is similarly docetic to treat day-to-day existence as if it were only apparently real, as if it were simply a mask for the eternal, unchanging realities of an unseen spiritual world. But these attitudes betray a fundamental misunderstanding of the very heart of Christianity, especially of how "the Word became flesh and made his dwelling among us" in order that we might perceive "his glory, the glory of the One and Only, who came from the Father, full of grace and truth" (John 1:14). Christianity is a religion that takes bodily existence with utter seriousness. With unbelief in his voice, Paul asked the Corinthians, "Do you not know that your bodies are members of Christ himself?" (1 Cor. 6:15). This is a religion that should stimulate, rather than retard, intense investigation into the realm inhabited by our physical bodies.

37. *Belgic Confession*, article 2; this translation, *Reformed Standards of Unity*, 2d ed. (Grand Rapids: Rose, 1952), 57–58. For general treatment of the "two books" idea, see James R. Moore, "Geologists and Interpretation of Genesis in the Nineteenth Century," in *God and Nature*, ed. David C. Lindberg and Ronald L. Numbers (Berkeley: University of California Press, 1986), 322–25.

The distinguished historian of the early church J. N. D. Kelly, speaking generally of the Gnostic invasion of Christianity, summarized aptly the deepest danger of the docetic tendency: "Because in general they disparaged matter and were disinterested in history, the Gnostics (in the narrower, more convenient sense of the term) were prevented from giving full value to the fundamental Christian doctrine of the incarnation of the Word."[38] It is the Word of God who became flesh that encourages Bible-believing evangelicals to look seriously at the realm of the flesh, for to learn about that realm is to learn about the sphere of God's fullest manifestation of himself.

Once again, however, the proper qualifications must be stated clearly. Scholarship is not the most important thing in the Christian life. It is self-evident for a religion to which not many are called from the "wise by human standards" (1 Cor. 1:26) that a believer may live and die an exemplary existence without pursuing the questions of a scholar.

But the intellectual life is still important. It is one of the arenas that God has made in which to live out our days. It is a legitimate sphere in which Christians may be active. It is one of the activities carried on in the body of Christ, all of whose members, as the apostle Paul teaches, deserve respect. As such — and no more — the life of the mind deserves the kind of cultivation that evangelicals regularly bestow upon their other business. If evangelicals acknowledge that it is appropriate, as a Christian, to be the best ball player or lawyer or bank executive or auto mechanic or operator of a janitorial service or owner of a retirement home or third-grade teacher that God has made it possible for a person to be, why do evangelicals find it difficult to believe that it is also appropriate, as a Christian, to cultivate the life of the mind as thoroughly as it can be cultivated?

The answer lies in the history of evangelicalism. Evangelicals do not, characteristically, look to the intellectual life as an arena in which to glorify God because, at least in America, our history has been pragmatic, populist, charismatic, and technological more than intellectual. In our past we have much more eagerly leaped to defend the faith than to explore its implications for the intellectual life. We have tended

38. J. N. D. Kelly, *Early Christian Doctrines* (New York: Harper, 1978), 27–28.

to define piety as an inward state opposed to careful thought, rather than as an attitude that might include attention to the mind. Although such tendencies are, by specifically Christian standards, indefensible, there are good historical reasons why American evangelicals have adopted them and so devalued the life of the mind.

PART 2

HOW THE SCANDAL
HAS COME TO PASS

CHAPTER 3

The Evangelical Mind Takes Shape — Revival, Revolution, and a Cultural Synthesis

To repeat, during the Reformation period the major Protestants, especially Luther and Calvin, defended the absolute necessity for higher education against populist anti-intellectual movements that expanded the attack on Roman Catholic dogma into an attack on education in general. During the seventeenth century, the Puritans who helped plant Protestantism in North America were equally insistent upon a comprehensive engagement with learning.

If the evangelical heritage began with the Reformation and then passed through the English Puritans, what happened to it? Why does the characteristic respect for the mind seen both in the sixteenth-century Reformers and in the seventeenth-century Puritans no longer prevail widely among modern evangelicals? The answer is found in our history. In his concise summation of developments for Canada, historian Michael Gauvreau has also described the United States: "The evangelical creed was forged in the transatlantic crucible of revival, revolution, and Enlightenment."[1] As modern American evangelicals, we are, first, the product of revivalism; second, we are the beneficiaries of the American separation of church and state, which, for all its blessings in other respects, did not do as much for the intellect; we are, third, the heirs of a Christian-American cultural synthesis created in the wake of the

1. Michael Gauvreau, *The Evangelical Century* (Montreal and Kingston: McGill-Queen's University Press, 1991), ix.

59

War for Independence; finally, our mental habits are profoundly influenced by the fundamentalist movement at the start of the twentieth century. Each of these influences is ambiguous — each preserved something essential in the Christian faith, but each also undercut the hereditary Protestant conviction that it was a good thing to love the Lord with our minds.

This chapter examines revivalism, the separation of church and state, and the broader cultural synthesis of American and Christian values. These subjects are worthy of full attention in their own right, but attending to them also puts us in a position to understand a genuine conundrum: Jonathan Edwards was the greatest evangelical mind in America in large measure because his thought was driven by the profoundest truths of evangelical Protestantism; yet Edwards also promoted with all his heart as the essence of evangelical Christianity a program that led to the eclipse of the evangelical mind in America.

After looking at the place of Edwards, we turn in the next chapter to examine in somewhat greater detail the evangelical appropriation of the Enlightenment. That examination will shed light on a second conundrum — how it was that the evangelical mind degenerated in America over the same period that evangelical Protestantism became the dominant cultural force in American civilization. Finally, chapter 5 treats the era of fundamentalism in order to observe how a series of innovative theologies rescued essential aspects of historic Christianity but did so at grievous intellectual cost.

Revivalism

Christian churches have always undergone periods of revival, so there is nothing new about the presence in America of revival as such. What was new after about the mid-eighteenth century was the way in which revival loomed as the dominant theme defining the nature and purposes of the church for Americans. On this continent, revivalism became prominent through the experiences of the First Great Awakening in the 1740s and the Second Great Awakening of the early nineteenth century. In the First Awakening lively preaching from the British spellbinder George Whitefield, learned defense of living faith by Jonathan Edwards, and the mobilization of a whole host of ministers and laypeople combined for a remarkable spiritual renewal. This revival was important for many reasons, but for long-standing impact on Christian thinking, two matters were most significant. The first was the way the revival promoted a new style of leadership — direct, personal, popular, and dependent much more on a speaker's ability to draw a crowd than upon that speaker's place in an established hierarchy. The second was the way the revival undercut the traditional authority of the churches. Ecclesiastical life remained important, but not nearly as significant as the decision of the individual close to Christ. The combined effects of these two matters originally had nothing to do with the life of the mind per se. The brilliant Jonathan Edwards was the most discriminating defender of the revival. But what they did do was to plant the seeds of individualism and immediatism that would eventually exert a profound effect on Christian thinking.

In many ways, the defining figure in the history of American evangelicalism is the eighteenth-century revivalist George Whitefield. As shown in the splendid recent biography by Harry Stout, Whitefield's style — popular preaching aimed at emotional response — has continued to shape American evangelicalism long after Whitefield's specific theology (he was a Calvinist), his denominational origins (he was an Anglican), and his rank (he was a clergyman) are long since forgotten.[2] Daniel Pals has well summarized Whitefield's career: "The very thing that . . . accounts for his success [was] a deeply populist frame of mind. Almost every one of Whitefield's sermons is marked by a fundamentally democratic determination to simplify the essentials of religion in a way that gives them the widest possible mass appeal."[3]

As it was in the days of Whitefield, so it has been in the two centuries since. The most visible evangelicals, with the broadest popular influence, have been public speakers whose influence rested on their ability to communicate a simple message to a broad audience. So it was in the nineteenth century in the era of Charles Finney and D. L.

2. Harry S. Stout, *The Divine Dramatist: George Whitefield and the Rise of Modern Evangelicalism* (Grand Rapids: Eerdmans, 1991).
3. Daniel L. Pals, "Several Christologies of the Great Awakening," *Anglican Theological Review* 72 (1990): 426.

Moody; so it has been in our own century of Billy Sunday and Billy Graham, Oral Roberts and Kenneth Copeland, Jimmy Swaggart and Jerry Falwell, John Stott and Martyn Lloyd-Jones.

The benefits of such self-definition are not insignificant. A religion defined by revivalists keeps the question of personal salvation uppermost. It is not prone to write off marginalized races or the poor as unimportant. And it is alert to the power of God. But if there are advantages to anti-institutional moralism, populist intuition, and democratic biblicism, there are grave weaknesses as well.

The way in which evangelicalism in America came to be defined by populist revivalism yielded one very important benefit. In sharp contrast to religious developments in western Europe, American evangelicals continued to make their messages heard in a society increasingly defined by the norms of democratic individualism. But for the life of the mind, there would be problems. The American experience might lead to the conclusion that, if one desires a Christian mind, then one must avoid revivals. If there are no revivals, however, there will be not many Christians around at all.

The impetus given by the colonial awakening to individualism and immediatism was accelerated by the revivals early in the new United States that are known collectively as the Second Great Awakening.[4] Inspired by doughty frontier preachers like James McGready and W. Barton Stone as well as respectable ministers from the eastern seaboard like the president of Yale, Timothy Dwight, the Second Great Awakening was the means by which a largely pagan America was evangelized. The passage of time from the 1740s to the early 1800s had witnessed a further loosening of institutional bonds and had further undercut the deference to tradition. Denominations like the Congregationalists, which relied upon their hereditary leadership of established society, had a greatly reduced impact on the early republic. Those like the Methodists and the Baptists, which exploited innovative revival techniques to carry the gospel to the people, flourished.

4. There is no satisfactory general study of the revivals lumped together as the Second Awakening. For good regional accounts, see Terry D. Bilhartz, *Urban Religion and the Second Great Awakening* (Rutherford, NJ: Fairleigh Dickinson University Press, 1986); and John B. Boles, *The Great Revival, 1787–1805: The Origins of the Southern Evangelical Mind* (Lexington: University Press of Kentucky, 1972).

The conversion of the population in the early United States by Methodists, Baptists, and like-minded innovators is one of the great stories in American Christian history. In 1790 something like only 10 percent of Americans professed membership in a Christian church. By the time of the Civil War, the proportion had multiplied several times. The active labors of the revivalists was the reason why.[5]

The problem with revivalism for the life of the mind, however, lay precisely in its antitraditionalism. Revivals called people to Christ as a way of escaping tradition, including traditional learning. They called upon individuals to take the step of faith for themselves. In so doing, they often left the impression that individual believers could accept nothing from others. Everything of value in the Christian life had to come from the individual's own choice — not just personal faith but every scrap of wisdom, understanding, and conviction about the faith. This dismissal of tradition was no better illustrated than in a memorable comment by two Kentucky revivalists early in the nineteenth century. When quotations from Calvin were used to argue against Robert Marshall and J. Thompson, they replied, "We are not personally acquainted with the writings of John Calvin, nor are we certain how nearly we agree with his views of divine truth; neither do we care."[6]

Revivalists, moreover, regularly challenged their hearers to seize the faith immediately. They insisted that what had gone on in the churches through the centuries was irrelevant to what must be done with respect to the faith *now*. Charles Grandison Finney, one of the most effective of nineteenth-century revivalists, put it sharply in describing the best form of conversion: "where a sinner is brought to see what he has to do, and he takes his stand at once, AND DOES IT."[7]

Revival does not necessarily have to be promoted in exactly these forms, but in antebellum America it was. The form of revivalism that

5. A recent, controversial account of this process is provided by Roger Finke and Rodney Stark, *The Churching of America, 1776–1990: Winners and Losers in Our Religious Economy* (New Brunswick, NJ: Rutgers University Press, 1992).

6. Quoted in Nathan O. Hatch, *The Democratization of American Christianity* (New Haven: Yale University Press, 1989), 174.

7. *Lectures on Revivals of Religion,* ed. William G. McLoughlin (Cambridge: Harvard University Press, 1960; orig. 1835), 380 (the capitalization is Finney's).

eventually came to prevail as the dominant mode of evangelical church life was activistic, immediatistic, and individualistic. As such, it was able to mobilize great numbers for the cause of Christ. But also as such — with its scorn for tradition, its concentration on individual competence, its distrust of mediated knowledge — American revivalism did much to hamstring the life of the mind.

The Separation of Church and State

By the early nineteenth century, American evangelicals were distinct not just because they promoted revival. They were distinct also because they enjoyed an unprecedented degree of religious freedom. This religious freedom, formalized in the separation of church and state, created the framework in which revivalists did their work in the early nation.[8] Although it was on balance a very good thing for the churches to be free of government, their very freedom from an establishment had an ironic result for Christian thinking.

The First Amendment to the United States Constitution, with its provision that "Congress shall make no law respecting an establishment of religion, or prohibiting the free exercise thereof," took effect in 1791. This provision would have a dramatic impact on the country's religious life, even though at the time there was, by modern standards, a great deal of intermingling between church and state. In 1791, five of the nation's fourteen states (Vermont had joined the Union in 1791) provided for tax support of ministers, and those five plus seven others had continued religious tests for state office. Only Virginia and Rhode Island enjoyed the sort of "separation of church and state" that Americans now take for granted, that is, where government provides no tax money for churches and poses no religious conditions for participation in public life. With scarcely a handful of exceptions, even the defenders of religious liberty in Rhode Island and Virginia did not object when Congress or the president proclaimed national days of prayer, when the

8. For the general story, see Thomas J. Curry, *The First Freedoms: Church and State in America to the Passage of the First Amendment* (New York: Oxford University Press, 1986).

federal government began its meetings with prayer, or when military chaplains were appointed and funded by law.

At the same time, the new nation was making an unprecedented move in the direction of disestablishment, of ending the formal ties between church and state. As part of the era's great fears about the potential for governmental tyranny, more and more Americans were affirming that religion was a matter of conscience between God and the individual and should be exempt from the meddling of government at any level. A growing number were also speaking out about the spiritual reasons demanding separation between church and state. Such a one was the leader of New England's Baptists, Isaac Backus (1724–1806). During the Revolution, which he supported, Backus asked Massachusetts and Connecticut why they maintained establishments of religion that forced Baptists and other non-Congregationalists to support forms of Christianity that these others conscientiously opposed. If the colonists were fighting Britain for liberty, Backus asked, why do the colonies themselves not grant religious liberty to their own residents?[9]

More practically, the possibility of establishing a national government seemed increasingly to hinge on leaving religious matters with the states. At both the Constitutional Convention and the first Congress, which was responsible for the First Amendment, leaders like James Madison realized that the question of religion was both explosive and complicated. Any effort to establish one particular faith would have drawn violent protests from adherents of other denominations. Yet any effort to deny the importance of religion would have deeply offended the substantial numbers who still believed that the health of a nation depended upon the health of its faith. The compromise chosen by the Founding Fathers was to avoid the issue. If they were going to have a Constitution for all of the people, they somehow were going to have to get the government out of the religion business. By leaving such matters to the states, it was hoped, they could establish a government for the nation without being forced to decide what the nation's religion should be.

9. *Isaac Backus on Church, State, and Calvinism: Pamphlets, 1754–1789,* ed. William G. McLoughlin (Cambridge: Harvard University Press, 1968).

The result was what sociologist Roger Finke has recently called "religious deregulation." The national government refused to support any particular denomination. The consequences for the churches were immense. They were now compelled to *compete* for adherents, rather than being assigned responsibility for parishioners as had been the almost universal European pattern. The denominations had to appeal directly to individuals. They had to convince individuals, first, that they should pay attention to God and, second, that they should do so in *their* churches and not elsewhere. The primary way the churches accomplished this task was through the techniques of revival — direct, fervent address aimed at convincing, convicting, and enlisting the individual. As Finke describes it, this process led to "a religious market that caters to the individual and makes religion an individual decision. Though religion is still a group phenomenon, which relies on the support, control and rewards of the local church, the open market stresses *personal* conversion and faith. Once again, the religious decision is an individual decision set in the context of a religious market with a wide array of diversity — a diversity that is assured by the diversity of the population and the lack of religious regulation."[10]

This combination of revivalism and disestablishment had effects whose importance cannot be exaggerated. Analyzed positively, the combination gave the American churches a new dynamism, a new effectiveness in fulfilling the Great Commission, and a new vitality in bringing the gospel to the people. Analyzed negatively, the combination of revivalism and disestablishment meant that pragmatic concerns would prevail over principle. What the churches required were results — new adherents — or they would simply go out of business. Thus, the production of results had to override all other considerations.

The combination of revivalism and disestablishment also predisposed believers to utilitarian apologetics, to functional theology. Now they tended to ask, What would most readily promote expansion of the church? What would most forcefully advance the cause of the church in the society?

This was the situation that ultimately created so much difficulty

10. Roger Finke, "Religious Deregulation: Origins and Consequences," *Journal of Church and State* 32 (Summer 1990): 609–25, quotation 625.

for the life of the mind. American evangelicals never doubted that Christianity was the truth. They never doubted that Christian principles should illuminate every part of life. What they did do, however, in the years between the Revolution and the Civil War, was to make most questions of truth into questions of practicality. What message would be most effective? What do people most want to hear? What can we say that will both convert the people and draw them to our particular church? The heavy pressure for results meant that very little time or energy was available to think about God and nature, God and society, God and beauty, or God and the shape of the human mind. In the context of the early United States, with the pragmatic challenge of subduing the wilderness and civilizing a barbarian society — these traditional issues of Christian learning, these matters of primary importance to a Christian mind, became largely irrelevant.

A Christian-Cultural Synthesis

When we turn to look at the content of evangelical thought, we see the same results, but for different reasons. Here the issue was the way that evangelicals exploited the events and the ideas of the new American nation. And here again we deal with a paradox. Evangelicals were successful in the early United States because they successfully adapted their Christian convictions to American ideals. This adaptation did involve remarkable savvy, remarkable displays of what might be called practical intelligence.[11] But at the same time, the formal thought of evangelicals — that is, the consideration of nature, society, history, and the arts — weakened throughout the early history of the United States because evangelicals adapted their Christian convictions uncritically to American ideals.

When in 1835 the Frenchman Alexis de Tocqueville published *Democracy in America,* a book that grew out of a lengthy tour in the states, he expressed the opinion that "there is no country in the world

11. Some of the general benefits and liabilities in this kind of thought are well sketched in Daniel Calhoun, *The Intelligence of a People* (Princeton: Princeton University Press, 1973).

where the Christian religion retains a greater influence over the souls of men than in America." (CMS, 7.9) Tocqueville was struck, however, not just by the simple fact of Christianity in the United States but by its character. "In France," he wrote, "I had almost always seen the spirit of religion and the spirit of freedom marching in opposite directions. But in America I found they were intimately united and that they reigned in common over the same country."[12]

Tocqueville put his finger on the essential matter. Unlike Europe — where Christian communities were often aristocratic, elitist, and traditional, and where the churches were increasingly alienated from the common people — in America, Christian churches were populist, democratic, and libertarian, and the churches were strongly identified with the common people.

The process by which evangelicals identified so thoroughly and, from one angle of vision, so successfully with American ideals is an involved one. But for the sake of simplicity we can speak about four dimensions: the way that evangelicals (1) adopted republican theories of politics, (2) took as their own democratic theories of society, (3) embraced liberal views of the economy (all discussed in this chapter), and (4) domesticated the Enlightenment for Christian purposes (examined in somewhat greater detail in the next chapter). In each of these areas a common procedure was at work. Evangelicals adopted concepts from American culture at large in order to evangelize or reform their culture more effectively. In each case that process of adoption was successful insofar as Christians, speaking the language of their culture, were able to present the gospel in such a way as to see individuals converted and to see changes in society. But in each case there was also a cost. Christian thinking, adapted so thoroughly to the norms of antebellum America, was neither as sound nor as durable as it appeared to be in the heyday of American evangelical culture.[13]

12. Alexis de Tocqueville, *Democracy in America*, ed. Thomas Bender (New York: Modern Library, 1981), 182, 185.

13. A profound meditation on the costs of such adaptation in the recent past is David F. Wells, *No Place for Truth; or, Whatever Happened to Evangelical Theology?* (Grand Rapids: Eerdmans, 1993).

A Republican Theory of Politics

Two crises dominated the political history of this era. The first was a crisis of the British Empire and was resolved by the American Revolution. The second was a crisis of government in the new United States and was resolved by the delegates who convened in Philadelphia during the summer of 1787 to write the Constitution. Both crises represented an effort by Americans to preserve the virtues of *republican* government.[14]

Christians and the Christian faith had played a substantial, if ambiguous, role in the shaping of republicanism, and American evangelicals continued to embrace republican thought as their own in the early period of the United States. In simple terms, republicanism was the concept of a commonwealth emphasizing the well-being of its people. In its many varieties, republicanism embraced the conviction that power defined the political process and that unchecked power led to corruption, even as corruption fostered unchecked power. Furthermore, the arbitrary exercise of unchecked power must by its very nature result in the demise of liberty, law, and natural rights. The United States' early republicans, therefore, tended to favor separation of power rather than its concentration. They usually held that a good government must mix elements of popular influence, aristocratic tradition, and executive authority, rather than be simply democratic, simply aristocratic, or simply monarchical.

Christians contributed their fair share to the formation of republicanism, though that process involved numerous individuals and groups over a long period of time. The Puritans who supported Oliver Cromwell or the Scottish Calvinists who agitated for the independence of their Presbyterian Kirk linked republican values with Scripture. They felt that republicanism represented a political recognition of the Bible's realistic teaching about human sinfulness and the ongoing struggle between Christ (who promoted true liberty) and Satan (who defined the worst possible tyranny). Others who contributed to the rise of

14. The material in this section receives fuller treatment in Mark A. Noll, *One Nation under God? Christian Faith and Political Action in America* (San Francisco: Harper & Row, 1988).

republicanism, however, were deists or agnostics. These included some of Britain's "real whigs" (opponents of the court party) of the early eighteenth century who had given up traditional Christian faith for a religion of nature with no place for miracles, the Incarnation, or special revelation.

Republicanism was critical for the bond between religion and politics in the Revolutionary era because the beliefs of American Christians paralleled republican principles in many particulars. This in turn led to the widespread assumption that republican principles expressed Christian values and that they could be defended with Christian fervor.

Together, the republican and the Puritan traditions shared many formal similarities. In the first place, each held to a view of human nature that recognized the human capacity for evil as well as for good. Puritans dwelt at length on the natural tendency toward evil that arose as a consequence of Adam's fall. Republicans dwelt at length on the natural tendency to abuse official power as a consequence of the corrupting nature of power itself.

Puritans and republicans also defined virtue, freedom, and social well-being in very similar terms. Both saw virtue primarily as a negative quality: Puritans as the absence of sin, republicans as the absence of corrupt and arbitrary power. Puritans looked on freedom as liberation from sin, republicans as liberation from tyranny. The Puritans defined a good society as one in which sin was vanquished and in which people stood vigilantly on guard against its reappearance. Similarly, republicans defined a good society as one in which political freedom from tyranny was preserved and in which citizens resolutely resisted any tendencies toward the corruption of power.

With similar views on virtue, freedom, and social well-being, it is not surprising that republican and Christian points of view began to merge during the Revolution, especially since a general Puritan influence remained strong in America. It was only a small step, for example, to expand concern for the glorious liberty of the children of God into concern for the glorious freedoms imperiled by Parliament.

Republicans and the heirs of the Puritans also shared a common view of history. Both regarded the record of the past as a cosmic struggle between good and evil. To American Christians good and evil were represented by Christ and Antichrist; to republicans, by liberty and tyranny. Both republicans and Puritans longed for a new age in which righteousness and freedom would flourish. Both hoped that the Revolution would play a role in bringing such a golden age to pass.

A lively tradition of millennialism also helped to forge a link between political freedom and Christian liberty. Speculation of this sort encouraged the notion that the great conflict between God and Satan was somehow being played out in the struggle with Britain, and that a victory over Parliament might signal the near approach of God's rule on earth, the millennium.

Republican and Christian points of view began to grow closer together after the French and Indian Wars (1756–63) as Britain and the Church of England replaced France and Roman Catholicism as the great terrors in colonial eyes. For many Americans, republican and Christian perspectives soon became almost indistinguishable as the crisis with the British Parliament grew more intense.

New England preachers had long stressed the special relationship between God and that region. As war approached, many of them cast the conflict with Great Britain in cosmic terms. God had called his people to religious and political freedom in the New World; certainly he would now sustain them as they fought off the tyrannical grasp of Parliament. New England was the scene of the sharpest early tensions with Britain, Boston patriots led in resisting parliamentary efforts to sustain a tax on tea (the Boston Tea Party), and the first actual battles of the war took place in Massachusetts (Lexington and Concord, Bunker Hill). It was thus of great significance for the whole American effort against Great Britain that a long New England tradition had perceived God as the Lord of Battles, actively intervening on behalf of "his people."

The long-term effect of evangelical republicanism in America was to short-circuit political analysis. So deeply entwined were republican and Christian themes that there seemed to be no need for reexamining the nature of politics itself. It could simply be assumed that the American way was the Christian way. That assumption is not necessarily baseless.[15] But as long as it functioned as an assumption, that belief

15. The strongest recent arguments for the basic compatibility between American political ideals and the Christian faith have come from Richard John Neuhaus,

was not conducive to the development of a Christian mind. For practical questions, the overwhelming evangelical commitment to this assumption created difficulties for missionary efforts in other political cultures, it made for problems in understanding the role of the United States in the world, and it led to confusion in the treatment of non-Protestants in the United States. Theoretically considered, however, the greatest damage from the assumption that linked Christian faith and republicanism was its very character as an assumption. If the Christian truth about politics was so clear, there was no need to *think* about politics at all.

A Democratic Understanding of Society

The American Revolution stimulated social changes almost as dramatic as the political changes it brought about.[16] As much as the winds of war offered a marvel to the world — an upstart band of provincials defying the greatest power in Western civilization — even more did the libertarian spirit, with its self-evident truths, inalienable rights, and the equal creation of all, harvest a democratic whirlwind at home. Historian Nathan Hatch has succinctly noted that the two generations after 1776 witnessed a "cultural ferment over the meaning of freedom."[17] What was true for America at large was no less true for its Christian churches.

The social changes of the Revolutionary period had much to do with a universal passion for liberty. Restraint — whether political from a corrupt Parliament, ecclesiastical from denominational traditions, or professional from the special prerogatives of lawyer, minister, or physician — was everywhere a cause for resentment. A Presbyterian minister in 1781 put it bluntly: "This is a time in which civil and religious

---

for example, in *The Naked Public Square: Religion and Democracy in America* (Grand Rapids: Eerdmans, 1984).

16. See especially Gordon S. Wood, *The Radicalism of the American Revolution: How Revolution Transformed a Monarchical Society into a Democratic One Unlike Any That Had Ever Existed* (New York: Knopf, 1992).

17. Hatch, *Democratization of American Christianity,* 6. This section depends heavily upon Hatch's work.

liberty is attended to. . . . It is a time in which a spirit of liberty prevails, a time in which the externals of religion may properly be new modeled, if needful, and fixed upon a gospel plan."[18]

One of the things this passion for liberty affected most was Bible reading.[19] Many of the new denominations that sprang to life in America between the War for Independence and the Civil War — Disciples and "Christians" of several varieties, Adventists, Mormons, Cumberland Presbyterians, offshoots of the Methodists, and more — did so in large part because there were so many unfettered interpretations of Scripture. Americans in the early nineteenth century took to an earlier battle cry of the Reformation, "the Bible alone," with a vengeance. The result was a blend of Christian fervor and democratic fragmentation.

Considered positively, this blend brought a Christian message, adapted to the shape of American social realities, to a wide circle of the previously unchurched. Leaders of the Restoration movement, for example, like Barton Stone or Thomas and Alexander Campbell, sought to roll back what they perceived as the corruptions of the centuries in order to restore the purities of primitive Christianity.[20] Their message, however, was a democratic one, thoroughly imbued with the American spirit. Barton Stone wrote as an old man that "from my earliest recollection I drank deeply into the spirit of liberty, and was so warmed by the soul-inspiring draughts, that I could not hear the name of British, or Tories, without feeling a rush of blood through the whole system."[21] When he and his followers broke with the Presbyterians of Kentucky, he called the move their "declaration of independence." For his part, Alexander Campbell, in an effort to encourage the hearts of his "Chris-

18. Jacob Green, *A View of the Christian Church and Church Government* (Chatham, NJ, 1781), 56.

19. See especially Nathan O. Hatch, "*Sola Scriptura* and *Novus Ordo Seclorum*," in *The Bible in America*, ed. Hatch and Mark A. Noll (New York: Oxford University Press, 1982).

20. See Richard T. Hughes and C. Leonard Allen, *Illusions of Innocence: Protestant Primitivism in America, 1630–1875* (Chicago: University of Chicago Press, 1988).

21. The quotations in this paragraph are from Hatch, *Democratization of American Christianity,* 70–71.

tian" followers, would one day write that July 4, 1776, was "a day to be remembered as with the Jewish Passover. . . . This revolution, taken in all its influences, will make men free indeed." The Disciples, Christian Churches, and Churches of Christ founded by these leaders effectively evangelized America because they had translated the Christian message into an indigenous American idiom. Their adjustment of the Christian message to the themes of democratic ideology also characterized many leaders in more traditional groups as well. The revival, for instance, became the dominant religious force in American Protestantism in large part because it was so effective in winning the unaffiliated, but also because it so effectively expressed the country's democratic spirit.

This democratic approach to society was in many respects a good thing. But again, the assumption that Christian faith can be expressed fully and properly only in a democratic setting was not conducive to shaping a Christian mind. Because evangelicals so thoroughly assumed the harmony of Christian faith and democratic America, they did not think comprehensively and foundationally about very real problems. Issues like the nagging political conflict between northern and southern states called out for fresh Christian thinking. Many other questions did too. How would this new land react to the growing numbers of immigrants? Was it a genuinely free country, or a land hospitable only to northern European Protestants? Even before the Civil War, outsiders from Catholic Ireland and from Asia had been made to feel unwelcome in "the land of the free." And this was to say nothing of the black population, whose bondage remained a gross contradiction to the lofty sentiments of the Declaration of Independence. Did American democracy have a place for one if one was black? Content as they were with the democratic assumptions of the United States, evangelicals gave very little *thought* to such matters.

A Liberal View of the Economy

Almost the same thing may be said about economic matters. Increasingly throughout the period before the Civil War, evangelicals came to assume the God-given character of liberal political economy.[22] By "liberal" in the context of the nineteenth century, historians mean the tradition of individualism and market freedom associated with John Locke and especially Adam Smith. (In one of the more interesting linguistic accidents of recent decades, many of the traits now associated with political "conservatives" were mainstays of the "liberal" economics of the nineteenth century.) For American public life after the Constitution, the language of liberalism — emphasizing the freedom of individuals from hierarchical restraint and the formation of community upon the unfettered choices of free individuals joined by contract — became the dominant assumption about proper economic life. The American System, which promoted internal trade through government financing of roads and canals; the rise of market capitalism as the favored means of producing goods and services at home and abroad; and, as historian Gordon Wood puts it, "the scrambling, individualistic, acquisitive society that suddenly emerged in the early nineteenth century"[23] — all bespeak the importance of liberal economic conceptions.

We can see the great importance of these ideas for the churches by noticing how many of the period's salient religious developments bear a formal resemblance to liberal themes.[24] Thus, the revival defined conversion as an unmediated choice made by individuals. The predominant form of action for religious causes was the voluntary society, where individuals joined together of their own free will to influence others toward the good. And the triumph of the believers' church, defined as the sum of its members, whose own choices brought it into existence, also may have benefited from liberal themes in American life.

The point again is not whether evangelicals should have embraced liberal economic practice, for a case can be made for the compatibility between evangelical Christianity and moderate forms of market

22. On the emergence of that economy, see Joyce Appleby, *Capitalism and a New Social Order* (New York: New York University Press, 1984); and Charles G. Sellers, *The Market Revolution: Jacksonian America, 1815–1846* (New York: Oxford University Press, 1991).

23. Gordon S. Wood, "Ideology and the Origins of Liberal America," *William and Mary Quarterly,* 3d ser., 44 (July 1987): 635.

24. Many of these resemblances are highlighted in Stout's biography of Whitefield, *The Divine Dramatist.*

economy. The point is rather *how* evangelicals embraced liberal economic practice. Again this was done without a great deal of thought. But precisely in the antebellum period, before attention was drawn to the economy as a moral problem, was when such thinking was needed. The most important economic questions of the day dealt with the early growth of industrialization. What kinds of obligations did capital and labor owe to each other? How would the growth of large industries, first in textiles and then in railroads, affect community life or provisions for the disabled, aged, and infirm? Each of these questions, and many more like them, posed a potential threat to Christian witness and to public morality. Each of them was also the sort that could be answered only by those who had thought through principles of Scripture, who had struggled to see how the truths of creation, fall, and redemption applied to groups as well as to individuals. Unfortunately, there was very little of such thinking. These problems developed pretty much under their own steam and received little specific attention from Christians wrestling with the foundations of economic thought and practice.

In sum, American evangelicalism arose out of the specific events of early American history. In the United States the religion of pietistic Protestantism took on a new look, especially due to the importance of revival, the freedom provided by the separation of church and state, and the adjustment to powerful political, social, and economic features in the new republic. As we will observe in the next chapter, it also made strategic adjustments to the major intellectual trends of the era. Each of these developments secured the place of evangelicals in America, but each also led to problems for the mind.

At the same time, the early history of evangelicalism in America is notable for the career of Jonathan Edwards, for Edwards was the most powerful intellectual in American evangelical history. Before moving on to study what became of evangelical intellectual life in the course of American history, it is more than appropriate to outline the range and depth of Edwards's intellectual labor, to show how he undertook that work from the most explicitly evangelical convictions, and finally to explore the irony whereby this greatest of evangelical thinkers was left without successors.

Jonathan Edwards: Evangelical Intellectual

Jonathan Edwards (1703–58), as a defender of the Great Awakening, always insisted that a living spirituality was the one indispensable thing. Yet Edwards also realized how vital it was to struggle toward distinctly Christian views of the world. To him there was no antithesis between heartfelt devotion and the most recondite labors of the mind.[25]

Edwards lived through a period of rapidly changing conceptions of the world, God, and humanity. The famous changes in scientific theories were only the most obvious signs of great alterations in general attitudes. By his day, the conventions of the Enlightenment had come to prevail widely on the Continent, in Great Britain, and also in America. In keeping with the spirit of the Enlightenment, almost all thinkers in Edwards's age, Christian or not, had come to assume that the fundamental reality was matter in motion. Almost all had concluded that the pursuit of happiness was the loftiest human goal. Almost all were agreed that the ability to understand the world depended ultimately on the activities of the human mind. From these assumptions, different movements were arising to challenge intellectual traditions, some of them in philosophy, some in science, some in religion, and some in politics.

The intellectual achievement of Jonathan Edwards was his refusal to admit that these assumptions were in fact the starting points of thought. His work was important for his own time and for later Christians precisely because it dealt constantly with ideas at their foundations. Edwards refused to acknowledge that matter in motion was

---

25. Among the best of the surge of outstanding works on Edwards in recent years are Conrad Cherry, *The Theology of Jonathan Edwards,* rev. ed. (Bloomington: Indiana University Press, 1990); Norman Fiering, *Jonathan Edwards's Moral Thought in Its British Context* (Chapel Hill: University of North Carolina Press, 1981); Iain H. Murray, *Jonathan Edwards: A New Biography* (Edinburgh: Banner of Truth, 1987); Nathan O. Hatch and Harry S. Stout, eds., *Jonathan Edwards and the American Experience* (New York: Oxford University Press, 1988); and Sang Hyun Lee, *The Philosophical Theology of Jonathan Edwards* (Princeton: Princeton University Press, 1988). The great Yale edition of Edwards's works, which is now approaching fifteen volumes, is a treasure, both for the learnedly edited texts and for their solid introductions.

the most basic thing in the physical world. He resisted the idea that the pursuit of happiness was the highest purpose of human life. He did not believe that human understanding depended ultimately upon humans. These positions, moreover, rested self-consciously on explicit Christian convictions. God was a more basic reality than matter in motion. The glory of God was a higher goal than human happiness. Human understanding of the world depended upon God's ordaining that the human mind could grasp the nature of things. In a word, for Edwards, God was the source of reality; God was the source of truth; human intellect and the world itself were ever and always dependent on him.

Edwards's beliefs about the world — what we could call his meta-physics, his ethics, and his epistemology — grew from his Christian convictions. He felt that all the world belonged to God, who had brought it into existence originally and who sustained it each moment by his loving providence. Edwards felt, furthermore, that humans were dependent on God's grace for the ability both to be truly virtuous and to understand the world correctly. To be sure, Edwards held that we could learn a great deal about ourselves and our world from those who do not honor God. But this knowledge was always secondary. Only a heart changed by God's grace would properly understand itself, God, the world of nature, and the proper potential of human existence.

The comprehensiveness of Edwards's thought, just as much as his desire to regard all questions from a distinctly Christian perspective, made him unusual in American Christian history. Over a lifetime of unceasing intellectual labor, Edwards worked out Christian responses to many of the troubling issues of his day. Even as he gave his primary attention to studying the Scriptures, to preaching, and to addressing the needs of his congregation,[26] he took time for a host of more general intellectual pursuits. These included theology, where Edwards wrestled with the relationship between divine sovereignty and human freedom.[27]

26. *The Works of Jonathan Edwards: Sermons and Discourses, 1720–1723,* ed. Wilson H. Kimnach (New Haven: Yale University Press, 1992); *The Works of Jonathan Edwards: The Great Awakening,* ed. C. C. Goen (New Haven: Yale University Press, 1972).

27. *The Works of Jonathan Edwards: Freedom of the Will,* ed. Paul Ramsey (New Haven: Yale University Press, 1957).

They involved questions in what we would call psychology, where he explored the components of genuine religious emotion.[28] They dealt with philosophy, where Edwards proposed ways of counteracting the drift toward scientific materialism.[29] And they included profound reflections on ethics, where Edwards drew distinctions between prudential self-love and true virtue.[30]

In each of these areas the structure of Edwards's thought was the same. The basis was always God's being and our understanding from Scripture of God's actions. Beyond this basis, Edwards was also eager to discover what others were learning about nature, whether physical or human. He thrilled, for example, to read the works of John Locke and Sir Isaac Newton for what those works told him about human nature and the physical world. But Edwards also always denied that this natural knowledge of the world was the highest or finest knowledge. That kind of understanding was received through faith in Christ by God's grace. Edwards's efforts to think in comprehensive terms about the world and humanity's place in the world enabled him to gain perspective on most of the major intellectual challenges of his day. The lesson he offers to later Christians lies partly in the actual conclusions he reached. Even more, it lies in his effort to think about the major questions of life distinctly as a Christian, from a Christian base, and with Christian principles.

The career of Jonathan Edwards shows us how fruitful it can be to love the Lord with the whole mind. His works on revival helped the church pick its way through complicated questions about the place of emotion in religious life. His theological works have helped many to work through questions about the nature of original sin and of the human will. In more recent years his philosophical writings have stimulated much serious reflection. Yet Edwards's career shows us something more. It is not simply advantageous to love the Lord with the mind;

---

28. *The Works of Jonathan Edwards: A Treatise concerning Religious Affections,* ed. John E. Smith (New Haven: Yale University Press, 1959).

29. *The Works of Jonathan Edwards: Scientific and Philosophical Writings,* ed. Wallace E. Anderson (New Haven: Yale University Press, 1980).

30. *The Works of Jonathan Edwards: Ethical Writings,* ed. Paul Ramsey (New Haven: Yale University Press, 1989).

it is also good, sweet, holy, beautiful, and honoring to God. The last reward to be had from the exercise of a Christian mind is to know God better, and that reward requires no other justification.

Once Edwards's most basic convictions are grasped, it is possible to resolve the conundrum about his place in evangelical history. Edwards was an *evangelical* thinker because he held strenuously to the conviction that God's action was the basis for human reaction in every area of life. His belief in evangelical conceptions of grace led him to the conclusion that people were dead in their trespasses and sins until God himself called them to life in Christ. The shape of his thought more generally followed exactly the shape of his theology. The reason that people could know something was the same for why they could be redeemed. If we are saved because of a prior action of God's grace, so also do we know because of conditions established by God. In other words, Edwards's theories of knowledge all presupposed the foundational activity of God, just as his theory of salvation presupposed God's initial action as the key.

The historical paradox occurred as Edwards's theology of salvation developed in the American context. As a theologian of grace, Edwards supported revivals because they were occasions when God graciously drew people to himself. But as the revival tradition developed in America, with the disestablishment of the churches, that revival tradition came to compromise the life of the mind. Where Edwards's thinking had grown out of his theology, the revivalism that Edwards promoted (because of his theology) eventually led to a decline of theology. Revivalism and disestablishment, in other words, set up a style of faith with scant use for patient, comprehensive Christian thinking about the world and life as a whole. So it was that the *context* for evangelical life in America, though that context had been promoted by America's greatest Christian thinker, was working against the development of a Christian mind.

Edwards, in a full range of metaphysical, psychological, and epistemological works, alongside a small library of theological and biblical writing, was responsible for the most God-centered as well as the most intellectually subtle reasoning in all of American evangelical history. Yet Edwards was also a promoter of the revival that pushed American evangelicalism in a direction that made it unable or unwilling to benefit from his own intellectual work. As a result, evangelicalism's most discriminating thinker is best known for one fairly untypical sermon, "Sinners in the Hands of an Angry God." Moreover, in the great recovery of Edwards's reputation that has taken place in the last generation, the lead was taken by secular scholars for secular purposes, while evangelicals have played only a secondary role in the recovery. Apart from a few noteworthy exceptions such as Richard Lovelace and John Piper,[31] evangelicals continue to neglect Edwards, with the result that the riches of his thought — as spiritually invigorating as it is intellectually challenging — remain virtually unknown among the hordes of evangelicals who are his religious descendants.

CREDIBILITY

PLAUSIBILITY UNDERMINED

31. Richard F. Lovelace, *Dynamics of Spiritual Life* (Downers Grove, IL: Inter-Varsity Press, 1979); John Piper, *Desiring God* (Portland, OR: Multnomah Press, 1986); John Gerstner, *Steps to Salvation: The Evangelistic Message of Jonathan Edwards* (Philadelphia: Westminster, 1968).

CHAPTER 4

The Evangelical Enlightenment

Jonathan Edwards was an "enlightened" evangelical, but he was not, in the terms of the eighteenth century, an "evangelical of the Enlightenment." In the generations following Edwards, however, most evangelicals who took an interest in science, philosophy, history, politics, and the arts adopted procedures of the Enlightenment by which to express their thought in these areas. They also used the same Enlightenment categories to express their theology. This evangelical embrace of the Enlightenment at the turn of the eighteenth century still remains extraordinarily important nearly two centuries later because habits of mind that the evangelical Enlightenment encouraged have continued to influence contemporary evangelical life. Of those habits, the most important were a particular kind of commitment to objective truth and a particular "scientific" approach to the Bible.

The way in which evangelicals became wedded to a particular form of the Enlightenment had very much to do with the wider social history of evangelicalism, which was sketched in the last chapter. That history helps explain how evangelicalism, a religion of marginal influence during the American Revolution, emerged as the nation's dominant faith by the early decades of the nineteenth century; how evangelicals put to use the forms of the Enlightenment to express their faith; and how intellectual crises in the period from the Civil War to World War I, especially the controversial issue of biblical criticism, were addressed along lines dictated by the earlier commitment to the Enlightenment. Finally, a brief historical overview will help us see why the principles of the nineteenth-century Enlightenment continue to shape evangelical thought to this day.

The Enlightenment to the Rescue of Evangelicalism

The key to understanding why there was a powerful *evangelical* Enlightenment in America is to remember that intellectual history on this side of the Atlantic was not the same as that on the European continent.[1] An important book by Henry May, *The Enlightenment in America,* is critical for this purpose, because it shows that eighteenth-century Americans perceived several Enlightenments, rather than just one.[2] Americans in general held in high regard, but from afar, what May calls the *moderate* Enlightenment exemplified by Isaac Newton and John Locke. By contrast, evangelicals in America came to repudiate two other forms of European Enlightenment — *skeptical,* as defined by Voltaire and David Hume; and *revolutionary,* as in the work of Rousseau, William Godwin, and (after 1780) Tom Paine. A fourth variety of Enlightenment, however, received a very different reception in Protestant America. This *didactic* Enlightenment, which has recently been the subject of fresh scholarly attention, was largely a product of Scotland.[3] There three generations of philosophers and moralists — among whom Francis Hutcheson, Thomas Reid, Adam Smith, and Dugald Stewart were the leaders — struggled to restore intellectual confidence and social cohesion to the Enlightenment ideal. They achieved these goals by arguing

1. The argument in this section is expanded in Mark A. Noll, "The American Revolution and Protestant Evangelicalism," *Journal of Interdisciplinary History* 23 (Winter 1993): 615–38.

2. Henry F. May, *The Enlightenment in America* (New York: Oxford University Press, 1976).

3. Among the most helpful of many recent books are S. A. Grave, *The Scottish Philosophy of Common Sense* (Oxford: Clarendon Press, 1960); Richard B. Sher, *Church and University in the Scottish Enlightenment: The Moderate Literati of Edinburgh* (Princeton: Princeton University Press, 1985); and Istvan Hont and Michael Ignatieff, eds., *Wealth and Virtue: The Shaping of Political Economy in the Scottish Enlightenment* (New York: Cambridge University Press, 1983).

that all humans possessed, by nature, a common set of capacities —
both epistemological and ethical — through which they could grasp
the basic realities of nature and morality. Moreover, these human capacities could be studied as scientifically as Newton studied the physical
world. Such rigorous study, especially of consciousness, would yield
laws for human behavior and ethics every bit as scientific as Newton's
conclusions about nature. In the United States this Scottish form of
Enlightenment came to dominate intellectual life for more than the
first half-century of the nation's history.

The influence of this didactic Enlightenment stretched broadly
in the population at large, from Jefferson and Madison in the White
House to the first professional scientists in the United States as well as
to the literary pioneers of the new nation.[4] But the most articulate
spokesmen for the common-sense principles of the American Enlightenment were Protestant educators and ministers. These principles provided the basis for collegiate instruction at Unitarian Harvard, Baptist
Brown, Congregationalist Yale, Presbyterian Princeton, and the rest of
the nation's rapidly growing network of colleges, still at this stage almost
exclusively the preserve of the churches. They defined mental habits
for evangelicals North and South, for dignified urban ministers and
enterprising preachers on the frontier, for sober doctrinal conservatives
and populist democratic polemicists.[5]

4. Garry Wills, *Inventing America: Jefferson's Declaration of Independence* (Garden
City, NY: Doubleday, 1978); as modified by Ronald Hamowy, "Jefferson and the
Scottish Enlightenment: A Critique of Garry Wills's *Inventing America*," *William and
Mary Quarterly* 36 (1979): 503–23; Roy Branson, "James Madison and the Scottish
Enlightenment," *Journal of the History of Ideas* 40 (1979): 235–50; Herbert
Hovenkamp, *Science and Religion in America, 1800–1860* (Philadelphia: University
of Pennsylvania Press, 1978); John C. Greene, *American Science in the Age of Jefferson*
(Ames: Iowa State University Press, 1984), 12–36, 411–12; and Terrence Martin, *The
Instructed Vision: Scottish Common Sense Philosophy and the Origins of American Fiction*
(Bloomington: University of Indiana Press, 1961).

5. The two most helpful general studies are Sydney E. Ahlstrom, "The Scottish
Philosophy and American Theology," *Church History* 24 (1955): 257–72; and
Theodore Dwight Bozeman, *Protestants in an Age of Science: The Baconian Ideal and
Antebellum American Religious Thought* (Chapel Hill: University of North Carolina
Press, 1977). For the colleges, see Daniel Walker Howe, *The Unitarian Conscience:
Harvard Moral Philosophy, 1805–1861* (Cambridge: Harvard University Press, 1970);

A wealth of outstanding writing has recently illuminated the way in which evangelicals made the Enlightenment their own. But still there is something of a mystery about it. How did a Protestant tradition rooted in the Reformation and recently renewed by the revivalism of John Wesley, George Whitefield, and Jonathan Edwards come to express itself so thoroughly in the language of the Enlightenment? Protestant traditions from the Reformation as well as the major themes of the revival had stressed human incapacities more than natural human abilities, and both had stressed the evil effects of sin on the mind more than confidence in human reason.

Jonathan Edwards, America's most important evangelical thinker of the eighteenth century, had called into question the notion of human nature that was so important to the ethics of the Scottish Enlightenment. He also resisted the Enlightenment tendency to let the scientific procedures practiced by Newton dictate an ideal way of working in theology and all other fields. Along with Edwards, all major evangelical leaders of the mid-eighteenth century defended the Reformation's view of human nature and denied that people had a "natural" moral sense by which they could understand what was both true and in their best interest. Yet this idea of humanity was critical for the didactic Enlightenment, and by the early nineteenth century it became a widely accepted assumption of America's evangelicals.

A problem, therefore, exists in explaining why American evangelicals came so rapidly and so thoroughly to embrace the Enlightenment in its Scottish form. The Reformation in which American Protestantism was rooted, the Puritan tradition that provided Americans their most articulate theological heritage, and the Great Awakening through the

Mark A. Noll, *Princeton and the Republic, 1768–1822: The Search for a Christian Enlightenment in the Era of Samuel Stanhope Smith* (Princeton: Princeton University Press, 1989), 36–43, 117–23, 188–91, 284–86; and for collegiate instruction generally, D. H. Meyer, *The Instructed Conscience: The Shaping of the American National Ethic* (Philadelphia: University of Pennsylvania Press, 1972). For the Scottish Enlightenment among southern Protestants, see E. Brooks Holifield, *The Gentlemen Theologians: American Theology in Southern Culture, 1795–1860* (Durham, NC: Duke University Press, 1978), 96–101 and 110–54; and Fred J. Hood, *Reformed America: The Middle and Southern States, 1783–1837* (University: University of Alabama Press, 1980), 1–67, 88–112.

writings of its leading exponents — all make it harder rather than easier to see why American evangelicals by 1800 would everywhere champion the naturalism, the optimism, and the scientific rationality that, albeit "pressed . . . into the service of traditional values,"[6] nonetheless still characterized their Enlightenment.

The answer to this puzzle is that the Scottish Enlightenment offered evangelicals and other Americans exactly what they needed to master the tumults of the Revolutionary era. In the midst of an era marked by a radical willingness to question the verities of the past, the intuitive philosophy provided by the Scots offered an intellectually respectable way to establish public virtue in a society that was busily repudiating the props upon which virtue had traditionally rested — tradition itself, divine revelation, history, social hierarchy, an inherited government, and the authority of religious denominations. As Norman Fiering once put it, the "moral philosophy" of the eighteenth-century Scottish Enlightenment "was uniquely suited to the needs of an era still strongly committed to traditional religious values and yet searching for alternative modes of justification for those values."[7] For evangelicals who wanted to preserve traditional forms of Christianity without having to appeal to traditional religious authorities, the common-sense reasoning of the Scottish Enlightenment (at least as that philosophy took on a life of its own in North America) was the answer.[8]

Two great political tasks confronted the Revolutionary generation, and a third equally great difficulty faced the Protestants who joined the patriot cause. The first was to justify the break with Great Britain. The second was to establish principles of social order for a new nation that was repudiating autocratic government, hierarchical political assumptions, and automatic deference to tradition. The third task, for evangelicals, was to preserve the hereditary position of Christianity in a culture that denied absolute sovereignty to any authority and that was

6. D. H. Meyer, *The Democratic Enlightenment* (New York: G. P. Putnam's Sons, 1976), xxvi.

7. Norman Fiering, *Moral Philosophy at Seventeenth-Century Harvard: A Discipline in Transition* (Chapel Hill: University of North Carolina Press, 1981), 300.

8. The contemporary philosopher Nicholas Wolterstorff has made the important point in conversation that the way Americans used the Scottish philosophy may have seriously altered the work of Thomas Reid, Dugald Stewart, and their colleagues, who cannot necessarily be held responsible for how their ideas were popularized in America.

turning against the structures of traditional religion (like the political episcopate or the establishment of Congregational churches in New England) as actively as it was turning against other inherited authorities.

For each of these tasks the reasoning of the Scottish Enlightenment proved irresistible. The general influence of the Revolution on American thought was such that the form of reasoning by which patriots justified their rebellion against the Crown instinctively became also the form of reasoning by which political and religious leaders sought a stable social order for the new nation and by which evangelical spokesmen defended the place of traditional faith in a traditionless society.

The particularly Enlightenment character of this reasoning was its trust in objectivity, its devotion to a principle of privileged scientific inquiry. Protestant commitment to this form of the Enlightenment was thoroughgoing because it seemed to work so well — it could justify the rebellion, it did establish social order through a Constitution infused with the principles of moral philosophy, and it did make way for nearly a century's triumphant vindication of traditional Protestantism. Evangelical commitment to this form of the Enlightenment became deeply ingrained, not only because it was so successful, but also because it was so intuitive, so instinctual, so much a part of second nature. For much of the history of the United States, evangelicals denied that they had a philosophy. They were merely pursuing common sense.[9]

The utility of this kind of Enlightenment reasoning was apparent. It was, most obviously, a mainstay of political argument. What weight could the traditional authority of the king in Parliament carry against the "self-evident truths," the "unalienable rights," or "the laws of nature" proclaimed by the Declaration of Independence? What need was there for a careful rebuttal of authorities, or even a careful perusal of Scripture, to justify rebellion, if it was transparent to the moral sense that such a rebellion was necessary?[10]

For evangelicals, Enlightenment patterns of thought had even

9. For an overview, see Mark A. Noll, "Common Sense Traditions and American Evangelical Thought," *American Quarterly* 37 (Summer 1985): 216–38.

10. For a fine discussion of the intellectual background of the political founders, see Daniel Walker Howe, "The Political Psychology of *The Federalist*," *William and Mary Quarterly* 44 (1987): 485–509.

more uses than they did for the politicians who had used common-sense arguments to establish a new government. Guardians of American public virtue could now rely on the "moral sense" to restate traditional morality in a scientific form without having recourse to the traditional props for ethics, including even the special revelation of the Bible. John Witherspoon, the president of Princeton College, who had migrated from Scotland in 1768, claimed that when we study our own minds, we end up with the proper principles for a just and stable society. He hoped that "a time may come when men, treating moral philosophy as Newton and his successors have done natural [philosophy], may arrive at greater precision" on ethical matters.[11]

Witherspoon's successor as president of Princeton, Samuel Stanhope Smith, was one of the most capable systematizers of the American Enlightenment. In a work from 1787 defending the unity of humanity, Smith left no doubts about his faith in the power of the new moral philosophy to move from an examination of one's own heart to universally valid principles of social order, a power that would be destroyed if humanity did not constitute a unified species:

> The science of morals would be absurd; the law of nature and nations would be annihilated; no general principles of human conduct, of religion, or of policy could be framed; for, human nature . . . could not be comprehended in any system. The rules which would result from the study of our own nature, would not apply to the natives of other countries who would be of different species. . . . Such principles tend to confound all science, as well as piety; and leave us in the world uncertain whom to trust, or what opinions to frame of others. The doctrine of one race, removes this uncertainty, renders human nature susceptible of system, illustrates the powers of physical causes, and opens a rich and extensive field for moral science.[12]

The paths marked out by Witherspoon and Stanhope Smith were followed by most of the country's major evangelical intellectual leaders

11. John Witherspoon, "Lectures on Moral Philosophy," in *The Works of the Rev. John Witherspoon*, 4 vols. (Philadelphia: William W. Woodward, 1802), 3:470.
12. Samuel Stanhope Smith, *An Essay on the Causes of the Variety of Complexion and Figure in the Human Species* (Philadelphia: Robert Aitkin, 1787), 109–10.

in the years before the Civil War.[13] Exceptionally able books by Wilson Smith, Daniel Walker Howe, and D. H. Meyer have shown how deeply ingrained this trust in Enlightenment procedure became.[14] Explicit in the lectures and textbooks of the nation's Protestant leaders was the Enlightenment belief that Americans could find within themselves resources, compatible with Christianity, to bring social order out of the rootlessness and confusion of the new nation.

The Enlightenment and the Shape of Evangelical Thought

The extent of evangelical incorporation of the Enlightenment, however, went much further than merely its utility for influencing the moral direction of society. In fact, when we observe how deeply this kind of Enlightenment entered into the fabric of evangelical thought, we begin to see why the tie between evangelicalism and the Enlightenment has been so enduring. At the levels of high culture that tie shaped apologetics and theology. For all major evangelical groups it influenced expectations concerning revival. And among both common people and the elite it provided the framework for appropriating Scripture.

Apologetics

For evangelical leaders, principles of the didactic Enlightenment arrived just in time. A modern, respectable defense of the faith seemed absolutely essential for the survival of Protestantism in Revolutionary America. The American Revolution differed from the later Revolution in

13. See Hood, *Reformed America*, 10–46, on the specific influence of Witherspoon and Smith in the South; and Robert M. Calhoon, *Evangelicals and Conservatives in the Early South, 1740–1861* (Columbia: University of South Carolina Press, 1988), 85, who suggests that Witherspoon fashioned "a kind of secularized Calvinism that filled a real need in early national political culture."

14. Wilson Smith, *Professors and Public Ethics: Studies of Northern Moral Philosophers before the Civil War* (Ithaca: Cornell University Press, 1956); Howe, *Unitarian Conscience;* and D. H. Meyer, *The Instructed Conscience: The Shaping of the American National Ethic* (Philadelphia: University of Pennsylvania Press, 1972).

France in part because of the ability of American evangelicals to align faith in reason with faith in God. The intellectual goal of evangelicals in the struggle against the irreligion and disorder of the Revolutionary period was, in Witherspoon's words, "to meet [infidels] upon their own ground, and to show them from reason itself, the fallacy of their principles."[15] In the 1790s and for several decades thereafter evangelicals relied heavily on the imported apologetics of William Paley to secure their case.[16]

Later, as they began to develop their own defenses for Christianity, evangelicals drew ever more directly on the methods of the didactic Enlightenment. Examples of apologetics grounded on scientific rationality abounded in the early national period. It was a part of Timothy Dwight's armament that proved immediately useful when he became president of Yale in 1795 and confronted undergraduate doubts about the veracity of the Bible.[17] Widespread as the recourse to scientific demonstration was among the Congregationalists, it was the Presbyterians who excelled at what T. D. Bozeman has called a Baconian approach to the faith.[18] In divinity, rigorous empiricism became the standard for justifying belief in God, revelation, and the Trinity. In the moral sciences, it marked out the royal road to ethical certainty. It also provided a key for using physical science itself as a demonstration of religious truths.[19] In every case the appeal was, as Stanhope Smith put it, "to the evidence of facts, and to conclusions resulting from these facts which . . . every genuine disciple of nature will acknowledge to

15. Witherspoon, "Moral Philosophy," 3:368.

16. Wilson Smith, "William Paley's Theological Utilitarianism in America," *William and Mary Quarterly* 11 (1954): 402–24.

17. Sereno E. Dwight, "Memoir," in *Theology Explained and Defended*, 4 vols., by Timothy Dwight (New Haven: S. Converse, 1823), 1:22–23.

18. Bozeman, *Protestants in an Age of Science*, 3–31.

19. For examples in divinity, see Witherspoon, "Lectures on Divinity," in *Works*, 4:22–75; Samuel Stanhope Smith, *A Comprehensive View of the Leading and Most Important Principles of Natural and Revealed Religion* (New Brunswick, NJ: Deare & Myer, 1815); Archibald Alexander, *A Brief Outline of the Evidences of the Christian Religion* (Princeton: D. A. Borrenstein, 1825); and Nathaniel W. Taylor, *Lectures on the Moral Government of God*, 2 vols. (New York: Clark, Austin & Smith, 1859). For harmonizations with science, see Bozeman, *Protestants in an Age of Science*, 71–159; Hovenkamp, *Science and Religion in America*.

be legitimately drawn from her own fountain."[20] Among both Congregationalists and Presbyterians, the most theologically articulate evangelicals in the early republic, this approach guided responses to Paine's *Age of Reason* in the 1790s and to other infidels thereafter.[21] This kind of "supernatural rationalism" was also useful for counteracting the impious use of science, by making possible the harmonization of, first, the Bible and astronomy and, then, Scripture and geology.[22]

Closely related to the evangelical reliance upon scientific reason was dependence upon intuitive common sense, which was everywhere considered the basis for reliable knowledge. Nothing worked better at squelching the deism that Tom Paine promoted, said the lay activist Elias Boudinot, than simply "the rules of common sense."[23] Timothy Dwight praised common sense as "the most valuable faculty . . . of man" and regularly used it to begin and sustain arguments.[24] The same faith in intuition served the New Haven Theology as it counterattacked the Unitarians and modified Edwards's theory of the will. To accomplish the latter, Nathaniel William Taylor urged, "Let a man look into his own breast, and he cannot but perceive . . . *inward freedom* — for if freedom be not in the *mind* it is nowhere. And liberty in the mind implies self-determination."[25]

20. Stanhope Smith, *Essay,* 3.

21. See Gary B. Nash, "The American Clergy and the French Revolution," *William and Mary Quarterly* 22 (July 1965): 402–4; and James H. Smylie, "Clerical Perspectives on Deism: Paine's *Age of Reason* in Virginia," *Eighteenth-Century Studies* 6 (1972–73): 203–20.

22. For a good discussion of "supernatural rationalism," see Bruce Kuklick, *Churchmen and Philosophers from Jonathan Edwards to John Dewey* (New Haven: Yale University Press, 1985), 87. On the harmonizations, see Ronald L. Numbers, *Creation by Natural Law: Laplace's Nebular Hypothesis in American Thought* (Seattle: University of Washington Press, 1977), 55–66; Bozeman, *Protestants in an Age of Science,* 96–97; and Hovenkamp, *Science and Religion in America,* 119–46.

23. Elias Boudinot, *The Age of Revelation; or, The Age of Reason Shewn to Be an Age of Infidelity* (Philadelphia: Asbury Dickens, 1801), 30.

24. Timothy Dwight, *Theology Explained and Defended,* 4 vols. (New Haven: S. Converse, 1823), 4:55, 260–61, as quoted in George M. Marsden, "Everyone One's Own Interpreter? The Bible, Science, and Authority in Mid-Nineteenth-Century America," in *The Bible in America,* ed. Nathan O. Hatch and Mark A. Noll (New York: Oxford University Press, 1982), 85.

25. N. W. Taylor, undocumented quotation from William G. McLoughlin, *Revivals, Awakenings, and Reform* (Chicago: University of Chicago Press, 1978), 119.

So basic did this reasoning become that even self-consciously orthodox evangelicals had no qualms about resting the entire edifice of the faith on the principles of the Scottish Enlightenment. Archibald Alexander, longtime professor at the confessional Presbyterian seminary in Princeton, year by year told the first-year students: "To prove that our faculties are not so constituted as to misguide us, some have had recourse to the *goodness* and *truth of God*, our creator, but this argument is unnecessary. We are as certain of these intuitive truths as we can be. . . . Besides, we must be sure that we exist, and that the world exists, before we can be certain that there is a God, for it is from these *data* that we prove his existence."[26] In a word, the basic principle of the Scottish philosophy — that people could reason naturally from the evidence of their own consciousness to the existence of God and the validity of traditional morality — had become very widespread by the early nineteenth century.

Theology Proper

The range and development of antebellum theology more generally is too complicated to sum up briefly. But even an abbreviated account of the New England tradition of trinitarian Congregationalism, which Bruce Kuklick calls "the most sustained intellectual tradition the United States has produced," may suggest the alterations that occurred when, even among those most solicitous of preserving historic faith, evangelicals became partners in the American Enlightenment.[27]

Jonathan Edwards's immediate heirs, Joseph Bellamy and Samuel Hopkins, clearly tried their best to preserve the master's teaching in the age of Enlightenment that was dawning about them. Yet the need they felt to defer to the impersonal, lawlike character of the universe or to stake everything on the importance of human happiness marked the path of the future. Bellamy, that is, was so moved by the Enlightenment

26. Archibald Alexander, "Theological Lectures, Nature and Evidence of Truth" (1812), in *The Princeton Theology, 1812–1921,* ed. Mark A. Noll (Grand Rapids: Baker, 1983), 65.
27. Kuklick, *Churchmen and Philosophers,* 222.

HUMAN HAPPINESS

IMPERSONAL, LAW LIKE UNIVERSE

demand for visible, public morality that he changed traditional Christian teaching on the Atonement to de-emphasize God's wrath at sin
and to emphasize the way that the death of Christ preserved God's
moral government of the world.[28] For his part, Hopkins was so influenced by the Enlightenment demand to show things working out for
good that he taught that God had willed the existence of sin as an
advantage to the universe.[29] Bellamy and Hopkins did not mean to
alter the truth they had learned from Jonathan Edwards; rather, they
were only substituting an Enlightenment mentality of celestial accounts
for Edwards's preoccupation with the prerogatives of deity.

In the next generation, Timothy Dwight and Jonathan Edwards,
Jr., came more explicitly to trust in natural intuition, the unacknowl-
edged source from which Bellamy and Hopkins's sense of universal
fitness had also emerged. Although Dwight was the most effective
experimental Calvinist in the early United States, he yet relied directly
on "common sense" to shape his beliefs about what was possible in the
moral world, and on "natural ability" to begin a course of action.[30] In
the mature thought of Dwight's most important successor, N. W. Taylor
of Yale, orthodoxy no longer stood on its own but was dependent upon
"reason . . . our only guide in religion, in examining the evidences of
revelation, in ascertaining its import, in believing its doctrines, and in
obeying its precepts."[31]

In the next generation, the last of the great defenders of the New
England theological tradition, Edwards Amasa Park, spelled out exactly
how that theology had developed. The context for his account was a
long argument with Charles Hodge of Princeton, who accused the New

28. Glenn Paul Anderson, "Joseph Bellamy (1719–1790): The Man and His
Work" (Ph.D. diss., Boston University, 1971), 737–48.

29. Joseph A. Conforti, *Samuel Hopkins and the New Divinity Movement* (Grand
Rapids: Eerdmans, 1981), 59–75.

30. Robert L. Ferm, *A Colonial Pastor: Jonathan Edwards the Younger, 1745–
1801* (Grand Rapids: Eerdmans, 1976), 55, 110–26; Timothy Dwight, *Theology,
Explained and Defended* (Middletown, CT, 1818), 1:407, 507, as quoted in Conrad C.
Cherry, *Nature and Religious Imagination from Edwards to Bushnell* (Philadelphia:
Fortress, 1980), 122.

31. N. W. Taylor, *Lectures on the Moral Government of God,* 2 vols. (New York:
Clark, Austin & Smith, 1859), 1:382.

England Congregationalists of giving away essential doctrines of traditional Calvinism. Park acknowledged that later New Englanders had
adjusted Jonathan Edwards's convictions concerning free will, the im-
putation of Adam's guilt, and the nature of human sinfulness, but he
felt they had good reason for doing so. After Edwards's day, "a philosophical theory, on the freedom and worth of the human soul" had
made a welcome contribution to New England theology. The New
England "scheme" was still rooted in Edwards, but its expression also
benefited, as Park put it, from "the philosophy of Reid, Oswald, Campbell, Beattie, Stewart . . . *the philosophy of common sense.*" These Scottish
philosophers had been able "to develop 'the fundamental laws of human
belief.'" Their contribution "has aided our writers in shaping their faith
according to those ethical axioms, which so many fathers in the church
have undervalued." The result was that "the metaphysics of New England Theology . . . is the metaphysics of common sense." As a follower
of this theology, Park could also take pride in the fact that "the New
England system is not only scriptural, but is scriptural *science.*"[32] The
end result of the sort of changes described by Park has been well
summarized by Bruce Kuklick: "Disinterested benevolence showed the
movement of Congregationalists away from a mysterious divine cosmos
to a human-centered one, just as the theology itself relied less on mystery
and more on what appeared reasonable for divines to believe. Hopkins's
ethics responded to the same forces as Paley's utilitarianism. In the
nineteenth century Congregational theology continued to grow
humanistic."[33]

Other evangelical traditions in America developed differently, but
in almost all of the major systems of the era — Princeton Presbyterianism, the Oberlin perfectionism of Asa Mahan and Charles Finney,
and the frontier Restorationism of Alexander Campbell and Barton
Stone — similar evidence was present, though often in contrasting
ways, to show the shaping significance of the didactic Enlightenment
on theology.[34]

32. E. A. Park, "New England Theology," *Bibliotheca Sacra* 9 (1852): 191–92,
210.

33. Kuklick, *Churchmen and Philosophers,* 53.

34. Noll, *Princeton Theology;* Edward H. Madden and James E. Hamilton,

Revivalism

Revivalism, perhaps the least likely feature of antebellum Protestantism to reflect the influence of the Enlightenment, nonetheless took on a new shape because of that influence. The push, even in the realms of the Spirit, was to rationality and scientific predictability.[35] Charles G. Finney, the greatest evangelist of the antebellum period and one of the most influential Americans of his generation, did not speak for all. But the elements of Enlightenment thinking in his revivalism suggest how pervasive its principles had become. His *Lectures on Revivals of Religion* (1835) summarized a new approach to evangelism. Since God had established reliable laws in the natural world, we know that he has also done so in the spiritual world. To activate the proper causes for revivals was to produce the proper effect: "The connection between the right use of means for a revival and a revival is as philosophically [i.e., scientifically] sure as between the right use of means to raise grain and a crop of wheat. I believe, in fact, it is more certain, and there are fewer instances of failure."[36] Because the world spiritual was analogous to the world natural, observable cause and effect must work in religion as well as in physics.

The Bible

Nowhere did the marriage between Protestantism and the Enlightenment produce more lively offspring than in the American appropriation of the Bible. Traditional interpretations of Scripture may have come under attack in the new United States, and traditions of biblical ex-

---

Freedom and Grace: The Life of Asa Mahan (Methuen, NJ: Scarecrow Press, 1982); and Richard T. Hughes and C. Leonard Allen, *Illusions of Innocence: Protestant Primitivism in America, 1630–1875* (Chicago: University of Chicago Press, 1988).

35. A good discussion of Enlightenment revivalism is found in C. Leonard Allen, Richard T. Hughes, and Michael R. Weed, *The Worldly Church* (Abilene, TX: Abilene Christian University Press, 1988), 27–31.

36. Charles G. Finney, *Lectures on Revivals of Religion,* ed. William G. McLoughlin (Cambridge: Harvard University Press, 1960; orig. 1835), 33.

position or elitist assumptions about how much study was necessary before a man (or even a woman) could publicly preach the Bible were gleefully disregarded, but there was no retreat from the Scripture itself. For reasons that have yet to be probed satisfactorily, the "Bible alone" (in both senses of the term — as the *supreme* religious authority but also as the *only* hereditary authority) survived the assault on tradition that characterized the era. What Nathan Hatch has written about populist religion in the early republic was true as well for almost all evangelicals: "In a culture that mounted a frontal assault upon tradition, mediating elites, and institutions, the Bible very easily became . . . 'a book dropped from the skies for all sorts of men to use in their own way.'"[37]

Virtually every aspect of the profound evangelical attachment to the Bible was shaped by the Enlightenment. Theological arguments, like the rebuttal in 1833 by Andover's Moses Stuart of the notion of innate, inheritable depravity, could rest on the fact that the erroneous view was "plainly at variance with the explicit declarations of the Scriptures . . . and with the first dictates of our unbiased feelings and our reason."[38] The orthodox Congregationalist Leonard Woods, Jr., wrote in 1822 that the best method of Bible study was "that which is pursued in the science of physics," regulated "by the maxims of Bacon and Newton." Newtonian method, Woods said, "is as applicable in theology as in physics, although in theology we have an extra-aid, the revelation of the Bible. But in each science reasoning is the same — we inquire for facts and from them arrive at general truths."[39] Southern Presbyterian Robert Breckinridge wrote in 1847 that theology derived from the Bible could be a science expressed as "uncontrovertibly as I would write geometry."[40] The best-known statement of Enlightenment biblicism appeared after the Civil War in Charles Hodge's *Systematic*

37. Nathan O. Hatch, *The Democratization of American Christianity* (New Haven: Yale University Press, 1989), 182; the quotation is from John W. Nevin.

38. Moses Stuart, *Commentary on Romans* (1832), 541, as quoted in John H. Giltner, *Moses Stuart: The Father of Biblical Science in America* (Atlanta: Scholars Press, 1988), 115.

39. Leonard Woods, as quoted in Hovenkamp, *Science and Religion in America,* 61; and Kuklick, *Churchmen and Philosophers,* 89.

40. Robert Breckinridge, as quoted in Holifield, *Gentlemen Theologians,* 203.

Theology: "The Bible is to the theologian what nature is to the man of science. It is his store-house of facts; and his method of ascertaining what the Bible teaches, is the same as that which the natural philosopher adopts to ascertain what nature teaches. . . . The duty of the Christian theologian is to ascertain, collect, and combine all the facts which God has revealed concerning himself and our relation to him. These facts are all in the Bible."[41]

Such attitudes were by no means limited to the established denominations with reputations to protect. A recent study of Alexander Campbell and the Restorationist movement, which led to the founding of the Disciples of Christ, the Churches of Christ, and the Christian Churches, argues convincingly that "the Campbell movement was as clear an expression of the spirit of Common Sense rationalism as one could hope to find in American religion in the early nineteenth century."[42] Nowhere does that rationalism appear more evidently than in Restorationist use of Scripture. At (Francis) Bacon College, which Disciples founded in 1836, students were instructed in how to study the Bible by the example of Campbell: "I have endeavored to read the Scriptures as though no one had read them before me." Other Restorationist leaders, like Tolbert Fanning, expressed the boundless methodological confidence of the age when he asserted that "the Scriptures fairly translated need no explanation." Another Restorationist, James S. Lamar, published in 1859 his *Organon of Scripture; or, The Inductive Method of Biblical Interpretation,* in which the impress of the Enlightenment was unmistakable: "The Scriptures admit of being studied and expounded upon the principles of the inductive method; and . . . when thus interpreted they speak to us in a voice as certain and unmistakable as the language of nature heard in the experiments and observations of science."[43]

So influential had principles of Enlightenment rationality become that it was increasingly easy for evangelicals to treat the Scriptures as a "scientific" text whose pieces were to be arranged by induction to yield the truth on any issue.

41. Charles Hodge, *Systematic Theology,* 3 vols. (Grand Rapids: Eerdmans, 1952; orig. 1872–73), 1:10–11.

42. Hughes and Allen, *Illusions of Innocence,* 143.

43. Quoted in ibid., 157, 161, 156.

Evangelical Nationalism

One final feature of early national affinities came powerfully into play as American evangelicals embraced the didactic Enlightenment. In ways that have been probed extensively by a wealth of historical works, the process that witnessed Protestant alignment with the Enlightenment witnessed also Protestant alignment with the United States.[44] The contrast with Revolutionary France could not have been greater. In France, liberty, the people, the Enlightenment, and the new sense of French national destiny stood over against the church. By contrast, in the United States, evangelicalism identified itself with the people, the Enlightenment, democracy, republicanism, economic liberalism, and the sense of American manifest destiny. Once again, Alexis de Tocqueville saw the difference clearly: "There is no country in the world where the boldest doctrines of the *philosophes* of the eighteenth century, in matters of politics, were more fully applied than in America; it was only the anti-religious doctrines that never were able to make headway."[45]

This identification between some aspects of eighteenth-century intellectual life and some critical elements of evangelical religion had profound effects. Evangelical identity in America could no more be separated from its commitment to Enlightenment rationalism than from its belief in the divine character of the country and in God's ordination of democratic liberalism. All of the elements that went into the making of an American evangelical Enlightenment were melted together indistinguishably in the crucible from which also emerged the American nation.

44. See Nathan O. Hatch, *The Sacred Cause of Liberty: Republican Thought and the Millennium in Revolutionary New England* (New Haven: Yale University Press, 1977); John F. Berens, "The Sanctification of American Nationalism," in *Providence and Patriotism in Early America, 1640–1815* (Charlottesville: University Press of Virginia, 1978), 112–28; and Ruth Bloch, *Visionary Republic: Millennial Themes in American Thought, 1756–1800* (New York: Cambridge University Press, 1985).

45. Alexis de Tocqueville, *L'ancien régime et la révolution* (1967 ed.), 252–53, as translated in Thomas L. Pangle, *The Spirit of Modern Republicanism: The Moral Vision of the American Founders and the Philosophy of Locke* (Chicago: University of Chicago Press, 1988), 284n.8.

The Enlightenment and the History
of Evangelicalism after the Civil War

If the antebellum bond between the Enlightenment and evangelicalism was as secure as I have suggested, the intellectual situation that developed by the early twentieth century looks like a puzzle. By that time a different kind of science had replaced the earlier doxological Baconianism, and the academy had grown inhospitable to the earlier cultural alliance between science and Protestantism. In this situation there was an unprecedented intellectual division among evangelicals caused in large part by contrasting opinions on the merits of the new science. Through a complicated set of maneuvers in which the role of the churches has never been adequately studied, the academy was encouraging new forms of science at the same time that it was replacing the traditional religious framework for a more secular one.[46] Nothing less than an intellectual revolution was underway. Nonetheless, despite very significant changes, the earlier habits of Enlightenment thought continued to shape the intellectual life of evangelicalism, even as evangelicalism itself broke apart into liberal and fundamentalist parties.

Several possible reasons may be given for the rapid shift in American intellectual life after the Civil War, including new scholars, new influences from Europe, new configurations in the American economy, and new social expectations for mass culture.[47] Whatever the exact role of Protestants in bringing about the altered state of affairs, it is abundantly clear that a new intellectual world had dawned. Views of science were changing from static and mechanistic to developmental and organic, attitudes toward academic work from teleological and doxological to progressive and functional, perspectives on religion from particularistic and theistic to universalistic and agnostic.

Painful decisions faced the heirs of those who before midcentury

46. For a fresh account of this process, see the new study by George Marsden, *The Soul of the American University* (New York: Oxford University Press, 1994).

47. On this massive subject, expert orientation and important arguments are found in Laurence R. Veysey, *The Emergence of the American University* (Chicago: University of Chicago Press, 1965); and Alexandra Oleson and John Voss, eds., *The Organization of Knowledge in Modern America, 1860–1920* (Baltimore: Johns Hopkins University Press, 1979).

DEVELOPMENTAL/ORGANIC
STATIC/MECHANISTIC

had operated from a base of Christian faith and scientific rationality in restful harmony. A threefold division of nineteenth-century evangelicalism came about in response to the new challenge. First, the more liberal evangelicals moved with the times, conceded the hegemony of the new science, and sought to preserve in a new form the old harmonies of the American Protestant Enlightenment.[48] From this move came theological modernism.

By contrast, populist evangelicals, the later fundamentalists, made a more complicated response.[49] They moved both with and against the times — with, by adopting the new applied technologies of mass media and public marketing,[50] against, by resisting the evolution of the old science into the new. They too attempted to preserve the American Protestant Enlightenment, but with its old content as well as its old form.

By far the majority of evangelical Protestants vacillated in the middle. They were nostalgic for the old intellectual harmonies, unsettled by the tendency of the new science to dismiss traditional Christian convictions, but unwilling to decide decisively for either the old paradigm with its harmony between science and theology or the new with its division between theology and science.[51]

Because of the general intellectual situation and the nature of evangelical responses to that situation, the evangelical-Enlightenment synthesis, though battered, did survive. The new American university threw up major problems of fact to evangelicals but did not call forth

48. William R. Hutchison, *The Modernist Impulse in American Protestantism* (Cambridge: Harvard University Press, 1976), especially 87–94 on accommodations with the new science.

49. George M. Marsden, *Fundamentalism and American Culture: The Shaping of Twentieth-Century Evangelicalism, 1870–1925* (New York: Oxford University Press, 1980), especially 55–62 and 212–21 on the scienticism of fundamentalists.

50. On the psychological and technological modernity of fundamentalism, see Douglas Frank, *Less Than Conquerors: How Evangelicals Entered the Twentieth Century* (Grand Rapids: Eerdmans, 1986); and Martin E. Marty, *Modern American Religion*, vol. 1: *The Irony of It All, 1893–1919* (Chicago: University of Chicago Press, 1986), 208–47.

51. A good account of this middle group is found in Grant A. Wacker, "The Holy Spirit and the Spirit of the Age in American Protestantism, 1880–1910," *Journal of American History* 72 (1985): 45–62.

LIBERALS / CONSERV.

WITH / WITH + AGAINST / AGAINST

reconsiderations of method. This set of circumstances — new problems within the context of old opinions about how to solve problems — set the intellectual framework in which fundamentalism developed. The problems created by this combination of loyalties — for "doxological science" as well as for traditional orthodoxy — were well illustrated in the evangelical responses to the rise of biblical criticism.

The consensus that had once prevailed among Protestants on the nature of the Bible began to change during the last third of the nineteenth century.[52] Conclusions from both "textual criticism" (comparative study of the manuscript evidence for the original words of the Old and New Testaments) and "higher criticism" (the application of modern philosophical notions to the Bible) were calling settled opinions into question. The appearance of new views on the American scene corresponded with a surge of professionalization in the country's universities. In the 1870s and 1880s, graduate study on the European model began to be offered at older universities like Harvard and newer ones like Johns Hopkins. At such centers, supposedly objective science was exalted as the royal road to truth, and the new professional academics reacted scornfully to what they perceived as parochial, uninformed, and outmoded scholarship. All fields, including the study of the Bible, were to be unfettered for free inquiry. In keeping with newer intellectual fashions, however, this scholarship relied heavily upon evolutionary science; proponents of the new ideas held that histories, stories, and writings all evolved over time, as did religious consciousness itself. They also tended to be skeptical about the miraculous and to reflect the view that the religious experience of the Jews and Christians was not essentially different from that of other peoples in the ancient world.

For our purposes the salient feature of Protestant responses to the new views of the Bible was their uniformly scientific character. The

52. On that consensus, see John D. Woodbridge, *Biblical Authority: A Critique of the Rogers-McKim Proposal* (Grand Rapids: Zondervan, 1982), as supplemented by Jack B. Rogers and Donald K. McKim, *The Authority and Interpretation of the Bible: An Historical Approach* (San Francisco: Harper & Row, 1979). The paragraphs that follow draw on Mark A. Noll, *Between Faith and Criticism: Evangelicals, Scholarship, and the Bible*, 2nd ed (Grand Rapids: Baker, 1991); and Noll, "Review Essay: The Bible in America," *Journal of Biblical Literature* 106 (1987): 493–509.

inaugural public discussion of the new views occurred between Presbyterian conservatives and moderates from 1881 to 1883 in the pages of the *Presbyterian Review*. Both sides, as would almost all who followed in their train, tried as if by instinct to secure for themselves the high ground of scientific credibility. The moderates, led by Charles A. Briggs, were committed to "the principles of Scientific Induction." Since Old Testament studies had "been greatly enlarged by the advances in linguistic and historical science which marks our century," it was only proper to take this new evidence into account. To these Presbyterian intellectuals the situation, as Briggs saw it, was clear: "The great majority of professional Biblical scholars in the various Universities and Theological Halls of the world, embracing those of the greatest learning, industry, and piety, demand a revision of traditional theories of the Bible on account of a large induction of new facts from the Bible and history."[53]

The conservatives were just as determined to enlist science on their side. As A. A. Hodge and Benjamin B. Warfield put it at the start of the exchange:

[We] . . . are sincerely convinced of the perfect soundness of the great Catholic doctrine of Biblical Inspiration . . . and hence that all elements [of Scripture] and all their affirmations are absolutely errorless, and binding the faith and obedience of men. Nevertheless we admit that the question between ourselves and the advocates of [modern criticism] is one of fact, to be decided only by an exhaustive and impartial examination of all the sources of evidence, i.e., the claims and the phenomena of the Scriptures themselves.

Their colleague William Henry Green chose not to examine the "presumptions" that led W. Robertson Smith to adopt critical views of the Old Testament but rather chose the way of induction: "We shall concern ourselves simply with duly certified facts." And Willis J. Beecher contended that the "mere hypotheses" of the new views proved nothing.

53. Charles A. Briggs, "Critical Theories of the Sacred Scriptures in Relation to Their Inspiration," *Presbyterian Review* 2 (July 1881): 558; Henry Preserved Smith, "The Critical Theories of Julius Wellhausen," ibid. 3 (Apr. 1882): 386; and Briggs, "Critical Theories," 557.

"Without some element of positive evidence, a hypothesis or a hundred hypotheses fail of themselves. . . . Any author is uncritical if he indulges in assertions which are based on mere hypotheses."[54] In this debate, both sides recognized the role of presuppositions — they were what kept the other side from practicing the proper procedures of science in studying the Bible.

Once the terms of the debate were set in this scientific form, there was little deviation. Just as liberal scholars put to use newer notions of scientific exactitude to the Bible, so evangelicals continued without hesitation to apply standards of the early American Enlightenment to the Bible. R. A. Torrey's *What the Bible Teaches* (1898), for example, followed a "rigidly inductive" method, where "the methods of modern science are applied to Bible study — thorough analysis followed by careful synthesis." The result was "a careful, unbiased, systematic, thorough-going, *inductive* study and statement of Bible truth."[55] More academic conservatives followed the same path. Robert Dick Wilson of Princeton Seminary, for instance, published a work entitled *A Scientific Investigation of the Old Testament* (1926) in which he chose not to use prophecy or miracles to support his traditional conclusions about the Old Testament. Rather, he would use "the evidential method . . . the Laws of Evidence as applied to documents admitted in our courts of law . . . the evidence of manuscripts and versions and of the Egyptian, Babylonian, and other documents outside the Bible" to demonstrate the truth of traditional opinions.[56]

In the end, therefore, questions on biblical criticism divided evangelicals. But they remained struggles over facts (and also over control of schools and denominations). These struggles left intact the traditional evangelical confidence in Enlightenment rationality. Because it was an age of unquestioned hegemony for science — an age that fully em-

54. A. A. Hodge and Benjamin B. Warfield, "Inspiration," *Presbyterian Review* 2 (Apr. 1881): 237; William Henry Green, "Professor W. Robertson Smith on the Pentateuch," ibid. 3 (Jan. 1882): 111; Willis J. Beecher, "The Logical Methods of Professor Kuenen," ibid. 3 (Oct. 1882): 706.

55. R. A. Torrey, *What the Bible Teaches* (Chicago: Fleming H. Revell, 1898), 1.

56. Robert Dick Wilson, *A Scientific Investigation of the Old Testament* (Philadelphia: Sunday School Times, 1926), 6–7.

bodied the optimism, this-worldliness, and scientific confidence of the early evangelical Enlightenment — and because evangelicals for a century had known no other world, it was second nature to address new problems with the old certainties of the first American Enlightenment. In the early American Enlightenment, evangelicals had been able to unite a commitment to democratic authority from the people and intellectual authority from science. In response to shifting academic conditions after the Civil War, conservative evangelicals tried to retain the old populist science, liberal evangelicals opted instead for an elite new science over against the old populism, but both, with the multitudes in between, did not challenge the older conceptions of self-justifying authority or the dictates of common sense.

The Intellectual Legacy of the Evangelical-American Cultural Synthesis

Evangelical adoption of the didactic Enlightenment was one of the measures that made evangelical Protestantism so dynamically powerful in the early history of the United States. Had evangelicals not done so, their fate would probably have been like the fate of Europe's established churches, which, as they continued to rely on tradition and hierarchy, increasingly lost touch with ordinary people and eventually forfeited their once-dominant place in Europe's intellectual life. It was, in its own terms, a tremendous achievement for American evangelicals to save both the reputation of the gospel and their own influence within society. That achievement should not be taken lightly. Unfortunately, however, the successful alliance of evangelicals with main currents of American culture left a weak intellectual legacy.

The main problem was that so much of the Christianized version of the Enlightenment depended on assumptions, and thus so little actual thought went into developing the philosophical, psychological, and ethical implications of these views. All was well as long as Christian energies guided the nation. But once those energies were frustrated by the new social conditions after the Civil War, once they were challenged by new ideas from Europe that also penetrated American life increasingly after that same conflict, there was very little intellectual strength to meet the new challenges. Common-sense philosophy, as well as republican politics, democratic social theory, and liberal economics — all have something to recommend them to Christians. For each a case can be made that they can be compatible with Christian ideals. The difficulty for evangelical intellectual history, however, was that so little went into making the case. Evangelicals mostly just took for granted a fit between their faith and these ideals of the American situation. Little need was felt to exercise the mind for Christ, since evangelism and fervent moral activism seemed so successful at meeting the church's immediate needs.

But eventually the chickens came home to roost. After the Civil War, a sense of cultural and intellectual crisis grew rapidly. Evangelism continued, with much good being done by leaders like D. L. Moody. But Christians also suffered many reverses. They were pressed beyond their intellectual resources. Within a generation, the cities had mushroomed; older churches no longer seemed able to preserve a vital witness in those cities; immigration brought vast numbers of new Americans and great problems of social cohesion; mammoth factories sprang up, and their owners achieved unrivaled influence in public life; freed slaves were forced back into inhumane conditions in the South and allowed a mere subsistence in the North; the Bible came increasingly under attack as a largely irrelevant, mythological book; and new views in biology challenged both divine creation and the uniqueness of the human species.[57]

When Christians turned to their intellectual resources for dealing with these matters, they found that the cupboard was nearly bare. Scripture, they believed, still had the answers to all of life's problems — but what were they? Who had been spending time thinking about these kinds of social and intellectual problems? Who had been devoting the energy to these issues that had been devoted to evangelism? The sad answer is that almost no one had been engaged in such a process of consistent Christian thinking.

57. These changes are well summarized in Robert H. Wiebe, *The Search for Order, 1877–1920* (New York: Hill & Wang, 1967); and Ferenc Morton Szasz, *The Divided Mind of Protestant America, 1880–1930* (University: University of Alabama Press, 1982).

The prominence of Bible-onlyism, at the expense of well-articulated theology, meant that when new conditions arose — first the great social changes at the end of the nineteenth century, and then the continuing series of twentieth-century changes: the Great Depression, extreme religious pluralism, World War II, the rise of Communism, the collapse of Communism — there was little ground from which to reason. Evangelicals throughout the nineteenth century had not worked very self-consciously at thinking about the best ways, consistent with the Bible itself, to push thinking from the Scripture to modern situations and back again. That is, habits of patient study were far less well exercised than habits of quick quotation. Proof-texting did not cause great damage so long as the culture as a whole held to general Christian values, but when those general Christian values began to weaken, the weakness in evangelical theologizing — even more, in thinking like a Christian about the world in general — became all too evident.

As a result the Christian cause suffered. The effective evangelism and moral fervor of an earlier age had not been matched by comparable Christian attention to the mind. The consequences were sobering. A theological liberalism emerged that had little concern for human sinfulness, God's grace, or the supernatural work of Christ. A secular spirit spread rapidly in the general culture. In response, the descendants of orthodox evangelicalism, many of whom would soon be called fundamentalists, did hold on to basic Christian truths, but in order to do so they fled from the problems of the wider world into fascination with inner spirituality or the details of end-times prophecy.

$$\frac{\text{LARGE CULTURAL STORY}}{\text{INDIVIDUAL STORIES}}$$

$$\frac{\text{CONTEXT}}{\text{DETAILS}} \qquad \frac{\text{PICTURE-ON-THE-BOX}}{\text{PUZZLE PIECES}}$$

$$\frac{\text{WHOLE}}{\text{PARTS}}$$

CHAPTER 5

The Intellectual Disaster of Fundamentalism

The story of evangelical thought in the decades surrounding the beginning of the twentieth century is a discouraging one. Yet in order to understand the nature of the problem, it is important to remember the larger cultural story. That larger picture featured two realities: the evolution of American society away from what had previously been the dominant Protestant (and usually evangelical) public ethos of the United States, and the introduction among conservative evangelicals of several important theological innovations.[1] A full history of religion in North America, or a full history of North American evangelicalism, would have to begin with that larger picture, since it provides the indispensable context for the more specific intellectual developments.[2]

---

1. Again at this point, fuller comparisons with Canada would be beneficial, for both English Canada and French Canada retained their different forms of Christian culture longer than did the United States. Among Canadian evangelicals, the new theologies of the late nineteenth century did not produce the same levels of intellectual antagonism as in the United States; see especially Michael Gauvreau, *The Evangelical Century: College and Creed in English Canada from the Great Revival to the Great Depression* (Montreal and Kingston: McGill-Queen's University Press, 1991); and Marguerite Van Die, *An Evangelical Mind: Nathanael Burwash and the Methodist Tradition in Canada, 1839–1918* (Montreal and Kingston: McGill-Queen's University Press, 1989).

2. The indispensable study is George M. Marsden, *Fundamentalism and American Culture: The Shaping of Twentieth-Century Evangelicalism, 1870–1925* (New York:

This account, however, will focus on the specifically intellectual story, one shaped externally by developments in the colleges and universities of the wider intellectual world and internally by the effects of the fundamentalist-modernist controversy. That controversy, in turn, has two parts — first, the more general legacies bequeathed to intellectual life by fundamentalism; second, the specific problems created for evangelical intellectual life by the widespread adoption of Holiness, pentecostal, and dispensational theologies. These external and internal developments would combine by the 1930s to leave American conservative evangelicals intellectually moribund.

The Transformation of the University

Few historical transitions have been more momentous for evangelical thinking in North America than the reorganization of higher education at the end of the nineteenth century, for this was a reorganization that saw the evangelicals, who had dominated college life to that time, utterly displaced as the intellectual arbiters of the nation. As we noted in the last chapter, evangelicals had successfully mastered the didactic Enlightenment and, with that mastery, had become a dominant intellectual force in the new United States.

During the period 1865 through 1900 all of this changed.[3] When

---

Oxford University Press, 1980). Other useful accounts that put the evangelical story in broader contexts are found in Sydney E. Ahlstrom, *A Religious History of the American People* (New Haven: Yale University Press, 1972), 731–872; Robert T. Handy, *A History of the Churches in the United States and Canada* (New York: Oxford University Press, 1977), 262–376; George W. Dollar, *A History of Fundamentalism in America* (Greenville, SC: Bob Jones University Press, 1973); Martin E. Marty, *Modern American Religion*, vol. 1: *1893–1919;* vol. 2: *1919–1941* (Chicago: University of Chicago Press, 1986–91); and Mark A. Noll, *A History of Christianity in the United States and Canada* (Grand Rapids: Eerdmans, 1992), 311–89.

3. Besides the general studies mentioned in chapter 4, nn. 47 and 57, also insightful on these large-scale transitions are Burton J. Bledstein, *The Culture of Professionalism: The Middle Class and the Development of Higher Education in America* (New York: Norton, 1976); and Bruce Kuklick, *The Rise of American Philosophy: Cambridge, Massachusetts, 1860–1930* (New Haven: Yale University Press, 1977). The

Charles Eliot became president of Harvard in 1869, he set that influential institution on a course of innovation and expansion. The Johns Hopkins University, founded in 1876, exercised leadership in the establishment of graduate education. Other major changes were also under way: new universities were founded like Cornell, Chicago, and Stanford; older private colleges like Yale, Princeton, and Columbia were transformed into universities with the addition of graduate and professional schools; major state universities like Michigan and Wisconsin grew up almost overnight in the Midwest and West.

It is of the greatest significance that the money for this academic explosion did not come from the Christian communities that had hitherto provided the financial wherewithal for American higher education. Rather it was first the wealthy new entrepreneurs and then the state governments that provided the funds for this expansion. Funding networks connected with churches and evangelical voluntary societies became less and less important with each passing year.

This period also saw an unprecedented rise in the number of students attending colleges and universities. While the country's population nearly doubled between 1870 and 1900 (from 40 million to 76 million), the number of college students increased nearly five times. Where less than 1 percent of college-age people attended higher education in 1860, by 1930 the proportion had risen to 12.4 percent.

Almost unnoticed in the great influx of dollars and students was the decline of Christian characteristics that had marked higher education to this time. Neither the new donors nor the new breed of administrators was overly concerned about the orthodoxy of their faculties. Visible signs of this change abounded. At Harvard compulsory chapel ceased in 1886. The opening ceremonies at Johns Hopkins in 1876 contained no prayer but did feature an address by British evolutionary theorist Thomas Huxley. As money from businessmen increased, so did their concern that boards of trustees and college administrators function in a businesslike way. Thus it was that industrialists and bankers replaced clergymen as trustees, and laymen replaced ministers as college presidents. In 1839, fifty-one of the fifty-four presidents of America's

paragraphs that follow modify Mark A. Noll, introduction to *The Christian College*, by William C. Ringenberg, (Grand Rapids: Eerdmans, 1984), 1–36.

colleges were clergymen, most evangelicals. By the end of the century the number was greatly reduced.

For its curriculum, the new universities took a German model of education to replace the older British standard. Not character but research, not the handing on of tradition but the search for intellectual innovation became the watchword. In the curriculum of the renovated universities, moreover, new ideals of science, modeled especially after the striking proposals of Charles Darwin's *Origin of Species,* took on an unprecedented importance.

Systematically, the new university replaced the traditional emphases of Christian higher education in America. That education had been deeply flawed, but it did attempt a reconciliation between Christian faith and the world of learning. Between the Civil War and World War I, that reconciliation became less and less important.[4] Excess capital generated by the industrialists after the Civil War arose from a widespread exploitation of new scientific technology. This excess wealth was generated by individuals who had largely laid aside the constraints of altruism that America's old Christian-cultural synthesis had tried to inculcate. American industrialists, to one degree or another, seemed to have favored the kind of social Darwinism popularized by Herbert Spencer. One of the reasons this new class of wealthy Americans funded education was to encourage more of the practical science and managerial theory coming from the new universities and less of the moralism coming from the old colleges. Whether through the direct influence of the industrialists or not, clergymen were replaced by businessmen on college boards of trustees, and ministers were replaced as college presidents by educators alert to management ideas and the demands of the new science. These new presidents, in turn, focused much more attention on academic reputation than on the preservation of orthodoxy. Furthermore, the new scholarship that these presidents encouraged was liberated from the old orthodoxies that once dominated American

---

4. Three good case studies of the change are David P. Potts, *Wesleyan University, 1831–1910* (New Haven: Yale University Press, 1992); John Barnard, *From Evangelicalism to Progressivism at Oberlin College, 1866–1917* (Columbus: Ohio State University Press, 1969); and Thomas H. A. Le Duc, *Piety and Intellect at Amherst College, 1865–1910* (New York: Arno Press, 1969).

colleges. The new work was increasingly naturalistic in science and pragmatic in philosophy. In turn — and this brings us full circle — the new naturalistic science and the new pragmatic philosophy encouraged industrial giantism by providing training and technique to the capitalists while at the same time offering few criticisms of the new industrial wealth.

It is not as though religious emphases faded away altogether in the transformation of the university. Religious emphases still remained, but the schools that flourished were those that made their peace with the new developments.[5] A type of moderately liberal Protestantism that championed the rise of America in the world, the spread of democracy at home, and the application of modern science to social problems retained its place in the new university. But this Protestantism turned away from several traditional evangelical convictions, such as the universal need for salvation in Christ and the supernatural character of the Incarnation. While accepting the authority of the Bible as an indispensable record of religious experience, liberal Protestants were eager to explain away what were held to be the cruder supernatural aspects of Scripture.

Against this combination of new money, social Darwinism, naturalistic science, and accommodating Protestantism, the old synthesis of evangelical convictions, American ideals, and a common-sense Baconian science faded rapidly away. The collapse of that synthesis signaled the collapse of the effort by conservative evangelicals to construct a Christian mind in America. From the point of view of the new university, the effort to view knowledge whole was increasingly abandoned under the assumption that discrete parts of truth, discovered through empirical science, could stand on their own. The effort to integrate religious faith with learning was either given up entirely, under the assumption that the pursuit of science carried with it no antecedent

5. See especially the essays by Bradley J. Longfield and Darryl G. Hart in *The Secularization of the Academy,* ed. George M. Marsden and Bradley J. Longfield (New York: Oxford University Press, 1992); George M. Marsden, *The Soul of the American University* (New York: Oxford University Press, 1994); and R. Laurence Moore, "Secularization: Religion and the Social Sciences," in *Between the Times: The Travail of the Protestant Establishment, 1900–1960,* ed. William R. Hutchison (New York: Cambridge University Press, 1989).

commitments to a worldview — or it was greatly modified, under the felt need to align religion with the certainties of modern thought. In the process, common-sense ethics and Baconian inductivism lost out almost entirely to new forms of thought less congenial to Christian exploitation.

The quality of Christian thinking may not have been high in antebellum America. But at least it was there. With the rise of the new university, evangelical thinking, which had previously existed in the tension between academic and populist styles, became almost exclusively populist.

Fundamentalism

The fundamentalist movement was a response to general changes in American life, of which the transformation of the universities was only one among many. Those who would become fundamentalists feared what the massive immigration of Roman Catholics, Jews, and the unchurched was doing to a United States they considered a Protestant country; they were bewildered by the burgeoning cities that were rapidly displacing small towns and the countryside (where Protestantism had thrived) as the centers of American civilization; and they were appalled by the vogue for naturalist philosophy, and with it the dismissal of the Bible, that extended far beyond the universities. So central were these general concerns that it is possible to view the intellectual impact of fundamentalism as a kind of historical by-product. Even as a by-product, however, that intellectual impact was profound.[6]

6. The best studies of the fundamentalist phenomenon are Marsden, *Fundamentalism and American Culture,* and Ernest R. Sandeen, *The Roots of Fundamentalism: British and American Millenarianism, 1800–1930* (Chicago: University of Chicago Press, 1970). But valuable insights are added from books written by latter-day upholders of fundamentalism, such as Dollar, *History of Fundamentalism,* and David O. Beale, *In Pursuit of Purity: American Fundamentalism since 1850* (Greenville, SC: Unusual Publications, 1986); and by considerations of fundamentalism in specific regions, of which William Vance Trollinger, Jr., *God's Empire: William Bell Riley and Midwestern Fundamentalism* (Madison: University of Wisconsin Press, 1990), is a model. Mark Ellingsen, *The Evangelical Movement* (Minneapolis: Augsburg, 1988),

For theologically conservative Christians, the fundamentalist episode in American church history must be ambiguous. Fundamentalists
of the early twentieth century defended many convictions essential to
a traditional understanding of Christianity. At a time when naturalism
threatened religion, when relativism assaulted social morality, when
intellectual fashions were turning the Bible into a book of merely
antiquarian interest, fundamentalists said what needed to be said about
the supernatural character of religion, the objectivity of Christian
morality, and the timeless validity of Scripture.

At the same time, fundamentalism created major problems in
several ways for the life of the mind. First, it gave a new impetus to
general anti-intellectualism; second, it hardened conservative evangelical commitments to certain features of the nineteenth-century evangeli-
cal-American synthesis that were problematic to begin with; and third,
its major theological emphases had a chilling effect on the exercise of
Christian thinking about the world. But before examining these effects,
it would be helpful to summarize briefly the major theological innovations of the fundamentalist era.

Theological Innovations

The theological energy behind the fundamentalist defense of traditional
beliefs, as well as the fundamentalist reaction to the perceived crises of
American civilization, came from several new theological emphases.
These were Holiness (or "higher life" or "Keswick") spirituality, pentecostalism, and premillennial dispensationalism.

The Holiness emphasis accentuated historic Christian concern for
the indwelling presence of the Holy Spirit, the need for personal sanc-
tity, and the possibility of growing in grace throughout human life.[7] It

---

contains much that is relevant to the concerns of this chapter from the vantage point
of European and American Lutheranism.

7. For orientation, see Thomas C. Oden, ed., *Phoebe Palmer: Selected Writings*
(New York: Paulist Press, 1988); Melvin Easterday Dieter, *The Holiness Revival of the
Nineteenth Century* (Metuchen, NJ: Scarecrow Press, 1980); and H. Vinson Synan, *The
Holiness-Pentecostal Movement in the United States* (Grand Rapids: Eerdmans, 1971).

had been promoted effectively by Methodists and Wesleyans like Mrs. Phoebe Palmer during the middle part of the nineteenth century, it was increasingly an emphasis at Oberlin College in the latter years of Charles Finney's work at that institution, and it drew strength from a general Protestant stress on the work of Holy Spirit that had come to dominate the influential Keswick retreat center in England. A concern for holiness was one of the major factors in the creation of denominations like the Church of the Nazarene. But its influences spread far beyond just the Wesleyan groups. The stock phrases of the Holiness movement — "to lay all on the altar," to be "clay in the potter's hands," to experience a "deeper walk of grace," a "closer walk" with Christ, the "baptism of the Holy Ghost," a "higher life," "victorious living," or "overcoming power" — bespoke a growing concern to experience the realities of Christian spirituality.[8]

Pentecostalism emerged fully at the Azusa Street revival of 1906 in Los Angeles, but it too was a culmination of emphases, many of them emerging from the Holiness movement and some more generally from the concerns of sectarian Protestants.[9] Variations on a fourfold gospel message — stressing salvation in Christ, divine healing, the baptism or fullness of the Holy Spirit (eventually thought to be manifest most clearly through speaking in tongues), and the imminent return of Christ — were flourishing throughout North America and western Europe in the decades before the turn of the century. After its formal emergence, Pentecostalism developed along several different lines, but its central feature remained the belief that the person of the Holy Spirit could be experienced — verbally, physically, spiritually — in this latter day.

Multiform and diverse as the expressions of early twentieth-cen-

8. An excellent guide for historical context is Grant Wacker, "The Holy Spirit and the Spirit of the Age in American Protestantism, 1880–1910," *Journal of American History* 72 (June 1985): 45–62.

9. For orientation, see Edith Waldvogel Blumhofer, *Restoring the Faith: The Assemblies of God, Pentecostalism, and American Culture* (Urbana: University of Illinois Press, 1993); Donald W. Dayton, *Theological Roots of Pentecostalism* (Metuchen, NJ: Scarecrow Press, 1987); and David Edwin Harrell, *All Things Are Possible: The Healing and Charismatic Revival in Modern America* (Bloomington: Indiana University Press, 1975).

tury Holiness and Pentecostalism were, those movements may be simpler to define than the dispensational theology that began to prevail among vast numbers of evangelicals at the end of the century.[10] As a set of theological emphases, dispensationalism had been brought to America in the mid-nineteenth century by John Nelson Darby, an early leader of the Plymouth Brethren. Dispensationalism soon developed a large following alongside other forms of evangelical biblical theology, particularly as it was featured in the prophecy movement, and especially the annual meetings held at Niagara-on-the-Lake, Ontario, toward the end of the century. With the publication of C. I. Scofield's annotated edition of the King James Version in 1909 (a second edition followed shortly thereafter in 1917), premillennial dispensationalism came to dominate those northern evangelicals who had left the mainline denominations and to exert a growing influence among evangelicals North and South who remained in the historic denominations.

10. The standard accounts illustrate the difficulty of definition, since they tend to reflect different emphases, depending on when they were written. For explanations by some of the main "insiders," see C. I. Scofield, *Rightly Dividing the Word of Truth* (Philadelphia: Philadelphia School of the Bible, 1921); Lewis Sperry Chafer, *Dispensationalism* (Dallas: Dallas Seminary Press, 1936); Chafer, *Systematic Theology,* 8 vols. (Dallas: Dallas Seminary Press, 1947); Charles Caldwell Ryrie, *The Basis of the Premillennial Faith* (New York: Loizeaux Brothers, 1953); and Ryrie, *Dispensationalism Today* (Chicago: Moody Press, 1965). Among the fairest of accounts by opponents are C. Norman Kraus, *Dispensationalism in America* (Richmond: John Knox, 1958); Clarence B. Bass, *Backgrounds to Dispensationalism* (Grand Rapids: Eerdmans, 1960); Daniel P. Fuller, *Gospel and Law: Contrast or Continuum? The Hermeneutics of Dispensationalism and Covenant Theology* (Grand Rapids: Eerdmans, 1980); and Vern Poythress, *Understanding Dispensationalists* (Grand Rapids: Zondervan, 1987).

Recent works by self-avowed "progressive dispensationalists" make the task of definition harder because they reject as essential to dispensationalism certain beliefs that earlier foes and proponents alike had featured as the essence of the theology. For examples, see Robert Saucy, "Contemporary Dispensational Thought," *TSF Bulletin* 7 (Mar.–Apr. 1984): 10–11; Saucy, "Dispensationalism and the Salvation of the Kingdom," *TSF Bulletin* 7 (May–June 1984): 1–2; Craig A. Blaising, "Doctrinal Development in Orthodoxy" and "Development of Dispensationalism by Contemporary Dispensationalists," *Bibliotheca Sacra* 145 (1988): 133–40, 254–80; and especially the essays by editors Craig A. Blaising and Darrell L. Bock in *Dispensationalism, Israel, and the Church: The Search for Definition* (Grand Rapids: Zondervan, 1992). I would like to thank Stephen Spencer and Stan Gundry for introducing me to much of this more recent material.

Dispensationalism is difficult to define because it has meant different things to its different exponents, and because outside observers and opponents have isolated different elements as its central teaching. In a classic statement from 1965, Charles Ryrie tried to isolate three beliefs as "the *sine qua non* of dispensationalism": (1) a strict distinction between Israel and the church (from which flows the concern for the various divine dispensations in history), (2) "a system of hermeneutics which is usually called literal interpretation" but that Ryrie thought could be better denominated "normal or plain"; and (3) a concern for the glory of God rather than simply the outworking of salvation as the "underlying purpose of God in the world."[11] Some later dispensationalists, however, have questioned Ryrie's effort in trying to provide an essentialist definition for a complicated pattern of beliefs that have never been stable since their first formulation by Darby in the nineteenth century.[12] Craig Blaising and Darrell Bock, who call themselves "progressive dispensationalists," have identified four distinct phases to dispensational teaching — the dispensationalism of the Niagara conferences, of Scofield (and his student Lewis Sperry Chafer), of Ryrie, and of the progressives. They also note that still other variations exist like the Brethren theology of Darby, the dispensationalism to be found in some branches of Pentecostalism that concentrate on the new dispensation of the Holy Spirit, and the date-setting "historicism" of those like Hal Lindsey, who identify current events as the fulfillment of biblical prophecies (early dispensationalists advocated "futurism," the belief that prophetic events would be fulfilled in the future, in order to escape the onus of Seventh-day Adventist "historicism," which claimed to find fulfillment of biblical prophecy in contemporary events).[13]

For this book, however, the altogether praiseworthy effort to trace the shifting center of gravity in dispensationalism and to extract from that history fruitful lines of theological inquiry for the present is a different

11. Ryrie, *Dispensationalism Today,* 44–46.

12. Blaising, "Dispensationalism: The Search for Definition," in *Dispensationalism, Israel, and the Church* (Grand Rapids: Zondervan, 1992), 23–30.

13. Blaising and Bock, "Dispensationalism, Israel, and the Church: Assessment and Dialogue," in *Dispensationalism, Israel, and the Church* (Grand Rapids: Zondervan, 1992), 379.

enterprise from that of describing the intellectual history of evangelical-ism. For the latter purposes, the features of the various dispensationalisms that seem most prominent are the ones that readers of Darby, Scofield, Chafer, Ryrie, and John Walvoord (Chafer's successor as president of Dallas Theological Seminary) encountered in their many and widely read publications. In these terms, dispensationalism is an understanding of the Bible that divides the relationship of God to humanity into sharply separated epochs. The Bible is taken to provide explicit divine interpreta-tion for these epochs, or dispensations, that extend from Adam to the end of the New Testament, as well as for the dispensation foretold in Scripture for the end of time. The intervening "age of the church" is sometimes treated as a parenthesis, where the ebb and flow of events serve primarily to prepare believers for God's final in-breaking upon human history. The method of dispensationalism is a literalism in which great care is taken to arrange passages of Scripture from throughout the whole Bible (as in the Scofield example quoted in note 24) to establish biblical truths, especially truths concerning the end of the world.

The key to dispensationalism's popularity has been an ability to render the prophetic parts of the Bible understandable to ordinary people and applicable to current circumstances. Today, the convictions of "progressive" dispensationalists sound increasingly like variations on time-honored historic Protestant themes concerning the covenant or the kingdom of Christ. But historically considered, dispensationalists have stressed the decline or apostasy of institutional churches, the consequent degeneration of civilization, and the need for Christians to separate from institutions of ungodliness. Dispensationalists tradition-ally viewed their task in the present epoch as rescuing unbelievers from sin and keeping themselves unspotted from the world. The supernat-uralism of dispensationalism has always been intense. The unmediated agency of God is thought to lie behind all wholesome activities on earth; the mediated agency of Satan is perceived behind all natural and human evil.[14]

14. This description comes more from the works of earlier dispensationalists and the summary-critiques of their opponents (such as Bass, *Backgrounds to Dispe-nationalism,* and Kraus, *Dispensationalism in America*) than from the recent interpreta-tions of "progressive dispensationalists."

The confluence of these dispensational influences with the rising tides of Holiness and pentecostal belief marked a momentous stage in the development of American evangelicalism. The three movements were never entirely aligned, and in fact dispensationalists frequently attacked the pentecostal emphasis on tongues speaking, even as Holiness advocates decried the complicated biblical arguments of the dispensationalists, and some pentecostals, as a distraction from godliness. Yet together these movements shared a stress on the dangers of the world, the comforts of separated piety, the centrality of evangelism, and an expectation of the End. These emphases, in turn, exerted a powerful effect on evangelical thought.

TRANSCENDENCE   PERSONAL   HOLY SPIRIT
IMMANENCE   MECHANICAL   PRAGMATIC

Why These Theological Innovations?

Several explanations are possible to account for the rise of dispensational premillennialism alongside the Holiness movement and Pentecostalism. To adherents, simple biblical truth is the heart of the matter. Each of the three innovations, moreover, emphasized features of Christianity that were increasingly being called into question by the cultural elites of North America. Where divine immanence loomed ever larger among the learned, dispensationalists defended the transcendent control of God over history. Where the trust in mechanistic science grew ever greater in the culture as a whole, pentecostals insisted upon the ability of God to break into the life of the most ordinary person. Where learned elites were proposing pragmatic, democratic, and social-scientific solutions to the gravest modern problems, Holiness advocates offered the Holy Spirit.

Others suggest different reasons for why huge numbers of evangelicals adopted the new religious beliefs. Leo Ribuffo, a historian with no stake in the religious issues under debate, has viewed the dispensational premillennialism of the early twentieth century as simply a recasting of religious ideas, populist strategies of communication, and habits of political morality that had existed time out of mind in the American experience.[15]

15. Leo P. Ribuffo, *The Old Christian Right: The Protestant Far Right from the Great Depression to the Cold War* (Philadelphia: Temple University Press, 1983).

These theological emphases may also have been ways of coping with the marginalization that evangelical Protestants were undergoing in North America. Evangelicals might have been losing their once-dominant role in American society, but because they studied their Bible, they knew where history was headed; because they "laid their all on the altar of sacrifice," they were protected from tumults of the day. Timothy Weber has phrased this possibility gently: "Premillennialism did not create the crises of the last century; it simply capitalized on them. In a world out of control, the premillennialist view of the future provided both a blessed hope and a way of understanding why things were going so badly. There is an ironic comfort in knowing that centuries ago, the Bible predicted the current mess."[16] But it is also possible to make the same assessment with a sharper edge, as Douglas Frank has done: "I tend to think that it was just this quality of dispensationalism — its rationalistic neatness and systematic comprehensiveness — that recommended it to the evangelicals who, during the perilous times at the turn of the nineteenth century, were casting about for some means to bring history back under their control."[17]

David Bebbington, a historian of British evangelicalism, illuminates the search for historical cause-and-effect by providing several reasons why dispensational premillennialism became so much more important in America than it did in Britain, despite the fact that evangelicals in the two regions shared much else in common.[18] Bebbington concludes that a number of factors created the difference. In the 1870s and 1880s Britain witnessed the publication of important

16. Timothy P. Weber, "Premillennialism and the Branches of Evangelicalism," in *The Variety of American Evangelicalism,* ed. Donald W. Dayton and Robert K. Johnston (Knoxville: University of Tennessee Press; Downers Grove, IL: InterVarsity Press, 1991), 17. Weber's *Living in the Shadow of the Second Coming: American Premillennialism, 1875–1982,* rev. ed. (Chicago: University of Chicago Press, 1987) is a fine general study of the main dispensational emphases.

17. Douglas W. Frank, *Less Than Conquerors: How Evangelicals Entered the Twentieth Century* (Grand Rapids: Eerdmans, 1986), 73.

18. David Bebbington, "Evangelicalism in Modern Britain and America: A Comparison," in *Amazing Grace: Evangelicalism in Australia, Britain, Canada, and the United States,* ed. George A. Rawlyk and Mark A. Noll (Grand Rapids: Baker; Montreal and Kingston: McGill-Queen's University Press, 1994).

historicist interpretations of the end times at the very moment when futurist dispensationalism was becoming important in America. In Britain, Darbyite premillennialism was viewed as the particular property of just one sect (that is, the Brethren) and so was not taken as seriously as it was in America, where dispensationalism first appeared at the ecumenical prophecy conferences. In the United States, the doctrine of biblical inerrancy, which was such a critical presupposition for the dispensationalist effort to interpret prophetic Scripture literally, received much more learned defense than in Britain.[19] Finally, the dispensationalist attack on the institutional church was an argument more likely to find a favorable audience in the United States, where evangelical churchmanship was relatively weak, than in Great Britain, where members of the state churches of England and Scotland exerted great influence in the evangelical movement.

The larger cultural reasons for the spread of dispensationalism, as well as for the spread of Holiness teachings and Pentecostalism, deserve much more serious study than they have received. Incontrovertibly, however, these innovations did take place. Just as incontrovertibly, they affected evangelical thinking dramatically.

The Meaning of the Innovations

The fundamentalist era remains critical for evangelical thinking, since it so thoroughly established habits of mind for looking (or not looking) at the world. It greatly encouraged a set of intellectual instincts that still, after a century filled with change, exert a pervasive influence over the thinking of evangelicals. Fundamentalism — especially as articulated in dispensationalism, the most self-conscious theological system supporting the movement — was important for encouraging several

---

19. An ironic situation is present at this point. The most learned defense in America of biblical inerrancy was made by B. B. Warfield of Princeton Theological Seminary, who, however, held that dispensationalism "is scarcely in harmony with the New Testament point of view"; Warfield, "The Gospel and the Second Coming," in *Selected Shorter Writings of B. B. Warfield*, vol. 1, ed. John E. Meeter (Phillipsburg, NJ: Presbyterian and Reformed, 1970), 348-55, quotation 355.

kinds of simple anti-intellectualism, for reinforcing some of the questionable features of the nineteenth-century American evangelical synthesis, and for promoting right conclusions with the wrong kind of thought. The result was a tendency toward a docetism in outlook and a gnosticism in method that together constitute the central intellectual indictment against the fundamentalist past.

A New Surge of Anti-Intellectualism

In the first instance, fundamentalism hurt the effort to use the mind for the glory of God and for a better understanding of the world he had made by indulging in new forms of anti-intellectualism. This problem may not have been as serious as it first seems, for, however much defenders of supernatural religion, especially pentecostals and advocates of Holiness, may have turned away from the world's learning, their emphasis on the practical presence of God did represent pursuit of an essentially Christian goal. The problem came not with the goal, but with the assumption that, in order to be spiritual, one must no longer pay attention to the world.

Martyn Lloyd-Jones, the Welsh physician turned preacher, addressed a conference in 1941 that was called to assess reasons for the intellectual weakness of British evangelicals that then seemed so obvious to its own leaders as well as to outside observers. In his remarks, Lloyd-Jones highlighted the effects of the new theological positions from the end of the nineteenth century. What he said about the British scene was perhaps even more applicable to the American. Lloyd-Jones first highlighted the kind of ardent supernaturalism, which was manifest in the United States through the mingled influence of Pentecostalism and dispensationalism, by noting "the enduring influence of movements in the early nineteenth century (particularly noticeable in Edward Irving's Catholic Apostolic Church and among the Brethren) which emphasized the imminence of the Second Advent or the availability of gifts of prophecy in a manner which lessened the need for scholarship." He then went on to a nuanced account of the effects of the Holiness movement:

The Keswick, "higher-life" movement . . . also contributed to a reduction of interest in biblical theology and deeper scholarship. No Christian in his right mind will desire anything other than true holiness and righteousness in the church of God. But Keswick had isolated *one* doctrine, holiness, and altered it by the false simplicity contained in the slogan, "Give up, let go and let God." If you want to be holy and righteous, we are told, the intellect is dangerous and it is thought generally unlikely that a good theologian is likely to be a holy person. . . . You asked me to *diagnose* the reasons for the present weakness and I am doing it. . . . If you teach that sanctification consists of "letting go" and letting the Holy Spirit *do all the work,* then don't blame me if you have no scholars![20]

One of the additional consequences from the dogmatic kind of biblical literalism that gained increasing strength among evangelicals toward the end of the nineteenth century was reduced space for academic debate, intellectual experimentation, and nuanced discrimination between shades of opinion. This situation also had an anti-intellectual effect by driving out of fundamentalism at least some intellectuals who, though entirely content with classical Christian orthodoxy, found the modes of fundamentalism a disgrace. The Irish historian David Hempton has noted this result among British evangelicals as a result of the vogue of eschatology that J. N. Darby and others eventually carried to North America: "An ultra-simplistic view of the Bible and its interpretation was offensive to some intellectuals, who started out as evangelicals, and it placed the millenarians in a very vulnerable position in the face of biblical criticism. . . . Millenarianism was but one element in the increasing narrowness of evangelicalism which made it so unattractive to its more thoughtful adherents. The hard biblical literalism of the prophetical speculators left evangelicalism wide open to the mid-century attacks from biblical criticism and science."[21] These same anti-intellectual features would later

20. Quoted in Iain H. Murray, *D. Martyn Lloyd-Jones: The Fight of Faith, 1939–1981* (Edinburgh: Banner of Truth, 1990), 72–74.
21. D. N. Hempton, "Evangelicalism and Eschatology," *Journal of Ecclesiastical History* 31 (Apr. 1980): 187, 194. Hempton was referring, among others, to John Henry Newman, who left his evangelical upbringing for high-church Anglicanism and

prompt E. J. Carnell to call American fundamentalism a "cultic" and "ideological" movement only partially connected with Christian orthodoxy.[22]

In addition, the fundamentalist movement reinforced the dogmatic power of populist teachers. With the universities and their formal learning suspect, the spokesperson who could step forth confidently on the basis of the Scriptures was welcomed as a convincing authority. John Wick Bowman, an opponent of the dispensational system, nonetheless caught accurately one of the traits that made the Scofield Bible such a powerful tool for teaching dispensationalism: "There is a certain quality of infallibility attaching to [Scofield's] numerous dicta on all sorts of subjects — a quality no doubt calculated to attract the uneasy and comparatively illiterate in biblical lore but wholly unimpressive to one looking for genuine scholarship."[23] It is not necessary to accept Bowman's assessment of those who read the Scofield Bible to realize that he captured something important about the intellectual style of fundamentalist leaders. When, for example, Scofield interpreted obscure, contested biblical passages — like the "weeks" of Daniel 9:24 — as if his interpretation was the only one possible and as if the bearing of his interpretation on the general meaning of the Bible was intuitively compelling, he modeled a style that had anything but beneficial effects on evangelical thinking.[24] If intellectual life involves a certain amount

---

then Roman Catholicism, and Newman's brother Francis, who moved from evangelicalism to agnosticism.

22. E. J. Carnell, *The Case for Orthodox Theology* (Philadelphia: Westminster, 1959), 53, 114–17.

23. John Wick Bowman, "Dispensationalism," *Interpretation* 10 (1956): 172.

24. The following is the entire note on the "weeks" of Daniel 9:24 from *The Scofield Reference Bible*, rev. ed. (New York: Oxford University Press, 1917), 914–15: "These are 'weeks' or, more accurately, sevens of years; seventy weeks of seven years each. Within these 'weeks' the national chastisement must be ended and the nation re-established in everlasting righteousness (v. 24). The seventy weeks are divided into seven = 49 years; sixty-two = 434 years; one = 7 years (vs. 25–27). In the seven weeks = 49 years, Jerusalem was to be rebuilt in 'troublous times.' This was fulfilled, as Ezra and Nehemiah record. Sixty-two weeks = 434 years, thereafter Messiah was to come (v. 25). This was fulfilled in the birth and manifestation of Christ. Verse 26 is obviously an indeterminate period. The date of the crucifixion is not fixed. It is only said to be 'after' the threescore and two weeks. It is the first event in verse 26. The second event

of self-awareness about alternative interpretations or a certain amount of tentativeness in exploring the connection between evidence and conclusions, it was hard to find any encouragement for the intellectual life in the self-assured dogmatism of fundamentalism.

Simple anti-intellectualism, however, was not the major problem in fundamentalism for the life of the mind. More serious damage was done by the way in which the fundamentalist movement reinforced nineteenth-century assumptions about the conduct of thinking itself.

Reinforcing the Nineteenth Century

A major impediment created by fundamentalism for a doxological understanding of nature, society, and the arts was its uncritical adoption of intellectual habits from the nineteenth century.[25] Especially dispensation-

---

is the destruction of the city, fulfilled in A.D. 70. Then, 'unto the end,' a period not fixed, but which has already lasted nearly 2000 years. To Daniel was revealed only that wars and desolations should continue (cf. Mt. 24.6–14). The N.T. reveals, that which was hidden from the O.T. prophets (Mt. 13.11–17; Eph. 3.1–10), that during this period should be accomplished the mysteries of the kingdom of Heaven (Mt. 13.1–50), and the out-calling of the Church (Mt. 16.18; Rom. 11.25). When the Church-age will end, and the seventieth week begin, is nowhere revealed. Its duration can be but seven years. To make it more violates the principle of interpretation already confirmed by fulfillment. Verse 27 deals with the last week. The 'he' of verse 27 is the 'prince that shall come' of verse 26, whose people (Rome) destroyed the temple in A.D. 70. He is the same with the 'little horn' of chapter 7. He will covenant with the Jews to restore their temple sacrifices for one week (seven years), but in the middle of that time he will break the covenant and fulfil Dan. 12.11; 2 Thes. 2.3, 4. Between the sixty-ninth week, after which Messiah was cut off, and the seventieth week, within which the 'little horn' of Dan. 7 will run his awful course, intervenes this entire Church-age. Verse 27 deals with the last three and a half years of the seven, which are identical with the 'great tribulation' (Mt. 24.15–28); 'time of trouble' (Dan. 12.1); 'hour of temptation' (Rev. 3.10). (See 'Tribulation,' Psa. 2.5; Rev. 7.14.)"

25. For background, see Marsden, *Fundamentalism and American Culture*, 55–62; Theodore Dwight Bozeman, *Protestants in an Age of Science: The Baconian Ideal and Antebellum Religious Thought* (Chapel Hill: University of North Carolina Press, 1977); and the section on scientific method in Mark A. Noll, "Common Sense Traditions and American Evangelical Thought," *American Quarterly* 37 (Summer 1985): 222–25.

alism was heavily dependent upon nineteenth-century views of the goals and systematizing purposes of science. This overwhelming trust in the capacities of an objective, disinterested, unbiased, and neutral science perhaps was excusable in the early nineteenth century, but by the early twentieth century it was indefensible. Fundamentalist naïveté concerning science was matched by several other nineteenth-century traits that also undercut the possibility for a responsible intellectual life. These included a weakness for treating the verses of the Bible as pieces in a jigsaw puzzle that needed only to be sorted and then fit together to possess a finished picture of divine truth; an overwhelming tendency to "essentialism," or the conviction that a specific formula could capture for all times and places the essence of biblical truth for any specific issue concerning God, the human condition, or the fate of the world; a corresponding neglect of forces in history that shape perceptions and help define the issues that loom as most important to any particular age; and a self-confidence, bordering on hubris, manifested by an extreme antitraditionalism that casually discounted the possibility of wisdom from earlier generations. During the nineteenth century the broader, more historical concerns of leading theologians and lay intellectuals held these features of evangelical intellectual life in check. But they were traits that emerged unfettered in the fundamentalist era, especially among the proponents of dispensational theology.

The influential popular leaders of dispensationalism, from the time of Cyrus Scofield through the era of Charles Ryrie, spoke with one voice in defending the scientific, objective character of theology and in making that defense entirely in the terms of the nineteenth century. Scofield, for example, justified the preparation of his study Bible by claiming that "the old system of references, based solely upon the accident of the English words, was unscientific and often misleading."[26] Chafer's *Dispensationalism* claimed to center on "the specific meaning of the Scriptures" and so to come to its conclusions by "the most exacting proofs."[27] In Chafer's *Systematic Theology*, the catchphrases of nineteenth-century mechanistic scienticism constantly recur whenever theological method is discussed. Thus,

26. *Scofield Reference Bible*, iii.
27. Chafer, *Dispensationalism*, 7.

> Systematic Theology is the collecting, scientifically arranging, comparing, exhibiting, and defending of *all* facts from any and every source concerning God and His work. . . . The student of the Scriptures . . . will discover that God's great time-periods, characterized as they are by specific divine purposes, fall into a well-defined order. . . . God's program is as important to the theologian as the blueprint to the builder or the chart to the mariner. . . . Theology, as a science, has neglected this great field of revelation [typology]. . . . Contemplation of the doctrine of human conduct belongs properly to a science which purports to discover, classify, and exhibit the great doctrines of the Bible. . . . [T]he science of interpretation [is] usually designated *hermeneutics*. . . . [L]ogical procedure and scientific method [are the keys to hermeneutics].[28]

The scientistic language is muted somewhat in Ryrie's *Dispensationalism Today* but still provides the methodological framework for this important book.[29]

Along with this confidence in Baconian procedure went the characteristic nineteenth-century tendency to deprecate insights from the past. Scofield's self-confidence is legendary, as when he asserted in the opening pages of his most important methodological tract that "*any study* of the Word which ignores those Divisions [including the dispensations] must be in large measure profitless and confusing."[30] But a brisk antitraditionalism also energized Lewis Sperry Chafer's efforts at understanding the Scriptures. Chafer reportedly felt that his lack of formal theological training was an asset to his work as a theologian, because by not examining what others had done, he was preserved from their errors. In Chafer's words, "The very fact that I did not study a prescribed course in theology made it possible for me to approach the subject with an unprejudiced mind and to be concerned only with what the Bible actually teaches."[31]

28. Chafer, *Systematic Theology*, 1:x, xiii (2nd and 3rd quotations), xix, xx, 115, 119.

29. For example: "Hermeneutics is the science which teaches the principles of interpretation" (Ryrie, *Dispensationalism Today*, 34).

30. Scofield, *Rightly Dividing the Word of Truth*, 8.

31. Quoted in C. F. Lincoln, "Biographical Sketch of the Author," in Chafer, *Systematic Theology*, 8:5–6.

The central problem with these traits of nineteenth-century intellectual life, which were accentuated by some of fundamentalism's most important leaders, has been well described by a contemporary dispensationalist, Craig Blaising. In his effort to reform the dispensational tradition, Blaising looks back regretfully over several generations infected by "a methodological deficiency in the very hermeneutic that it proposed." Blaising accurately notes that,

> like most of fundamentalism and evangelicalism at the time [into the 1960s], [dispensationalism] possessed no methodological awareness of the historicity of interpretation. . . . Furthermore, this hermeneutical deficiency was structured into the very meaning of dispensational thought and practice in its advocacy of clear, plain, normal, or literal interpretation. . . . We have, then, a generation of theologians who find identity in a self-conscious hermeneutic that lacks methodological awareness of the historical nature of interpretation — a situation that under the pressures of apologetical exigencies seems particularly vulnerable to the danger of anachronism.

In more general terms, Blaising observes that "the problem is the failure to recognize that all theological thought, including one's own theological thought, is historically conditioned by the tradition to which that theologian belongs as well as personal and cultural factors such as education or experience. These factors condition an interpreter to think in a certain way. Awareness of them can be a step towards recognizing and rectifying misunderstanding."[32]

The difficulty perpetuated by the objectivist language of nineteenth-century Baconian science is not with the notion that theology must proceed carefully, systematically, and by giving thorough attention to all relevant evidence — that is, in "scientific" fashion. The difficulty is rather that the lack of self-consciousness characteristic of the nineteenth century's confidence in science continued in full force among some of the most influential popularizers of evangelical theology well into the late twentieth century.

For the purposes of this book, the most important concern is not even with what such habits of mind do to theology itself, but rather

32. Blaising, "Dispensationalism: The Search for Definition," 29–30, 22n.28.

how they affect the effort to bring a theological understanding to all other objects of study.

For Christian thinking about the world, the key question is what happens to a community when it tries to work out a Christian orientation to, say, the conundrums of modern nuclear physics, to the complexities of health care reform, to the meaning of traditional legal principles for a pluralistic society, to the interpretation of classic texts, to efforts at evaluating Communism in the twentieth century, to the issue of how music reinforces or subverts traditional morality, to the debate over which books should be assigned as the literary canon — that is, to the whole range of modern questions in which it is absolutely essential to exercise sensitivity concerning the interpreter's stance over against the data being interpreted, self-criticism about the way pre-commitments influence conclusions, and critical awareness of the symbiotic connections between methods and results. If that community's habits of mind concerning those things to which the community pays most diligent attention and accords highest authority — that is, to the Bible and Christian theology — are defined by naive and uncritical assumptions about the way to study or think about anything, so will its efforts to promote Christian thinking about the world be marked by naïveté and an absence of rigorous criticism.

In these terms, the problem of fundamentalism was that the worst features of the nineteenth-century intellectual situation became the methodological keystones for mental activity in the twentieth century. If this analysis is correct, it means that fruitful evangelical thinking at the end of the twentieth century must come to grips not only with the excesses of the fundamentalist past but with the compounded damage done when those excesses were grafted on to even longer-lived intellectual weaknesses.

Questionable Theological Guidance

An even more troubling difficulty with the legacy from earlier this century concerns the theological guidance offered by fundamentalist theology for the effort to understand nature, society, and the arts for the glory of God. Systems of Christian theology quite rightly begin with such matters as the nature of the Trinity, the ways God has revealed himself in the Bible, how humans may be saved from their sins through Christ, or how the church should model the realities of salvation. But Christian theologies also provide orientation for understanding the world and for carrying out practical tasks in the world — for making or appreciating music, for understanding the body, for stewarding the environment, for defining the purposes of gainful employment, for contemplating the way the past shapes the present, and so on.

Dispensational theology — especially when combined with the piety of "victorious living," "the higher life," or "the consecrated life" — posed a particular problem in providing that kind of orientation. Whether dispensationalism must always have the same negative effects on Christian thinking is not clear. In addition, the excesses of dispensationalism that worked themselves so deeply into habits of evangelical thinking do not necessarily characterize many modern dispensationalists, some of whom have done a great deal during the last decade to trim away the excesses of historic dispensationalism.[33] The point here, however, is not how dispensationalism is changing at the end of the twentieth century but the effect it has had on evangelicals throughout the century.

In specifically theological terms, the efforts of the fundamentalists were by no means totally without value. For a theological conservative, it is in fact intensely painful to catalog the intellectual vacuity of twentieth-century evangelicalism, precisely because of how faithfully fundamentalists, pentecostals, Holiness advocates, and conservative evangelicals passed on essential elements of the Christian faith. It is important to repeat what has been said before. If this book were a

---

33. At the same time, however, it is by no means clear that the "progressive dispensationalists" of the sort mentioned in n. 10 speak for all dispensationalists today. While these progressives appeal for "a new approach to defining dispensationalism" (ibid., 30), other dispensationalists seem entirely satisfied with older formulations. Thus, a recently published work that argues for excluding certain emphases of J. N. Darby from "normative dispensational theology" repeats the sine qua non of Charles Ryrie's *Dispensationalism Today* from 1965 as still providing the "essential factors of dispensationalism" in the 1990s; see Larry V. Crutchfield, *The Origins of Dispensationalism: The Darby Factor* (Lanham, MD: University Press of America, 1992), quotations from the extensive table of contents.

complete history of twentieth-century evangelicalism, the emphasis would be different. The preservation of supernaturalism — although not the excesses to which fundamentalist supernaturalism led — would be at the center of the picture. Were this an effort to write that kind of book, observations like the one made by Nels Ferré in 1948 would feature much more prominently: "Fundamentalism, as the defender of supernaturalism, has . . . a genuine heritage and a profound truth to preserve. . . . We shall some day thank our fundamentalist friends for having held the main fortress while countless leaders went over to the foe of a limited scientism and a shallow naturalism."[34]

This book, however, is not about the entire history of evangelicalism but about evangelical intellectual life, especially evangelical efforts to think in a Christian manner about society, the arts, the human person, and nature. For that kind of thinking the habits of mind fundamentalism encouraged can only be called a disaster. Because dispensationalism was the most intellectual form of fundamentalism, it was responsible for the most disastrous effects on the mind.

Dispensationalism promoted a kind of supernaturalism that, for all of its virtues in defending the faith, failed to give proper attention to the world. The supernaturalism of dispensationalism, especially in the extreme forms that were easiest to promote among the populace at large, lacked a sufficient place for the natural realm and tended toward a kind of gnosticism in its communication of truth. Adherents were instructed *about* nature, world events, ethics, and other dimensions of human existence, but almost always without studying these matters head-on. Bible verses were quoted to explain conditions and events in the world, but with very little systematic analysis of the events and conditions themselves.

The gnostic tendency was most evident in the authority accorded to elaborate charts and diagrams (often purporting to outline the whole future course of the world) by which Scripture was supposedly clarified. These efforts, however, amounted to interpretations of "the times" that were produced without going to the inconvenient work of ever looking at the times themselves. Under the influence of dispensationalism —

34. Nels F. S. Ferré, "Present Trends in Protestant Thought," *Religion in Life* 17 (1948): 336.

and to a lesser extent "victorious living" and pentecostalism as well — evangelicals pushed analysis away from the visible present to the invisible future. Under these influences, evangelicals almost totally replaced respect for creation with a contemplation of redemption.

When evangelicalism passed through dispensational premillennialism, the result was a fundamentalism that passionately defended the Book, the Blood, and the Blessed Hope.[35] Fundamentalist contentions for these doctrines took a common form that, as a by-product, created great difficulties for a more general intellectual life. For matters involving Scripture, redemption, and the last days — that is, for the matters that monopolized dispensationalist attention almost entirely — fundamentalists tried to read experience from the divine angle of vision. In each case they tried to understand the contemporary world as the divinely inspired authors of Scripture had understood their experience. In each case fundamentalists denied that historical processes — networks of cause and effect open to public analysis by all and sundry — had anything significant to contribute.

Thus, when fundamentalists defended the Bible, they did so by arguing for the inerrancy of Scripture's original autographs, an idea that had been around for a long time but that had never assumed such a central role for any Christian movement.[36] This belief had the practical effect of rendering the experience of the biblical writers nearly meaningless. It was the Word of God pure and simple, not the Word of God as mediated through the life experiences and cultural settings of the biblical authors, that was important.

Similarly, fundamentalist use of Scripture manifested the same denial of a natural or human element in the inspired text. For decades a much-practiced fundamentalist liturgy was the "Bible Reading," in which leaders selected verses from throughout the Scripture to illustrate

35. The next several paragraphs expand upon the schema of Joel A. Carpenter, "Contending for the Faith Once Delivered: Primitivist Impulses in American Fundamentalism," in *The American Quest for the Primitive Church,* ed. Richard T. Hughes (Urbana: University of Illinois Press, 1988), 99–119, as well as my response to Carpenter, in ibid., 121–22.

36. This interpretation follows Sandeen, *Roots of Fundamentalism,* as modified by Mark A. Noll, "A Brief History of Inerrancy, Mostly in America," in *The Proceedings of the Conference on Biblical Inerrancy* (Nashville: Broadman, 1987), 9–25.

a particular truth. James Brookes, one of the founders of the Niagara Prophecy Conferences, provided a codified instruction for this very common practice: "Have your leader select some word, as faith, repentance, love, hope, justification, sanctification, and with the aide of a good Concordance, mark down before the time of the meeting the references to the subject under discussion. These can be read as called for, thus presenting all the Holy Ghost has been pleased to reveal on the topic."[37]

The same procedure was followed by those who wrote the most popular dispensational literature, beginning with Scofield's *Rightly Dividing the Word of Truth* which, for example, expounded upon the seven dispensations he found in Scripture by making brief prefatory remarks before providing a series of biblical references that were supposed to define the existence and character of the individual dispensations. Following brief exposition, the fifth dispensation, "man under law," was demonstrated like this:

Exodus 19:1–8	2 Kings 17:1–18
Romans 10:5	2 Kings 25:1–11
Galatians 3:10	Acts 2:22, 23
Romans 3:19, 20	Acts 7:51, 52[38]

Lewis Sperry Chafer gave this procedure formal shape in his systematic theology. It was necessary, he wrote, to consider "all Scripture bearing on any given theme. . . . A right interpretation will also depend very largely on an induction being made of *all* that the Bible presents on a given subject."[39] It is clear from the expositions in his theology that Chafer meant all the *verses* that bore on the particular theme.

One of the most obvious problems of this approach to the Bible, a problem especially keen for those who wished to follow "the Bible only," is the versification of Scripture. Concordances cannot work

37. James H. Brookes, in *Truth* 5 (1879): 314, as quoted in Timothy P. Weber, *Living in the Shadow of the Second Coming* (New York: Oxford University Press, 1979), 37.

38. Scofield, *Rightly Dividing the Word of Truth*, 22–23.

39. Chafer, *Systematic Theology*, 1:117.

without verses, yet the division of the Bible into verses was not completed until the sixteenth century.[40] That ordinary human beings not inspired by the Holy Spirit had cut up the Bible into verses and that other ordinary human beings not inspired by the Holy Spirit were rearranging those verses to extract large-scale truths from the Scriptures meant that both the fundamentalist Bible Reading and the most important fundamentalist theological books partook fully in thoroughly natural and thoroughly human activity, even as they attempted to understand divine truth. To deny the natural and human character of the most widely practiced fundamentalist way of putting the Bible to use — as George Needham did in 1877 by claiming that "little that is human is introduced" by such a procedure[41] — was intellectual self-delusion. It was also the worse kind of intellectual legacy for later evangelicals who hoped to think about nature or humanity by following the message of Scripture.

Fundamentalist convictions about the miraculous character of redemption through the blood of Christ also reflected age-old Christian beliefs but likewise expressed them with a heightened concern for nonhistorical elements. When fundamentalists spoke of the new birth, they stressed the unmediated activity of the Holy Spirit. Although in practice they employed a wide variety of means to encourage conversion — family worship and nurture, earnest preaching, the example of holy lives — in theory they continued to stress the immediacy of the Holy Spirit's action. This too reflected a negation of historical process.

Finally, the fundamentalist fixation upon the end of the world treated current global history with a similarly cavalier spirit. If current events were important primarily because they fulfilled biblical prophecy, then the relationships that people in general could study between contemporary cause and contemporary effect paled into insignificance. Again, fundamentalists were reading history as if they were inspired like the authors of Scripture had been inspired, rather than as believers

40. *The Cambridge History of the Bible*, 3 vols. (Cambridge: Cambridge University Press, 1963–70), 3:436–37.

41. George Needham, introduction to James Brookes, *Bible Reading on the Second Coming of Christ* (Springfield, IL, 1877), viii, as quoted in Weber, *Living in the Shadow of the Second Coming* (1979 ed.), 37.

BIBLICAL PROPHECY

CONTEMPORARY CAUSE/EFFECT

whom God had commissioned to participate in the ongoing nurture of the church in a time between the times.

Dispensational writing on eschatology consistently spelled out how study of biblical prophecy would benefit the believer. Right at the start of his systematic theology, Chafer made much of what could be learned about the past and the future from studying prophecy.[42] Charles Ryrie likewise took care to show the "importance of studying prophecy . . . in relation to God . . . in relation to the Scriptures . . . in relation to the believer."[43] Ryrie also showed how dispensationalism offers a more adequate philosophy of history than other competing hermeneutical schemes by providing "(1) the recognition of 'historical events and successions,' or a proper concept of the progress of revelation; (2) the unifying principle; and (3) the ultimate goal of history."[44] Conspicuous by its absence from such advertisements for the virtues of studying prophetic literature is any sense of how such study might help the believer to find a biblical understanding of the world in which the believer lived. Chafer even went so far as to say that such an effort was beside the point: "The divine program of events so faithfully set forth in the Scriptures of truth and as faithfully revealed to the attentive heart by the Spirit of truth is little concerned with an ever shifting and transitory now."[45]

Fundamentalist belief in the supernatural was by no means unique in Christian history. But the way in which dispensationalism concentrated its energies upon the transcendent at the expense of the natural was distinct. When Lewis Sperry Chafer wrote, "The natural capacities of the human mind do not function in the realm of spiritual things,"[46] he defined himself and all those who followed after him as (to use Ronald Knox's terms) an "enthusiast," for whom grace had destroyed nature. With such an orientation, not only was the exploration of nature and ordinary human affairs suspect, but every possible barrier had been

42. Chafer, *Systematic Theology,* 1:xxxii–xxxiv.
43. Ryrie, *Basis of Premillennial Faith,* 15.
44. Ryrie, *Dispensationalism Today,* 17.
45. Chafer, *Systematic Theology,* 1:xxxiii–xxxiv.
46. Ibid., vi. For Knox's definition of "enthusiasm," see "Anti-Intellectual" in chapter 1, p. 10.

erected against the attempt to let the deep riches of Christian theology guide human understanding of the world.

CHRISTIAN THEOLOGY

The Intellectual Indictment   HUMAN UNDERSTANDING OF THE WORLD

For the purposes of Christian thinking, the major indictment of the fundamentalist movement, and especially of the dispensationalism that provided the most systematic interpretation of the Bible for fundamentalists and many later evangelicals, was its intellectual sterility. Under its midwifery, the evangelical community gave birth to virtually no insights into how, under God, the natural world proceeded, how human societies worked, why human nature acted the way it did, or what constituted the blessings and perils of culture. To be sure, fundamentalists and their descendants had firm beliefs about some of these matters — beliefs, moreover, that were backed up by citations from Scripture. Some of those beliefs were entirely correct. What even the laudably scriptural beliefs lacked, however, was profound knowledge of the divinely created world in which those beliefs were applied.

As a result of following a theology that did not provide Christian guidance for the wider intellectual life, there has been, properly speaking, no fundamentalist philosophy, no fundamentalist history of science, no fundamentalist aesthetics, no fundamentalist history, no fundamentalist novels or poetry, no fundamentalist jurisprudence, no fundamentalist literary criticism, and no fundamentalist sociology. Or at least there has been none that has compelled attention for insights into the way God has made the world and situated human beings on this planet. And because evangelicals, though often dissenting from specific features of fundamentalism, have largely retained the mentality of fundamentalism *when it comes to looking at the world*, there has been a similarly meager harvest of evangelical intellectual life.

What J. S. Bach gained from his Lutheranism to inform his music, what Jonathan Edwards took from the Reformed tradition to orient his philosophy, what A. H. Francke learned from German Pietism to inspire the University of Halle's research into Sanskrit and Asian literatures, what Jacob van Ruisdael gained from his seventeenth-century Dutch Calvinism to shape his painting, what Thomas Chalmers took from Scottish Presbyterianism to inspire his books on astronomy and political economy, what Abraham Kuyper gained from pietistic Dutch Calvinism to back his educational, political, and communications labors of the late nineteenth century, what T. S. Eliot took from high-church Anglicanism as a basis for his cultural criticism, what Evelyn Waugh found for his novels in twentieth-century Calvinism, what Luci Shaw, Shirley Nelson, Harold Fickett, and Evangeline Paterson found to encourage creative writing from other forms of Christianity after they left dispensationalism behind — precious few fundamentalists or their evangelical successors have ever found in the theological insights of twentieth-century dispensationalism, Holiness, or Pentecostalism.

As we will see in chapter 8, a fair number of American evangelicals raised in fundamentalist or postfundamentalist environments have in fact made significant intellectual contributions, especially since World War II. But when the work of these thinkers is examined, it is evident that in almost every case where theology has provided guidance for broader intellectual work, that theology has featured insights, not from dispensationalism or other twentieth-century evangelical innovations, but from classical traditions like Anglicanism, Calvinism, Roman Catholicism, Anabaptism, Lutheranism, or even Eastern Orthodoxy.

The major exceptions to these generalizations about the sterility of fundamentalist theology for broader intellectual questions are matters having to do with the origin of the earth and with contemporary political action. But as will be suggested in the next two chapters, the guidance of fundamentalist theology in those areas has done more harm than good.

The chief concern of this chapter is with the damage done by fundamentalist habits of thought to general intellectual life. But a word is also in order about their effect on theology per se. Into the early twentieth century America's best evangelical theologians regularly pushed core Christian insights out into penetrating exploration of broader intellectual matters. The work, for example, of New School Presbyterian Henry Boynton Smith or Northern Baptist A. H. Strong on conceptions of history,[47] Southern Baptist E. Y. Mullins on the

---

47. Henry B. Smith, *Faith and Philosophy* (New York: Scribner, Armstrong, 1877); and Grant Wacker, *Agustus H. Strong and the Dilemma of Historical Consciousness* (Macon, GA: Mercer University Press, 1985).

nature of the person,[48] or Old School Presbyterian B. B. Warfield on evolution[49] did not overwhelm the American intellectual community. But, though different from each other in many ways, all of these theologians were alike in that they meaningfully engaged vital contemporary questions and drew with careful discrimination from the best learning of the secular world, while maintaining their solid evangelical convictions. Much the same thing can be said for Canadian theologians, like the Methodist Nathanael Burwash or the Presbyterian George Monro Grant, who provided solidly intellectual, as well as spiritually discerning, theology into the early years of this century.[50] For the constituencies served by these theologians, the result was both stabilizing interaction with the best modern learning as well as continuing examples of how the mind in its most rigorous exercises could function for the glory of God. Since the fundamentalist era, however, no evangelical theologian has spoken with the same combination of theological depth and intellectual acuity.

The Lingering Effects of the Innovations

But surely the author doth protest too much. Surely we are flogging a dead horse by being so preoccupied with beliefs and practices from the early twentieth century that must now exert only a residual effect on the evangelical community. To be sure, the specific theological propositions of dispensationalism probably do not have quite the importance across the evangelical spectrum that they once did. Fundamentalist intellectual habits, however, have been more resilient than fundamentalism itself. Several matters from recent evangelical history indeed illustrate the continuing sway of those early patterns of thought.

48. Edgar Young Mullins, *The Christian Religion in Its Doctrinal Expression* (Nashville: Broadman, 1917), 12–24, 49–81.

49. B. B. Warfield, "Creation versus Evolution," *Bible Student* 4 (July 1901): 1–8, and "Calvin's Doctrine of Creation," *Princeton Theological Review* 13 (Apr. 1915): 190–255.

50. Van Die, *Evangelical Mind: Nathanael Burwash;* Barry Mack, "George Monro Grant: Evangelical Prophet" (Ph.D. diss., Queen's University, Ontario, 1992).

On predispositions in the use of Scripture, we should remember that, after the Bible, the best-selling book of any sort in the United States during the 1970s was Hal Lindsey's *Late Great Planet Earth,* a populist interpretation of world events in terms of historicist dispensationalism.[51] The evangelical predilection, when faced with a world crisis, to use the Bible as a crystal ball instead of as a guide for sorting out the complex tangles of international morality was nowhere more evident than in responses to the Gulf War in early 1991. Neither through the publishing of books nor through focused consideration in periodicals did evangelicals engage in significant discussions on the morality of the war, the use of the United Nations in the wake of the collapse of Communism, the significance of oil for job creation or wealth formation throughout the world, the history of Western efforts at intervention in the Middle East, or other topics fairly crying out for serious Christian analysis. Instead, evangelicals gobbled up more than half a million copies each of several self-assured, populist explanations of how the Gulf crisis was fulfilling the details of obscure biblical prophecies. The systems of biblical interpretation promoted in those best-sellers were all variations on dispensational theology.

The same sort of conclusion must be made for characteristic evangelical predilections for looking at the world. For the last half-decade, two sensationally popular novels by Frank Peretti — *This Present Darkness* (1986) and *Piercing the Darkness* (1989) — have consistently topped religious best-seller lists, they have spawned dozens of imitations, and they have set the tone for evangelical assessment of cause-and-effect connections in the world. These novels present a nearly Manichaean vision of life where conflicts on earth are paralleled by conflicts between angels and demons in the heavens, and where the line between good and evil runs, not as Solzhenitsyn once wrote,

51. Theologically considered, it may be correct, as "progressive dispensationalists" argue, that Lindsey represents an eccentric deviation from dispensationalism (Blaising, "Dispensationalism: The Search for Definition," 14–15n.3; Blaising and Bock, "Dispensationalism, Israel, and the Church: Assessment and Dialogue," 379). Simply the magnitude of sales, however, seems to show that the kind of dispensationalism represented by *The Late Great Planet Earth* reflects a much wider swath of evangelical thinking than the carefully qualified theological conclusions of the progressive dispensationalists.

through the heart of every individual, but between the secular forces of darkness on one side and the sanctified forces of light on the other. To the extent that Peretti's vision reflects evangelical perceptions more generally, it shows an evangelical community unwilling to sift the wheat from the chaff in the wisdom of the world, unprepared to countenance the complexity of mixed motives in human action, and uninterested in focusing seriously on the natural forces that influence human behavior. Although formally connected to the scriptural command to resist the devil, the stark dialectic of spiritual warfare found in these books can be traced directly to heightened language concerning Satan and the Holy Spirit that came to prominence in the first decades of the twentieth century. They reflect new prominence given to angels and demons in both the informal instincts of Pentecostalism and the formal theologies of dispensationalists.[52]

In general responses to crises, evangelicals in the late twentieth century still follow a pathway defined at the start of the twentieth century. When faced with a crisis situation, we evangelicals usually do one of two things. We either mount a public crusade, or we retreat into an inner pious sanctum. That is, we are filled with righteous anger and attempt to recoup our public losses through political confrontation, or we eschew the world of mere material appearances and seek the timeless consolations of the Spirit. The political analysis of the New Christian Right and the polemical activity of the biblical creationists (both of which are treated briefly in chapters that follow) illustrate the first stance. The evangelical silence on so many of the real-life complexities of the present age testify eloquently to the second. Not since the mid-nineteenth century have evangelicals characteristically tried to meet crises with a combination of voluntaristic activism, personal spirituality, and hard theological effort.

In sum, the specific tenets of dispensational, Holiness, and pentecostal theologies are not the exact point at issue for a more general consideration of the intellect. It is, rather, the patterns of thinking

---

52. Chafer, *Systematic Theology,* 1:xxvi–xxix; 2:3–124. For comment concerning Chafer's stress on angels and demons, see Jeffrey J. Richards, *The Promise of Dawn: The Eschatology of Lewis Sperry Chafer* (Lanham, MD: University Press of America, 1991), 195.

encouraged by these theologies. Whatever the contemporary fate of individual parts of those theologies, their habits of mind still loom large among evangelicals as the twentieth century draws to a close.

Conclusions

It is obvious that a person's assessment of how the theological innovations of fundamentalism affect intellectual life depends on how the person evaluates the theologies. In my case, as one who does not believe that the distinctive teachings of dispensationalism, the Holiness movement, or Pentecostalism are essential to Christian faith, it is not surprising that I find the intellectual consequences of these theologies damaging. Against dispensationalism, I believe that the major point of biblical prophecy is to reveal affective and cosmological dimensions of redemption in Christ and not to provide believers with a complete and detailed preview of the end of the world; and I believe that the Bible should be interpreted historically (with full attention to the human circumstances of each book), naturally (with full attention to the use of symbols, the imagination, and modes of discourse lying beyond the realm of nineteenth-century science), and Christocentrically (with the unity of Scripture resting in the determination of God to rescue sinners in Christ). With respect to Holiness theology, I believe that Christians grow in grace through following God into the world, embracing their vocations as gifts from God, and not by "letting go and letting God." With respect to Pentecostalism, I believe that every believer, as an essential element of being a Christian, is baptized with the Holy Spirit and that it is not necessary for believers to seek the extraordinary sign gifts.

With such convictions, my most serious difficulty with the theological innovations adopted by many evangelicals at the start of this century is theological. But because theological convictions provide one of the frameworks through which we analyze the world, it is also my conviction that specifically theological convictions have intellectual consequences. Thus, for example, any theology that encourages Bible reading as puzzle solving, instead of Bible reading as an occasion for the reader to examine his or her own soul, or that encourages Bible reading primarily to understand a "world out there," instead of "the world for me," is not only bad theology but a theology prejudicial to the intellectual life. The prejudice is the barrier set up by such Bible reading to the entrance of scriptural reality into the deepest parts of the personality, engagement of which is most urgently required for an intellectual life that would honor both God and the world in which he has placed us.

In a similar fashion, the tendency of dispensationalists to stress the rescue of believers through a secret rapture before the cataclysms of the end is not only questionable theology (because of a wooden interpretation of 1 Thessalonians 4 proposed by Darby only in the nineteenth century) but also a bad influence on the use of the mind more generally. The evidence presented by Paul Boyer and other scholars of apocalyptic literature is conclusive, that apocalyptic speculation can degenerate into a way of upbraiding opponents.[53] At least some practitioners of apocalyptic speculation do teach their views with the attitude described by George Eliot in the nineteenth century for some millenarians of her day: "Advertizing the pre-millenial Advent, is simply the transportation of political passions on to a so-called religious platform; it is the anticipation of the triumph of 'our party,' accomplished by our principal men being 'sent for' into the clouds."[54] This erroneous theological attitude also fosters damaging intellectual attitudes. Learners need to learn from whatever source they can, but the extreme partisanship fostered by doctrines like the secret rapture of the church make it all but impossible to think about learning something from other people throughout history, Christian or otherwise.

Whatever theological conclusions are reached about the desirability of pursuing the intellectual life, the historical picture seems relatively clear. Evangelicals in the nineteenth century enjoyed modestly successful efforts to think with at least limited Christian depth about life in general. Descendants of those evangelicals who have been influenced by one of the various forms of fundamentalism have had less success. The image employed by historian Nathan Hatch is very close to the

53. Paul Boyer, *When Time Shall Be No More: Prophecy Belief in Modern American Culture* (Cambridge: Harvard University Press, 1992), 136.
54. George Eliot, "Evangelical Teaching: Dr. Cumming," *Westminster Review* 64 (Oct. 1855): 455, as quoted in Hempton, "Evangelicalism and Eschatology," 181.

mark: "Let me suggest somewhat whimsically that the heritage of fundamentalism was to Christian learning for evangelicals like Chairman Mao's 'Cultural Revolution' [was] for the Chinese. Both divorced a generation from mainline academia, thus making reintegration [into larger worlds of learning] a difficult, if not bewildering task."[55]

Evangelical hymnody, often a sensitive barometer to shifting deep structures, well illustrates the intellectual history. Two lovely hymns, separated by only two generations, bespeak the momentous influence of fundamentalism. Both are, in their own terms, entirely appropriate expressions of piety. Both can be sung with a clear conscience. But the use of metaphor is revealing. Shortly before he died in 1860, George Croly penned the prayer "Spirit of God, Descend upon My Heart." In its second stanza Croly described what he felt would happen if he were to experience a deeper walk with the Spirit:

> I ask no dream, no prophet ecstasies,
> No sudden rending of the veil of clay,
> No angel visitant, no opening skies;
> But take the dimness of my soul away.

For Croly, to know God better would make our vision of the world *clearer*.

In 1922, Helen H. Lemmel wrote the words and music to a gospel song that is as moving as it is characteristic of the fundamentalist-Holiness outlook:

> Turn your eyes upon Jesus,
> Look full in His wonderful face,
> And the things of earth will grow strangely dim
> In the light of His glory and grace.

While the essentially Christian motivation of this song is clear, its ironic meaning can be understood better now than when it was written — under the influence of fundamentalism, evangelicals turned their eyes to Jesus, and the world grew very dim indeed.

55. Nathan O. Hatch, "Evangelical Colleges and the Challenge of Christian Thinking," *Reformed Journal*, Sept. 1985, p. 12.

Dispensationalism, the Holiness movement, and Pentecostalism were responses to real crises. They are systems of theology that deserve commendation from anyone who believes that Christianity is a supernatural religion. They deserve commendation as well for maintaining fidelity to the Bible in an age whose intellectual leaders assumed that they knew more about the world than did the authors of Scripture. They deserve serious respect for maintaining, as C. I. Scofield put it in the preface to his study Bible, that "the central theme of the Bible is Christ."[56]

But in their defense of the supernatural, fundamentalists and their evangelical heirs resemble some cancer patients. In facing a drastic disease, they are willing to undertake a drastic remedy. The treatment of fundamentalism may be said to have succeeded; the patient survived. But at least for the life of the mind, what survived was a patient horribly disfigured by the cure itself.

COGNITIVE   LIFE OF THE MIND: MORE THOUGHT...THINKING.

AFFECTIVE   LIFE OF THE EMOTIONS: MORE PRAISE - FEELING

VOLITIONAL LIFE OF THE WILL: - MORE OBEDIENCE - DOING

56. *Scofield Reference Bible*, vi.

PART 3

WHAT THE SCANDAL
HAS MEANT

CREDIBILITY

PLAUSIBILITY - DETERMINED

CHAPTER 6

Political Reflection

The character of American evangelical thinking is especially well illustrated in politics and science. In this chapter I try to show how an informal, populist, but not insubstantial tradition of nineteenth-century political thought was sidetracked by the fundamentalist habits described in the last chapter, and how those habits continue to influence evangelical political reflection to the present moment. In the next chapter the story will be roughly the same for evangelical thinking about science, except that the issues attracting evangelical scrutiny were fewer and the firestorms created around controversial issues were hotter. Both areas illustrate the practical damage done by fundamentalism to evangelical thought, but also the resilience of evangelicalism in surviving that damage. Thus, both chapters end with brief comment on signs of a more fruitful intellectual life that could be observed from the 1940s onward. These signs, in turn, provide the bridge to chapter 8, which offers a fuller account and assessment of efforts over the last half-century to recover an evangelical mind in America.

During the nineteenth century, evangelical thinking about politics was rough-and-ready, shaped by the rhetorical styles of an expanding democracy, and rarely theoretical as such. But it also was often careful, sometimes surprisingly conversant with important political and social theories from Britain and the Continent, and regularly engaged in the effort to let the Bible speak to the political environment (even as that environment regularly dictated the way the Bible would be heard).

Without papering over the very real problems of political reflection revealed by the partisanship of the Civil War era, it still can be said that, at least in an informal way, nineteenth-century evangelicals were *thinking* about politics even as they engaged in the multiple political activities for which they were renowned (and lampooned) throughout the Western world.[1]

The career of William Jennings Bryan, three-time nominee for president of the Democratic party, provides an especially apt illustration of the character of this earlier evangelical engagement with politics. Of all Bryan's multitudinous political activity, his famous speech in 1896 during the platform debate of the Democratic National Convention in Chicago provides the quickest and the liveliest entry into his thought. To view that speech in context has the added value of showing how it compared with other Christian approaches to politics at the end of the nineteenth century, especially Pope Leo XIII's significant encyclical from 1891, "On Capital and Labor" (usually called by the first two words of its Latin original, *Rerum Novarum*). Such a comparison highlights some of the most important features of evangelical political reflection, but it also puts us in position to trace the stages of evangelical political reflection in this century. As a baseline for considering evan-

1. Two outstanding books are essential for understanding the dimensions of nineteenth-century evangelical politics: Daniel Walker Howe, *The Political Culture of the American Whigs* (Chicago: University of Chicago Press, 1979); and Richard J. Carwardine, *Evangelicals and Politics in Antebellum America* (New Haven: Yale University Press, 1993). Excellent supplements for the South, where relations between evangelicalism and public life differed substantially from such relations in the North, are Robert M. Calhoon, *Evangelicals and Conservatives in the Early South, 1740–1861* (Columbia: University of South Carolina Press, 1988); and James Oscar Farmer, Jr., *The Metaphysical Confederacy: James Henley Thornwell and the Synthesis of Southern Values* (Macon, GA: Mercer University Press, 1986). I have provided an evaluation of some aspects of nineteenth-century evangelical politics in *One Nation under God? Christian Faith and Political Action in America* (San Francisco: Harper & Row, 1988). Extensive reference to much of the most important literature on the general subject is provided in the notes to the various essays in *Religion and American Politics from the Colonial Period to the 1980s*, ed. Mark A. Noll (New York: Oxford University Press, 1990). Some of the material in this chapter appeared in an earlier form as my contribution to *Being Christian Today*, ed. Richard John Neuhaus and George Weigel (Washington, D.C.: Ethics and Public Policy Center, 1993).

gelical thought more generally in the twentieth century, the career of William Jennings Bryan is an excellent place to begin.

William Jennings Bryan and Nineteenth-Century Evangelical Political Thought

When he gave his famous speech in Chicago, William Jennings Bryan of Nebraska was already, at age thirty-six, a former Congressman. Bryan had been addressing political crowds for a long time, but not as long as he had been preaching to congregations as a lay Presbyterian.[2] The speech in Chicago did not have a biblical text, but in style it resembled a sermon. Its character as an *evangelical* exposition of political thought was manifest in the metaphors of its unforgettable conclusion: "If they dare to come out in the open field and defend the gold standard as a good thing, we will fight them to the uttermost. Having behind us the producing masses of this nation and the world, supported by the commercial interests, the laboring interests, and the toilers everywhere, we will answer their demand for a gold standard by saying to them: You shall not press down upon the brow of labor this crown of thorns, you shall not crucify mankind upon a cross of gold."[3] Reflecting on the convictions that undergirded this address, Garry Wills recently argued that Bryan is "the most important evangelical politician of this century," and the Cross of Gold address "the greatest speech at any political convention."[4]

The proposition that this speech should also be considered a grand finale to nineteenth-century political reflection is supported by both its form and its content. In the first instance, the speech was a fine example of evangelical immersion in Scripture, as in Bryan's artful use of metaphors like the cross in his peroration, or his adaptation of

2. See especially Paolo E. Colletta, *William Jennings Bryan,* vol. 1: *Political Evangelist, 1860–1908* (Lincoln: University of Nebraska Press, 1964).

3. William Jennings Bryan, "Speech Concluding Debate on the Chicago Platform," in *The First Battle: The Story of the Campaign of 1896* (Chicago: W. B. Conkey, 1896), 206.

4. Garry Wills, *Under God: Religion and American Politics* (New York: Simon & Schuster, 1990), 97, 67.

1 Samuel 18:7, "If protection has slain its thousands, the gold standard has slain its tens of thousands."[5] It also summed up the public witness of a nineteenth-century Protestantism that had, in the words of Leonard Sweet, "created a *de facto* establishment of evangelicalism whose security lay in a common ethos, a common outlook on life and history, a common piety, and common patterns of worship and devotion."[6] In addition, the speech exemplified the evangelical habit of regarding each new national crisis as a cataclysm of world-historical importance. "Never before in the history of this country," said Bryan, "has there been witnessed such a contest" as that taking place over monetary policy.[7] Finally, Bryan's speech was a dramatic statement that applied treasured evangelical traditions to the crisis of the hour.

This speech also recapitulated one important set of political convictions that had been prominent among at least some evangelicals throughout the nineteenth century. In a fashion that had become commonplace in democratic, evangelical America, Bryan championed ordinary people: "The man who is employed for wages . . . the attorney in a country town . . . the merchant at the cross-roads store . . . the farmer who goes forth in the morning and toils all day . . . [and] the miners who go down a thousand feet into the earth . . . are as much business men as the few financial magnates who, in a back room, corner the money of the world."[8] He rose to speak, in other words, on behalf of "the struggling masses . . . the toilers everywhere."[9]

In pronouncements throughout his public career, moreover, Bryan made no secret of the specifically evangelical principles that drove this vision of politics.[10] But as he did so, he also attempted to make a distinction between the relatively effective potential of politics and the

5. Bryan, "Speech," 204.

6. Leonard I. Sweet, "Nineteenth-Century Evangelicalism," in *Encyclopedia of the American Religious Experience*, 3 vols., ed. Charles Lippy and Peter Williams (New York: Scribner's, 1988), 2:896.

7. Bryan, "Speech," 199.

8. Ibid., 200.

9. Ibid., 205-6.

10. On the consistency of Bryan's career from populist politician to fundamentalist champion, see especially Lawrence W. Levine, *Defender of the Faith: William Jennings Bryan, the Last Decade, 1915–1925* (New York: Oxford University Press, 1965).

[handwritten annotation: absolute potential of GOSPEL / relative potential of politics]

absolutely effective principles of the gospel. Throughout his career Bryan delivered a speech entitled "The Prince of Peace," in which this distinction was central: "Christ has given us a platform more central than any political party has ever written. . . . When He condensed into one commandment those of the ten which relate of man's duty toward his fellows and enjoined upon us the rule, 'Thou shalt love thy neighbor as thyself,' He presented a plan for the solution of all the problems that now vex society or hereafter arise. Other remedies may palliate or postpone the day of settlement but this is all-sufficient and the reconciliation which it effects is a permanent one."[11]

For Bryan, the greatest danger from modern secularism was not an attack on this or that particular Christian doctrine but the demeaning of the person implied by much modern thought. His increasingly strident opposition to evolution arose not so much from a threat to traditional interpretations of Genesis 1 but because evolution threatened human dignity. A godless theory of evolution was "an insult to reason and shocks the heart. That doctrine is as deadly as leprosy; . . . it would, if generally adopted, destroy all sense of responsibility and menace the morals of the world."[12]

Bryan's analysis of industrial strife illustrated his concern for the general health of communities. "The strike and the lockout are to our industrial life what war is between nations, and the general public stands in much the same position as neutral nations. The number of those actually injured by a suspension of industry is often many times as great as the total number of employers and employees in that industry combined."[13]

Bryan's speech in 1896, and even more the general shape of his political career, amounted to a passionate application of evangelical principles to the exigencies of his American hour. What those principles meant, and did not mean, is brought into sharper focus by comparing

11. Bryan, "The Prince of Peace," in *William Jennings Bryan: Selections,* ed. Ray Ginger (Indianapolis: Bobbs-Merrill, 1967), 148–49.

12. Bryan, *The Last Message of William Jennings Bryan* (New York: Fleming H. Revell, 1925), 51. The conclusion that Bryan attacked evolution for broadly humanistic rather than narrowly doctrinal reasons is well argued in Levine, *Defender of the Faith,* 261–70; and Wills, *Under God,* 97–106.

13. Bryan, *In His Image* (New York: Fleming H. Revell, 1922), 231.

them with another of the significant Christian pronouncements of the day, the encyclical from Leo XIII in 1891, which was a well-considered response by the Catholic Church to more than a century of social, economic, and political turmoil in Europe.[14]

Nineteenth-Century Evangelical Political Reflection in Comparative Perspective

Leo XIII and William Jennings Bryan were both compassionate and creative communicators. They both thought that traditional Christian faith had an answer to contemporary public crises, not as the faith was reinterpreted by the conventions of the moment, but as its hereditary truths were redirected to encompass modern situations. Both also felt that the resources of traditional Christianity were especially necessary for redressing the grievances suffered by ordinary people from economic modernization.

If there is much that links Leo's *Rerum Novarum* and Bryan's "Cross of Gold," however, there is also much that divides them. Precisely those aspects that were different reveal what was most deeply characteristic of nineteenth-century evangelical public thought and most directly anticipatory of evangelical politics in the twentieth century. An examination of how Bryan's speech differed from Leo XIII's encyclical, therefore, moves us closer to understanding the character of evangelical political reflection and also to assessing its strengths and weaknesses.

The most obvious of these differences may also be the most important. *Rerum Novarum* was an encyclical; Bryan's speech was a speech. As it had developed since the revivals of the mid-eighteenth century, American evangelicalism did include a tradition of serious written reflection. But that reflection tended to influence only a narrow slice of the evangel-

14. For the text, see Leo XIII, *Rerum Novarum*, in *The Papal Encyclicals, 1878–1903*, vol. 2, ed. Claudia Carlen (n.p.: McGrath, 1981). For enlightening centennial commentary, see George Weigel and Robert Royal, eds., *A Century of Catholic Social Thought: Essays on "Rerum Novarum" and Nine Other Key Documents* (Washington, D.C.: Ethics and Public Policy Center, 1991).

ical constituency. Political persuasion as well as experiential religion, in contrast, were primarily matters of public speaking. Puritan experience, with its central focus on the sermon, pointed in this direction. As we have seen, George Whitefield's sermonic power defined much of what American evangelicalism became.[15] Evangelicalism was a tradition in which its greatest speculative theologian, Jonathan Edwards, is best known for a sermon, "Sinners in the Hands of an Angry God." Evangelicals have no exclusive claim to the religion of Abraham Lincoln, whose faith seems to have been as generally Hebraic as it was specifically Christian. But it is nonetheless significant that the most profound statement of Christian, or at least theistic, political theology in the evangelical nineteenth century was Lincoln's second inaugural *address.*

After the sermon, nineteenth-century evangelicals looked next to the popular press for their inspiration, instruction, information, and guidance on public issues.[16] It was thus entirely in keeping with American evangelical tradition that the most impressive statement of evangelical political sentiment at the end of the century came from Bryan, "The Boy Orator of the Platte," who, when he was not speaking on the road, earned his living as a newspaper editor.

Throughout its history, the most visible evangelicals, those with the broadest popular influence, have been public speakers. The fact that twentieth-century evangelicals were in the lead exploiting both radio and television for religious purposes grows out of that earlier history.[17] It is also a fitting chapter in the evangelical story that Carl Henry's *Uneasy Conscience of Modern Fundamentalism,* a book influential in the

15. Essential for understanding the power of the spoken word in the Puritans and the Great Awakening are two books by Harry S. Stout: *The New England Soul: Preaching and Religious Culture in Colonial New England* (New York: Oxford University Press, 1986) and *The Divine Dramatist: George Whitefield and the Rise of Modern Evangelicalism* (Grand Rapids: Eerdmans, 1992).

16. David Paul Nord, "The Evangelical Origins of Mass Media in America, 1815–1835," *Journalism Monographs* 88 (1984): 1–30; and Nathan O. Hatch, *The Democratization of American Christianity* (New Haven: Yale University Press, 1989), 125–26, 141–46.

17. Quentin J. Schultze, "Evangelical Radio and the Rise of the Electronic Church, 1921–1948," *Journal of Broadcasting and Electronic Media* 32 (Summer 1988): 289–306.

awakening of public concern among northern, postfundamentalist neo-evangelicals, originated in 1947 as a series of talks, and at a time when Henry was more a journalist than a theologian. Remembering that the place of black Protestants in evangelical history is an ambiguous one, it is still noteworthy that the nation's most profound confrontation with Christian public testimony in the twentieth century was precipitated by the sermons/speeches of Martin Luther King, Jr., and his colleagues, in which evangelical themes were prominent.

The evangelical predilection for the sermon and the speech fits well with the urgency that has defined the evangelical movement as a whole. Evangelicals have not promoted a faith of word and sacrament, but one of word preached, word studied, and word shared. By the time Leo XIII issued *Rerum Novarum,* a tradition of pastoral letters from the popes, addressing specific issues from the standpoint of general Christian teaching and for the benefit of the whole church, was well established among Catholics. Just as firmly established was the evangelical reliance on public speech, addressing gathered audiences on specific issues with the powerful conventions of revivalistic fervor.

Second, *Rerum Novarum* was a statement issued by the head of the Catholic Church in which the church itself was assigned a critical role in meeting the contemporary social crisis. By contrast, Bryan's "Cross of Gold" speech, as well as the countless addresses that made up his life's oeuvre, were promulgated on his own authority, and they made their strongest appeal to individuals. The American evangelical tradition may not be as "liberal," in the nineteenth-century or classical meaning of the term, as it sounds, but the focus on individual action — sans church, sans family, sans social structures of whatever sort — has predominated since the days of Whitefield. The enduring contribution to evangelicalism of the republicanism of the Revolutionary era was the undermining of hereditary trust in institutions.[18] The enduring contribution of the Great Awakenings in the colonial and early national periods was to substitute the voluntary society for the church.[19]

18. For a summation of this argument, see Hatch, *Democratization of American Christianity,* 5–9.

19. Donald G. Mathews, "The Second Great Awakening as an Organizing Process," *American Quarterly* 21 (1969): 23–43.

The result — with Charles Finney's revivals, Theodore Dwight Weld's abolition, Frances Willard's temperance, and William Jennings Bryan's campaign for the silver standard — was to transform the mechanism of Christian social action. Insight for analyzing the public sphere and guidance for political action came not from authoritative pronouncements handed down from on high but from inner conviction springing up from within. The great men and women of American evangelicalism have been those who both recognized this reality and knew best how to persuade.[20] In his speech, Bryan bypassed the inherited institutions that Leo promoted in *Rerum Novarum* as the agents for addressing the modern economic crisis. Rather, he urged the Silver Democrats to adopt "a zeal approaching the zeal which inspired the crusaders who followed Peter the Hermit."[21] A call to symbolic battle took the place of the renovation of institutions.

Sometimes the evangelical ecclesiology and the voluntarism with which it is associated are styled democratic.[22] The democratic element is unmistakable, but more precisely it is not a democratic situation as such but one where authority has been transferred from heredity to charisma, from a power *commanding* assent to a power *eliciting* assent. Bryan's speech and the more general evangelical tradition of public political reflection have been, in other words, not just Protestant but dissenting or congregationalist Protestant. During the last fifteen years of his life, Bryan took an increasing interest in the affairs of his Presbyterian denomination. But it was for him, as churches have most often been for American evangelicals, only one more arena in which to campaign for votes.[23] It was not just American convictions about the separation of church and state but also an entire tradition of voluntary organization that kept Bryan from saying what came naturally to Leo XIII with his claim in *Rerum Novarum* that "no practical solution of this [economic] question will be found apart from the intervention of religion and of the Church."[24]

20. For critical background, see Harry S. Stout, "Religion, Communications, and the Revolution," *William and Mary Quarterly* 34 (1977): 501–41.

21. Bryan, "Speech," 199.

22. See especially Hatch, *Democratization of American Christianity.*

23. See the sections on Bryan in Bradley J. Longfield, *The Presbyterian Controversy: Fundamentalists, Modernists, and Moderates* (New York: Oxford University Press, 1991).

24. Leo, *Rerum Novarum*, 245, par. 16.

Third, Bryan's use of history in the "Cross of Gold" speech also marked a difference with *Rerum Novarum*. Where the encyclical made careful use of ancient authorities, especially Thomas Aquinas, both to define a proper method for examining public issues and to provide answers for specific economic questions, Bryan's history was ritualistic and mythic. His evocation of "the hardy pioneers who braved all the dangers of the wilderness" was moving, but it was not analytical. Bryan knew the importance of the past but recognized that for his audience that importance was mostly emotive. So he took time to enlist history — "the pioneers away out there [pointing to the West], who rear their children near to Nature's heart, where they can mingle their voices with the voices of the birds — out there where they have erected school-houses for the education of their young, churches where they praise their Creator, and cemeteries where rest the ashes of their dead." But it was a picture drawn for the purpose of moving rather than instructing — "these people, we say, are as deserving of the consideration of our party as any people in this country."[25] Bryan referred to historical authorities, but these references were mythic — to Thomas Jefferson, who opposed the political influence of banks, and to Andrew Jackson, "who did for us [what Cicero did for Rome] when he destroyed the bank conspiracy and saved America."[26]

In such use of history, Bryan was merely extending an evangelical tradition. The American Revolution had taught evangelicals that the past was corrupt and that ardent effort in the present might even usher in the millennium.[27] An intense surge of primitivism in the early republic reenergized selective Puritan motifs, created several new Christian denominations like the Disciples and the Churches of Christ, powered the new religion of Joseph Smith, and also had an impact on almost all American denominations (including the Catholics).[28] This

25. Bryan, "Speech," 200.

26. Ibid., 203.

27. See especially Ruth H. Bloch, *Visionary Republic: Millennial Themes in American Thought, 1756–1800* (New York: Cambridge University Press, 1985).

28. Richard T. Hughes and Leonard Allen, *Illusions of Innocence: Protestant Primitivism in America, 1630–1875* (Chicago: University of Chicago Press, 1988); and T. D. Bozeman, *To Live Ancient Lives: The Primitivist Dimension in Puritanism* (Chapel Hill: University of North Carolina Press, 1988). For hints of Catholic prim-

primitivism sought to dispense with history almost entirely in its effort to recapture the pristine glories of New Testament Christianity.

Because it draws strength from evangelicals' devotion to the Bible generally and to the illuminating examples of the New Testament specifically, the primitivist influence in American evangelicalism remains very strong. But for evangelicals, the record of the centuries after the New Testament era is dim at best, corrupting at worst. Responding to the crises of the moment, therefore, requires, as in the example of Bryan, an application of absolute principles along with a fervent appeal to millennial possibilities. The aeon between the first and second Advents has never been the object of systematic evangelical attention. For William Jennings Bryan, as for evangelical commentary on public life more generally, there has been no Thomas Aquinas, no deference to a tradition such as Aquinas represented for Leo XIII, and no felt need for such deference.

The tradition that Bryan epitomized was populist (and so preferred spoken argument over published treatises), activistic (and so sought to protect community values through the exertion of individuals), and myth making (and so preferred ideals from the primitive past instead of patient examination of history in general). The political reflection nurtured by these characteristics was not well rounded or extensive, but neither was it inconsequential. It possessed potential both for solid development (as in the concern for justice to individuals along with dignity for communities) and for dangerous degeneration (as in the propensity to mythologize the past). In the subsequent history of American evangelicals both kinds of potential would be realized.

Evangelical Political Reflection and Evangelicalism

An examination of Bryan's career, as exemplified in the "Cross of Gold" speech and the major themes of his career, provides an epitome of nineteenth-century evangelical political reflection. The most obvious

itivism, see the sections on Romanticism and the Enlightenment in Patrick W. Carey, ed., *American Catholic Religious Thought* (New York: Paulist Press, 1987).

thing about the nature of that reflection is that it mirrors the characteristics of evangelical life more generally. Evangelical political reflection
has depended upon moralism that we could call antiecclesiastical (or
at least an-ecclesiastical) because evangelicalism in America has been a
movement stressing moral activism without providing a major role for
the church. Evangelical political reflection is oriented in a populist
direction because evangelicalism has been a populist movement. Evangelical political reflection has drawn upon intuitive conceptions of
justice because evangelicals in general have trusted their sanctified common sense more than formal theology, systematic study of history, or
deliverances from academically trained ethicists. Evangelical political
reflection is nurtured by a common-sensical biblicism for the same
reasons that a "Bible only" mentality has flourished more generally
among evangelicals.

The common evangelical framework for political reflection in the
twentieth century, as well as for political action, has been determined
by this legacy from the previous century. The legacy consists of four
elements: moral activism, populism, intuition, and biblicism. If, however, there is a common framework, it does not mean that evangelical
political action has been entirely uniform or predictable. Over the
course of this century evangelicals have, in fact, differed widely among
themselves concerning specific political actions and principles. These
differences sometimes arise when particular aspects of the common
evangelical framework are given special prominence at specific times or
in response to specific crises. (For example, *Roe v. Wade* called forth a
resurgence of traditional moral activism, whereas in the 1930s an intuitive uneasiness about the evils of politics nurtured a widespread
evangelical quietism.) Sometimes special emphases in the theologies or
religious practices of groups making up the evangelical mosaic have led
to political differences. For example, after World War II the Mennonites
and the Dutch-American Christian Reformed were two immigrant
groups that began to introduce new political ideas to the broader
evangelical constituency. Differences among evangelicals also arise when
a formerly quiescent segment of the mosaic — for example, Southern
Baptists in the last two decades — begins to look outward from their
previously parochial concerns.

The fate of William Jennings Bryan's specific political agenda among his evangelical successors illustrates the magnitude of these political differences. Bryan was a populist who favored measures like the direct election of Senators and the enfranchisement of women, which gave as much power as possible directly to the people. But at least some prominent evangelicals since Bryan have been much more solicitous than he was of constitutional checks on democratic power. Bryan was a progressive who championed the income tax, prohibition, and other measures dramatically increasing the role of the central government in the lives of individual citizens. Although evangelicals favored prohibition, and so gave tacit support to increasing the authority of the federal government, they have tended more generally to argue against the growth of centralized power. Bryan's defense of silver coinage put him at odds with later evangelicals who describe inflation as a moral evil. Bryan was also a near pacifist, who in 1915 resigned as secretary of state from Woodrow Wilson's cabinet when he thought that Wilson's policies were needlessly pushing the nation into the world war. And of course Bryan was a Democrat. As such, he was typical of most American evangelicals for much of the twentieth century, since the heirs of nineteenth-century revivalism were as likely to be Democrats as Republicans until sometime in the 1960s. Since then, however, one of the century's most dramatic shifts in political allegiance has been the move of hereditary evangelicals to the Republican party.[29]

All this is to say that no major group of twentieth-century evangelicals has shared Bryan's specific positions. But the way Bryan promoted his political convictions is still the way evangelicals have pursued politics in this century — activistic, intuitive, populist, and biblicistic. That evangelical framework has been remarkably constant throughout the twentieth century. To be sure, hints of alternative approaches have appeared. Yet the set of characteristics inherited from the nineteenth century has been the dominant shaping force for evangelical political reflection to the present hour.

29. Lyman A. Kellstedt and Mark A. Noll, "Religion, Voting for President, and Party Identification, 1948–1984," in *Religion and American Politics,* ed. Noll (New York: Oxford University Press, 1990), 372–76; and James Guth, John Green, Lyman Kellstedt, and Corwin Schmidt, "Evangelicals and God's Own Party," *Christian Century,* Feb. 17, 1993, pp. 172–76.

Stages in Evangelical Political Reflection

A brief survey of twentieth-century political reflection among evangelicals cannot capture the diversity of the movement or make the necessary
nuances about dominant positions. Nor is it easy with evangelicals to
disentangle political reflection from political action, especially in light
of the way that activism dominates the evangelical response to the public
sphere. Nonetheless, a tentative division of twentieth-century evangelical political reflection into five periods may reveal how the common
framework has been sustained through shifting theological emphases
and a changing public landscape. What such a survey shows is that the
intuitive and populist elements in the framework have been the most
constant. Only in the last two or three decades have they been challenged from within evangelicalism, and with as yet only minimal results.
In contrast, evangelical activism and evangelical biblicism have varied
more dramatically. Shifts in what they meant and how they have been
applied account for the most important changes in the nature of political reflection.

The Age of Bryan

The age of Bryan, 1896–1925, witnessed mostly a continuation of
nineteenth-century themes. Evangelicals were not as yet distinguished
clearly from the mainline Protestants, and so the instincts of cultural
propriety were especially strong. American Protestants produced very
little reflection as such on politics, but their actions implied a full
freight of theory from the nineteenth century. To summarize an
excellent survey of the period by Robert Handy, Protestants in the
Progressive Era relied instinctively on the Bible to provide their ideals
of justice. They believed in the power of Christ to expand the
kingdom of God through the efforts of faithful believers. They were
reformists at home and missionaries abroad who felt that cooperation
among Protestants signaled the advance of civilization. They were
thoroughly and uncritically patriotic. On more specific issues, they
continued to suspect Catholics as anti-American, they promoted the
public schools as agents of a broad form of Christianization, and they

were overwhelmingly united behind prohibition as the key step toward a renewed society.[30]

The more self-consciously evangelical groups within American Protestantism had begun to make a distinction between the application of the gospel to society and a gospel defined by the social needs of the period. They were, that is, beginning to be suspicious of what Walter Rauschenbusch would call the Social Gospel. But as a fine book by Norris Magnuson has shown, they were by no means withdrawing from social activity such as the promotion of prohibition and other reforms.[31] In the United States, and even more so in Canada, leaders of deeply ingrained evangelical convictions continued to promote a social agenda for the churches.[32]

Evangelical reflection of the period also took for granted the propriety of active political involvement. Bryan never doubted for a moment that a career in politics was a fitting Christian vocation. Woodrow Wilson, who in the phrase of George Marsden was "as Puritan as any New Englander who ever held the office" of president, just as easily carried Christian instincts over into public service.[33] The ease with which the realms of evangelical faith and political activity could merge for Wilson is indicated by an address he gave on the Bible to a Denver audience of twelve thousand in May 1911 as he prepared the groundwork for seeking the Democratic nomination for president. Wilson closed the address by urging his listeners to "realize that the destiny of America lies in their daily perusal of this great book. . . . If

30. Robert T. Handy, "Protestant Theological Tensions and Political Styles in the Progressive Era," in *Religion and American Politics,* ed. Mark A. Noll (New York: Oxford University Press, 1990), 283–88. In his own era, the religious, civil, and social concerns of evangelist Billy Sunday were broadly typical of Protestantism in general; see Lyle Dorsett, *Billy Sunday and the Redemption of Urban America* (Grand Rapids: Eerdmans, 1991).

31. Norris Magnuson, *Salvation in the Slums: Evangelical Social Work, 1865–1920* (Grand Rapids: Baker, 1990; orig. 1977).

32. See Richard Allen, *Religion and Social Reform in Canada, 1914–1928* (Toronto: University of Toronto Press, 1971).

33. George M. Marsden, "Afterword: Religion, Politics, and the Search for an American Consensus," in *Religion and American Politics,* ed. Mark A. Noll (New York: Oxford University Press, 1990), 385.

they would see America free and pure they will make their own spirits free and pure by this baptism of the Holy Scripture."[34]

In sum, evangelical political reflection in the age of Bryan was intuitive in its reliance upon the Bible, its confidence in reform, and its assumptions about a Catholic threat. It was also intuitive in its use of history. Even when written by a professional like Woodrow Wilson, the history of the West in general and of the United States in particular functioned primarily to illustrate the ideals of American Christian civilization. Evangelical political reflection of the period was also populist, as the prominence of Bryan and Wilson indicate (although there are evangelical echoes also in the pronouncements of Republicans like William McKinley and Theodore Roosevelt). Its activism was of a piece with the kind of biblicism that Timothy Smith has described as such a powerful agent for reform in the nineteenth century.[35] Evangelicals expressed that biblicism passionately, but also vaguely in a theology that was Reformed in outline, Methodistic in practice, and perfectionistic in piety.

The Age of Fundamentalism

Distinct changes appeared in evangelical political reflection when the age of Bryan gave way to the age of fundamentalism, 1925–41. The year 1925 marked an important transition, not so much because of the Scopes trial, a largely symbolic event that has been more useful for historians interested in finding a turning point than it was for participants battling over whether and how to teach evolution in the public schools.[36] Rather, 1925 was important because in that year Bryan, the last great exemplar of nineteenth-century evangelical political activism,

---

34. *The Papers of Woodrow Wilson, 1911–1912,* vol. 23, ed. Arthur S. Link (Princeton: Princeton University Press, 1977), 20.

35. Timothy L. Smith, *Revivalism and Social Reform: American Protestantism on the Eve of the Civil War,* expanded ed. (Baltimore: Johns Hopkins University Press, 1980); and Smith, "Righteousness and Hope: Christian Holiness and the Millennial Vision in America, 1800–1900," *American Quarterly* 31 (Spring 1979): 21–45.

36. See Paul M. Waggoner, "The Historiography of the Scopes Trial: A Critical Re-evaluation," *Trinity Journal* 5 (1984): 155–74.

died. The third decade of the century also marked the emergence of a more self-conscious evangelicalism (at least in the North) when Baptist and Presbyterian defenders of traditional evangelical beliefs were marginalized by denominational inclusivists or were driven out altogether. It was also the decade when Keswick Holiness and premillennial dispensationalism, which had been gaining strength for some time, assumed a new prominence. These more general matters, rather than the Scopes trial, pushed evangelical political reflection into a new era.

In terms of the hereditary evangelical framework for political reflection, evangelicals continued to be as intuitive and as populist as ever. Among evangelicals of all varieties, there was little evidence of any felt need for systematic theoretical reflection, for a theology applied self-consciously to politics, or for critical-historical studies in aid of political theory. Evangelicalism was still overwhelmingly a religion of the people. In the North, fundamentalism was flourishing because leaders like William Bell Riley, Mark Mathews, T. T. Shields, James Gray, Will Houghton, and a host of other dynamic personalities could attract crowds by making good sense face-to-face. Preachers-cum-editors like Donald Barnhouse, Arno Gaebelein, and Charles Trumbull successfully expanded the influence of their popular periodicals. On the airwaves, pioneers like Charles Fuller discovered how to adapt the old-time religion to the newfangled means of mass communication. The same may be said for the situation in the South, where, like northern fundamentalists, Southern Baptists, Churches of Christ, and other sectarian evangelicals grew measurably throughout the darkest days of the depression.

Whatever account is made for the rise of these tendencies, their combined impact on evangelical politics was unmistakable. Under their influence, William Jennings Bryan's optimistic prospects for reform and his support for active government gave way to cultural pessimism and a fear of governmental encroachment. Concern for political involvement was replaced with an almost exclusive focus on personal evangelism and personal piety. Current events evoked interpretations of prophecy instead of either reforming activism or political analysis.

So it was that James M. Gray, president of Moody Bible Institute from 1925 to 1935, analyzed the League of Nations and the Interchurch World Movement primarily as signs anticipating the end of the age.

When in the 1930s Gray watched the rise of dictatorships in Italy and Germany, he took comfort from the fact that biblical prophecy gave the assurance that humanity's "darkest hour" would come "just before the dawn."[37] Donald Barnhouse, a popular pastor, editor, and radio speaker in Philadelphia, in 1939 reassured the readers of his periodical *Revelation* about the rush of current events, since they were among "those of us who read the Bible and who know the general lines of Bible prophecy." Because they had studied the book of Ezekiel, they knew more about what was going around them than did those who read the *Saturday Evening Post.*[38] For *Revelation,* Barnhouse wrote a regular column entitled "Tomorrow: Current Events in the Light of Bible Prophecy." Because of dispensational teaching concerning the importance of a ten-nation Roman federation for the last days, evangelicals of many sort, including speakers at Moody Bible Institute and writers for the *Sunday School Times,* conjectured that Mussolini might be the Antichrist or at least a stalking horse for him.[39] More than one evangelical saw the Blue Eagle, the logo of the National Recovery Administration, as related in some way to the sign of the beast described in the book of Revelation.[40] Charles Trumbull, editor of the *Sunday School Times* and leader of the American Keswick movement, regarded the world-shaking events of the 1930s as signs of the End. He once wrote that, after an individual's personal salvation, the most important thing in life was to gain "a knowledge of God's prophetic program for the age in which we are living, and for the age to come."[41] A few

37. This example and guidance for this whole section come from a splendid manuscript by Joel A. Carpenter, "Revive Us Again: The Recovery of American Fundamentalism, 1930–1950."

38. Donald Grey Barnhouse, "Russia Wins the War!" *Revelation* 9 (Dec. 1939): 477, 499–500, quotation 477.

39. L. Sale-Harrison, "Mussolini and the Resurrection of the Roman Empire," *Moody Bible Institute Monthly* 29 (Apr. 1929): 386–88; Ralph C. Norton and Edith F. Norton, "A Personal Interview with Mussolini: Fascism, the Bible, and the Cross," *Sunday School Times* 74 (Aug. 13, 1932): 423, 426.

40. "The Blue Eagle," *Revelation* 3 (Sept. 1933): 329; Walter B. Knight, "The Mark of the Beast; or, Is the Antichrist at Hand?" *Moody Bible Institute Monthly* 34 (July 1934): 493.

41. Charles G. Trumbull, introduction to Louis S. Bauman, *Light from Bible Prophecy As Related to the Present Crisis* (New York: Fleming H. Revell, 1940), 3.

evangelicals, inspired by dispensationalism's focus on the role of the Jews in the latter days, were easy prey for conspiratorial anti-Semites.[42] Many times more were enthusiastic proponents of the Zionist movement.[43] In both cases, however the stance toward the Jews arose from prophetic interpretation much more than from contemporary analysis or more general theological reflection on nations, international justice, or the recent history of the Middle East. These illustrations come from self-conscious fundamentalists in the North, but they are representative of the most visible political commentary of any sort from evangelicals during the 1930s.

Thus, a long evangelical tradition in which biblicistic forms of theology undergirded political activism and a rough-and-ready intuitive political reflection gave way to a period when a new form of biblicism undermined political activism as well as political reflection. This is the historical situation that led Garry Wills to conclude about the political action of contemporary evangelicals: "The problem with evangelical religion is not (so much) that it encroaches on politics, but that it has so carelessly neglected its own sources of wisdom. It cannot contribute what it no longer possesses."[44] With the shift in evangelical political emphases during the fundamentalist era, the scene was set for the prophetic best-sellers of the Gulf War.

In the South, where fundamentalism of the premillennial dispensational type had not advanced as far, another set of circumstances worked against political reflection. Southern evangelicalism in Baptist, Methodist, Restorationist, and pentecostal varieties was always very much a social phenomenon. But only rarely, after the early decades of the nineteenth century, was it a self-consciously political phenomenon. A doctrine of "the spirituality of the church," which held that bodies of believers in their corporate life should eschew political involvement, also had the effect of discouraging reflection on politics. The doctrine as a theological principle may have offered interesting possibilities for

42. Timothy P. Weber, "Finding Someone to Blame: Fundamentalism and Anti-Semitic Conspiracy Theories in the 1930s," *Fides et Historia* 24, 2 (Summer 1992): 40–55.
43. David A. Rausch, *Zionism within Early American Fundamentalism* (New York: Edwin Mellen, 1979).
44. Wills, *Under God*, 164.

political thought. But in the actual outworking of events it was, in the words of John Leith, "corrupted by the pressures of racial and economic issues into an escape from social responsibility."[45] Southern evangelicals could mobilize for specific political causes like prohibition, but they did so without elaborate theoretical justification and as part of populist crusades. The most general attitude toward Christian political activity and, by implication, political reflection was illustrated by the words of a Methodist spokesman who in 1844 defended the creation of a separate southern denomination by claiming that the "peculiar mission of the Methodist Episcopal Church, South, is that it alone stands for the Christian principle of staying out of politics."[46]

Political activism went into eclipse among evangelicals during the 1930s at the same time that political reflection reached an absolute nadir. Out of fairness, however, we need to mention the qualifying facts and mitigating circumstances. A few evangelicals did remain active politically. Most unhappily, conspiratorialists like Gerald Winrod were able to enlist some fellow evangelicals for their anti-Semitic campaigns of the 1930s.[47] More ambiguously, a dispensational premillennialist radio preacher in Alberta, William Aberhart, overcame the inactivism implied by his theology to mount a populist campaign that led to his service as premier from 1935 to 1943.[48] And throughout the country, countless unnoticed acts of kindness were being done in rescue missions, soup kitchens, and settlement houses by Salvationists, pentecostals, Baptists, Church of the Brethren, independents, and other evangelicals.[49]

45. John H. Leith, "Spirituality of the Church," in *Encyclopedia of Religion in the South,* ed. Samuel S. Hill (Macon, GA: Mercer University Press, 1984), 731.

46. Quoted in Samuel S. Hill, Jr., *The South and the North in American Religion* (Athens: University of Georgia Press, 1980), 128; this book is an excellent introduction to its theme.

47. Weber, "Fundamentalism and Anti-Semitic Theories"; Leo P. Ribuffo, *The Old Christian Right: The Protestant Far Right from the Great Depression to the Cold War* (Philadelphia: Temple University Press, 1983).

48. David R. Elliott and Iris Miller, *Bible Bill: A Biography of William Aberhart* (Edmonton, Alberta: Reidmore, 1987).

49. For one example, see Paul Boyer, *Mission on Taylor Street: The Founding and Early Years of the Dayton Brethren in Christ Mission* (Grantham, PA: Brethren in Christ Historical Society, 1987).

If exceptions existed to the general turn by evangelicals from political action, there were few, if any, exceptions to the turn from political reflection.[50] But mitigating factors do remove some of the onus from this absence. First, the evangelical substitution of apocalyptic speculation for serious political analysis was no more irresponsible and considerably less dangerous than the swooning for Stalinism that infected large swaths of American learned culture in the 1930s. Second, it can be said in defense of the premillennial dispensationalists that they were not entirely wrong. The tumults of the 1930s no doubt reflected momentous spiritual realities; the trends could, in fact, not be analyzed satisfactorily if the spiritual character of human beings was neglected. Third, whatever damage an excessive supernaturalism exerted upon evangelical political reflection, that same supernaturalism did keep alive an awareness of transcendence and so passed on to succeeding evangelical generations the critical starting point for meaningful Christian thought.

Significant changes followed the fundamentalist era, but many of the emphases of that period have remained influential. On the whole, however, evangelicals eventually returned to the more traditional relationship between activism and biblicism and so overcame the apolitical impetus of both dispensationalism and the southern concept of "the spirituality of the church." Yet since evangelicalism has remained a deeply populist movement, the most visible forms of political reflection have still been intuitive — carried on without serious recourse to self-conscious theological construction, systematic moral philosophy, thorough historical analysis, or careful social scientific research. At the same time, however, from the 1940s there have been a growing number of exceptions to the intuitive character of evangelical politics. For several reasons having to do with the evangelical mosaic itself, significant, if still preliminary, steps have been taken toward self-conscious, critical, and theologically informed political thought.

50. Joel Carpenter, in "Revive Us Again," draws attention to a slim pamphlet by Judson E. Conant, *The Growing Menace of the "Social Gospel"* (Chicago: Bible Institute Colportage, 1937), but this work is no more than a rudimentary effort.

An Era of New Beginnings

The year in which the National Association of Evangelicals was established is a convenient signpost to mark a transition from the age of fundamentalism to an era of new beginnings. From 1941, that is, until the reemergence of evangelical activism, which might be marked by *Roe v. Wade* in 1973, a number of subterranean stirrings began to redirect the political energies of evangelicals. We will expand upon these stirrings at greater length in chapter 8, but one other development of this period had at least an indirect influence on evangelical political thought.

The civil rights movement of this period had less of an immediate effect on white evangelicals than one might expect, given the substantial contribution to that movement of biblical and evangelical themes. The cultural distance between black activists and white evangelicals North and South was simply too great for the whites to recognize how much revivalistic evangelicalism contributed to the civil rights movement. Early evangelical responses, even in the moderate *Christianity Today,* were never more than grudgingly supportive.[51] But soon a more discriminating stance prevailed. For most evangelicals, the movement remained extrinsic to their most basic concerns, but it did provide a rallying point for a few young evangelicals, and in only a few years' time it became a model for political engagement by evangelicals eager to agitate on behalf of other causes.

In short, the postwar decades were moving evangelicals in two directions politically — back toward a traditional balance between activism and biblicism and out toward a more thoughtful engagement with political thought itself.

Era of the New Right

Evangelical responses to *Roe v. Wade* in 1973 ushered in a distinct period of political thought and action for evangelicals that extended at least

51. Mark G. Toulouse, "*Christianity Today* and American Public Life: A Case Study," *Journal of Church and State* 35 (Spring 1993): 255-57, 272-74.

until the dissolution of the Moral Majority in 1989.[52] During this period the central story was certainly the reassertion of moral activism in response to the perceived crises of the day. With the New Christian Right, we have returned, mutatis mutandis, to William Jennings Bryan. Although the podiums had become electronic, still the main actors were once again dynamic public speakers like Jerry Falwell or D. James Kennedy. Injustice to the unborn replaced injustice to debtors, but campaigns for at least some classes of unrepresented oppressed were nonetheless again respected as Christian service. Although the political party of choice for restoring Christian morality was now the GOP, evangelicals beyond doubt had returned to the fray. Mass mailings and mass demonstrations replaced the whistle-stop tour as the preferred means for enlisting the public, but evangelical politics of the 1970s and 1980s depended as much on mobilizing the masses as ever it did in the days of Bryan.

An intriguing variant to this main story was the rise of a "New Christian Left," which, with nearly the same stock of evangelical phrases and emotions, promoted a public agenda almost completely opposed to the platforms of the Christian Right.[53]

For this main story, whether the large Right or the small Left, it was the old-time evangelical politics brought back to life in virtually the same form as in the days of William Jennings Bryan. It was a biblicistic politics that (notwithstanding lingering effects of dispensationalism to the contrary) supported vigorously a broadening activism. It was also a populist politics whose leaders were the ones who

52. Among many worthy studies, the following are some of the most informative: Jerry Falwell, with Ed Dobson and Ed Hindson, *The Fundamentalist Phenomenon: The Resurgence of Conservative Christianity* (Garden City, NY: Doubleday, 1981); Robert C. Liebman and Robert Wuthnow, eds., *The New Christian Right: Mobilization and Legitimation* (New York: Aldine, 1983); Richard John Neuhaus and Michael Cromartie, eds., *Piety and Politics: Evangelicals and Fundamentalists Confront the World* (Washington, D.C.: Ethics and Public Policy Center, 1987); and Richard John Neuhaus, ed., *The Bible, Politics, and Democracy,* Encounter Series, no. 5 (Grand Rapids: Eerdmans, 1987).

53. For a learned summary of a full spectrum of positions, see Craig M. Gay, *With Liberty and Justice for Whom? The Recent Evangelical Debate over Capitalism* (Grand Rapids: Eerdmans, 1991).

could mobilize the hinterlands most effectively. And it was still largely an intuitive politics in which the mythic virtues of an Edenic past and the self-evident responses of a born-again people were the bases for argument.

After the Christian Right

If recent commentators are correct in concluding that the age of the New Christian Right is past, or is entering into a new phase, we are currently in a largely uncharted situation.[54] The uncertain future for evangelicalism as a whole, as well as more specifically for evangelical politics, means that there can be no assured predictions. It is, in fact, possible to construct contrasting scenarios for every specific variable. It is conceivable, for example, that intramural evangelical differences over the exact nature of biblical authority, the precise role of women in the church, or the exact nature of God's creation of the world could further fragment evangelicalism to the point of losing even the vestiges of theological cohesion. Or a renewal of commitment to the Bible and the cross of Christ might lead to a new era of spiritual insight. It is altogether probable that the future course of the Southern Baptist Convention, which has been much more the evangelical sleeping giant than the leader its numbers and wisdom qualify it to be, will become ever more influential among evangelicals.[55] But whether that influence comes from importing Southern Baptist squabbles or by learning from positive Southern Baptist examples, no one knows. It is also not out of the question that the pentecostal-charismatic surge will so come to dominate the evangelical mosaic that its inner spiritual dynamic will take an entirely new shape.

54. See Steve Bruce, *The Rise and Fall of the New Christian Right: Conservative Protestant Politics in America, 1978–1988* (New York: Oxford University Press, 1988); and the essays by George Marsden, Robert Wuthnow, and Robert Booth Fowler in *No Longer Exiles: The Religious Right in American Politics,* ed. Michael Cromartie (Washington, D.C.: Ethics and Public Policy Center, 1992).

55. Though sometimes seeming merely to echo the themes of the New Right, the periodical of the Southern Baptists' Christian Life Commission, *Light,* contains increasingly thoughtful, if still populist, commentary on modern politics.

In the political sphere, the forces of the New Right could regroup and go on to more influential political action, or they may sputter and vanish. Evangelicals could be co-opted by Republican leaders with their own agendas, or perhaps come meaningfully to influence Republican strategy and maybe even begin once again to be heard among the Democrats. They perhaps may be able to convince more Americans of the need for supporting a pro-life policy and other evangelical concerns. On the specific question of social thought, it is possible that the push toward self-conscious Christian theorizing on the nature and ends of politics will move from the margin to the center of evangelical consciousness, but it is just as possible that it might be thoroughly swamped by new waves of pietistic anti-intellectualism.

Style and Content

Whatever happens in the practicalities of American political development, however, evangelicals will almost certainly continue to exhibit, in one form or the other, the activism, biblicism, intuition, and populism that have defined evangelicals for more than two centuries. If they repeat the imbalances of their history, evangelical political action may be destructive and their political reflection nonexistent. For example, if evangelicals continue to be influenced by historicist dispensationalism (the dispensationalism that goes in for identifying specific current events as the fulfillment of biblical prophecy), there is little intellectual hope for the future.

Historicist dispensationalism, first, has a track record that simply cannot inspire confidence as a basis for political analysis. Historian Dwight Wilson has expertly summarized a dismal tale:

> The current crisis was always identified as a sign of the end, whether it was the Russo-Japanese War, the First World War, the Second World War, the Palestine War, the Suez Crisis, the June War, or the Yom Kippur War. The revival of the Roman Empire has been identified variously as Mussolini's empire, the League of Nations, the United Nations, the European Defense Community, the Common Market, and NATO. Speculation on the Antichrist has included Napoleon, Mussolini, Hitler, and Henry Kissinger. The northern

confederation was supposedly formed by the Treaty of Brest-Litovsk, the Rapallo Treaty, the Nazi-Soviet Pact, and then the Soviet Bloc. The "kings of the east" have been variously the Turks, the lost tribes of Israel, Japan, India, and China. The supposed restoration of Israel has confused the problem of whether the Jews are to be restored before or after the coming of the Messiah. The restoration of the latter rain has been pinpointed to have begun in 1897, 1917, and 1948. The end of the "times of the Gentiles" has been placed in 1895, 1917, 1948, and 1967. "Gog" has been an impending threat since the Crimean War, both under the Czars and the Communists.[56]

This dismal record has inspired the witticism known as "Murphy's Armageddon Observation: Those who don't learn from the past are condemned to write end-times books. *Corollary:* God doesn't read prophecy books."[57] The sad fact remains that an awful lot of evangelicals still do.

The theological problem with this kind of hit-or-miss application of biblical apocalyptic to current events is even worse. The evangelical tendency to exalt the supernatural *at the expense of the natural* makes it nearly impossible to look upon the political sphere as a realm of creation ordained by God for serious Christian involvement. The same tendency also makes it very difficult to search for norms in this life that combine reverence for God with respect for the variety of political institutions that God has ordained.

Modern difficulties created by speculating on prophecy resemble the problems created by the penchant for conspiratorial thinking, which also has a long history among evangelicals.[58] Both prophetic speculation and conspiracy thinking depend preeminently on the mind of the observer for their understanding of the world. Prophecy buffs apply a

56. Dwight Wilson, *Armageddon Now! The Premillenarian Response to Russia and Israel since 1917* (Grand Rapids: Baker, 1977), 216.

57. From Steve Dennie, *Murphy Goes to Church* (Downers Grove, IL: InterVarsity Press, 1993), as quoted in an InterVarsity Press newsletter, Apr. 12, 1993, p. 1.

58. David Brion Davis, ed., *The Fear of Conspiracy: Images of Un-American Subversion from the Revolution to the Present* (Ithaca: Cornell University Press, 1971); Marsden, *Fundamentalism and American Culture,* 141–70, 206–11; Weber, "Fundamentalism and Anti-Semitic Conspiracy"; and Carpenter, "Revive Us Again," chap. 5.

grid from Scripture to their understanding of the world; conspiracy theorists bring a similar grid from what they know to be true in general to what they are experiencing about the world. Neither takes seriously the information presented from the world itself. Both have much more confidence in their minds than in the evidence of their senses. This situation, however, reverses the scale of confidence communicated by Scripture, where we are taught, first, to respect God and what he has done (including his creation of the world, his guidance of all human affairs, and his preservation of the human ability to learn something about the world) and, second, to mistrust our own deceiving hearts.

Thankfully, more fruitful approaches to political thought have appeared among evangelicals in the last half-century. In chapter 8 we will spend some time noting how over the last decade a more hopeful kind of political reflection has contributed to a reinvigoration of the evangelical life of the mind.

CHAPTER 7

Thinking about Science

Evangelical thought about science has followed the same general path as evangelical reflection on politics. As we saw in chapter 4, nineteenth-century evangelicals effectively adopted the then-popular notions of science for their own purposes. Although that adoption took place more for utilitarian purposes than for intellectual reasons, it still led to fruitful evangelical engagement with science. But then the same combination of forces that crippled evangelical political reflection came into play for science. In the wider university world, aggressive secularization, often supposedly based on an exalted place for science, trampled traditional Christian concerns. Within the evangelical movement the major emphases of fundamentalism led, by a very different route, to a similar attack on the nineteenth-century harmony of science and evangelicalism. The reversal for evangelical scientific thinking was more profound than was the reversal in political reflection because the fundamentalist alternative to the main culture's science was more deeply embedded in the whole fundamentalist rejection of secularism, and because, in their opposition to the newly popular views of science, fundamentalists were remarkably successful in winning over the evangelical populace to their way of seeing the problem. To be sure, evangelicals have continued to train as scientists — in fact, over the last half century many evangelicals have become relatively distinguished in their respective scientific fields. But evangelicals who pursue science in the universities, who are employed as scientific experts for industry and government, or who teach science at the Christian colleges have usually approached their subjects as carefully segregated fields of knowledge rather than with the intent of studying scientific concerns in relation to theology or other spheres of thought. In other words, to be an evangelical scientist has been to hold a vocational rather than an intellectual position. With some notable exceptions, the way for most evangelical scientists to get along was to go along in silence about the contested, highly controversial theoretical issues that dominated scientific discussion in the evangelical movement. The result has been a catastrophe for scientific thinking among evangelicals. The havoc wrecked by this twentieth-century deluge has been particularly damaging, since it directly affected a central intellectual crux for the evangelical faith — how best to understand the wisdom of Scripture in relation to knowledge about the world.

The Nineteenth-Century Heritage

The commitment American evangelicals displayed to the pursuit of science in the decades after the founding of the country included the following range of convictions: theologians and properly trained laypersons should harmonize the most respected results of modern science with acceptably traditional interpretations of the Bible; at least some evangelical leaders should show how scientific conclusions might function as an apology for traditional Christian beliefs; and scientific procedure itself afforded the best general method for approaching all intellectual questions, even in theology. For nineteenth-century evangelicals, science usually meant "Baconianism," or the belief that strict induction from verified individual facts to more general laws offered the best way to understand the data of any subject.

Responses to Darwin

This approach to science shaped evangelical responses to the publication of Charles Darwin's *Origin of Species*.[1] In light of modern controversy

1. The following paragraphs rely heavily on the analysis of Jon H. Roberts, *Darwinism and the Divine in America: Protestant Intellectuals and Organic Evolution,*

over evolution, it may seem difficult to believe that early responses to the debated issues involving human origins were marked by both a plurality of evangelical conclusions and a relatively restrained climate of discussion. Until the American scientific community itself embraced a version of organic evolution (i.e., the development of new species out of already-existing species), Protestant leaders of widely varying theological persuasions (including advanced thinkers like Congregationalist Horace Bushnell, moderates like Episcopalian Phillips Brooks, and conservatives like Presbyterian Charles Hodge) could unite in rejecting Darwin's transmutation hypothesis as simply bad science. The few Americans who felt they could reconcile Darwinism with a reasonably evangelical theology were in a distinct minority during the 1860s.

Interestingly enough, however, the leading Darwinian in North America, who did more than any other scientist to get Americans to take Darwin seriously, was Asa Gray, a Congregationalist with fairly conservative theological views. Gray was a naturalist at Harvard who maintained a traditional theological position. In 1880, he described himself as "one who is scientifically, and in his own fashion, a Darwinian, philosophically a convinced theist, and religiously an acceptor of the 'creed commonly called the Nicene,' as the exponent of Christian faith."[2] At the same time, Gray argued with Darwin himself that the theory of natural selection could be interpreted as supporting God's providential design and maintenance of the world. Darwin was not convinced, but Gray never seems to have had a doubt.[3]

When, however, American scientists accepted the broad outlines

---

1859–1900 (Madison: University of Wisconsin Press, 1988); as supplemented by three other outstanding books: James R. Moore, *The Post-Darwinian Controversies: A Study of the Protestant Struggle to Come to Terms with Darwinism in Great Britain and America, 1870–1900* (Cambridge: Cambridge University Press, 1979); David N. Livingstone, *Darwin's Forgotten Defenders: The Encounter between Evangelical Theology and Evolutionary Thought* (Grand Rapids: Eerdmans; Edinburgh: Scottish Academic Press, 1987); and John C. Greene, *Darwin and the Modern World View* (Baton Rouge: Louisiana State University Press, 1961).

2. Quoted in A. Hunter Dupree, *Asa Gray* (Cambridge: Harvard University Press, 1959), 365.

3. On the Darwin-Gray correspondence, see Adrian Desmond and James Moore, *Darwin* (New York: Time Warner, 1991).

of organic evolution in the 1870s, the situation changed dramatically. Now evangelicals had to decide whether to follow time-honored Christian practice — by adjusting traditional conclusions to evolution as they had earlier done in response to proposals about the age of the earth and the nebular hypothesis — or to draw the line against this new challenge.[4] Three positions developed in the last quarter of the century. Conservative opponents rejected evolution out of hand, primarily for religious reasons, because it did not square with their understanding of the Bible. In the words of Presbyterian John T. Duffield from 1878, evolution as described by Darwin was "irreconcilable with what the Scriptures teach as to man's original and present spiritual condition"; its disregard for Christianity's description of redemption meant that the theory undercut the "central idea of religion in the Bible."[5] Such rejection of evolution was also shaped, however, by earlier American commitments to Baconian science (with the common-sense antagonism to speculation about origins) and eighteenth-century formulations of the argument from design (with the need to show how each feature of nature could provide edification for humans).

Those who found it possible to align evolution with their Protestant faith divided into two additional groups. Theologically conservative evolutionists, of whom James McCosh of Princeton University, George Frederick Wright of Oberlin College, and B. B. Warfield of Princeton Seminary were the preeminent examples, thought it was possible to affirm evolution within the boundaries of historic Christian doctrines.[6] Because fundamentalists by the 1930s had so thoroughly

4. See especially Martin J. S. Rudwick, "The Shape and Meaning of Earth History," and James R. Moore, "Geologists and Interpreters of Genesis in the Nineteenth Century," both in *God and Nature: Historical Essays on the Encounter between Christianity and Science,* ed. David C. Lindberg and Ronald L. Numbers (Berkeley: University of California Press, 1986); and Ronald L. Numbers, *Creation by Natural Law: Laplace's Nebular Hypothesis in American Thought* (Seattle: University of Washington Press, 1977).

5. Quoted in Roberts, *Darwinism and the Divine,* 108–9.

6. James McCosh, "Religious Aspects of the Doctrine of Development," in *History, Essays, Orations, and Other Documents of the Sixth General Conference of the Evangelical Alliance,* ed. Philip Schaff and S. Irenaeus Prime (New York: Harper & Brothers, 1874), 264–71; Ronald L. Numbers, "George Frederick Wright: From

rejected the choice made by McCosh, Wright, and Warfield, it will be necessary to return to the question of why these evangelical evolutionists took the path they did.

The majority who embraced evolution, however, did so as part of a major adjustment in theology. The reinterpretation that evolutionary ideas entailed for them often accompanied favorable views on the higher criticism of the Bible, a new trust in religious consciousness (understood generally), and a growing confidence in the progressive advancement of the human race. Following these trends, modernist Protestant evolutionists came to defend an immanent conception of God, to redefine the Bible as an expression of evolving religious consciousness, and to recast Christian notions of redemption in terms borrowed from organic evolution.[7]

The debate over evolution in the last third of the nineteenth century was momentous because of the importance science had previously assumed for evangelicals in post-Revolutionary, democratic America. The ability to demonstrate scientifically the existence of God and the truths of the Bible had become far more important for American evangelicals than for their counterparts in Europe, where traditional authorities continued to support, in varying degrees, traditional Christianity. Hence, conservative British and European Protestants never divided over evolution in the same way that Americans did.[8] In these terms, the intellectual debate over evolution was also a debate over the role of Protestantism in a culture that had forsworn tradition. The failure of either proponents or opponents to question historic Protestant commitments to that bond between Enlightenment notions of science and traditional conceptions of Christianity testified to the deep historical commitment of evangelicals to the scientific enterprise, but also to an unself-conscious commitment to the assumptions of Baconian science.

Christian Darwinist to Fundamentalist," *Isis* 79 (1988): 624–45; and David N. Livingstone, "B. B. Warfield, the Theory of Evolution, and Early Fundamentalism," *Evangelical Quarterly* 58 (Jan. 1986): 68–83.

7. William R. Hutchison, *The Modernist Impulse in American Protestantism* (Cambridge: Harvard University Press, 1976), 88–90.

8. See George M. Marsden, "Fundamentalism as an American Phenomenon: A Comparison with English Evangelicalism," *Church History* 46 (1977): 215–32.

The "Two Books" of Nineteenth-Century Evangelical Science

Despite the deficiencies created by that lack of critical self-awareness, nineteenth-century American evangelicals nonetheless developed a fairly sophisticated conception of how to integrate science and theology. Evangelicals continued to hold firmly to the idea that the Bible should provide the overarching framework for understanding anything, even the deliverances of scientists. Although this feature of nineteenth-century evangelical intellectual life was passed on successfully to the twentieth century, evangelicals in this century have had more difficulty understanding how their predecessors could believe that the deliverances of scientists should aid in understanding the Bible. Theologians at Princeton are useful for illustrating this second feature of nineteenth-century evangelical science, since later evangelicals have continued to use their definitions of biblical authority. In 1812 in his inaugural address as the first professor at Princeton Seminary, Archibald Alexander intimated the reasons for being open to scientific conclusions: "Natural history, chemistry, and geology have sometimes been of important service in *assisting the Biblical student to solve difficulties contained in Scripture;* or in enabling him to repel the assaults of adversaries which were made under cover of these sciences."9

Alexander's successor, Charles Hodge, went even further in arguing for a limited autonomy for science within a framework of divine creation. In January 1863, Hodge's journal, the *Biblical Repertory and Princeton Review,* published an essay by Joseph Clark entitled "The Skepticism of Science." In this article Clark contended that, since science was becoming ever more important in Western civilization, Christians should adopt a twofold strategy of dealing with scientific questions: first, maintain the full trustworthiness of the Bible; second, allow scientists to pursue the proper inductive procedures of their disciplines without precommitments to conclusions thought to be found in the Bible. Clark pointed out how earlier interpretations of

9. *The Sermon, Delivered at the Inauguration of the Rev. Archibald Alexander . . . To Which Are Added, the Professor's Inaugural Address* (New York: J. Seymour, 1812), 84 (emphasis mine).

Scripture (like the belief that the Bible taught a flat earth) had been revised in response to later scientific conclusions. He concluded by suggesting that the church might have to make further adjustments of this kind, but that no damage would result to the church or to doctrines of biblical inspiration if believers allowed scientists to pursue their investigations and if Christians themselves became better acquainted with scientific work.[10]

To the editorial writer of the *New York Observer,* however, it seemed as if Clark was giving too much away. As the editor defended traditional interpretations of Scripture (e.g., that humanity was six thousand years old), he also charged that Clark was advancing on dangerous theoretical ground: "If we are to accept the teachings of *Science* and set *revelation* aside when the deductions of the former conflict with the latter, where are we?"[11]

Charles Hodge responded that, if only the editor's question were rephrased slightly, we would be exactly where the Christian should be. In response to the editor's comments, Hodge held firmly to a doctrine of biblical inerrancy, and he also urged scientists to beware of advancing cosmological speculations that contradicted the central teachings of Scripture. But he also defended "the proposition that the Bible must be interpreted by science." To Hodge, it was "all but self-evident" that the tested conclusions of scientific enterprise should be brought to bear on the interpretation of Scripture. Hodge is worth quoting at length at this point, because he breathed a spirit that became lamentably difficult to find in fundamentalism and its wake:

> Nature is as truly a revelation of God as the Bible; and we only interpret the Word of God by the Word of God when we interpret the Bible by science. As this principle is undeniably true, it is admitted and acted on by those who, through inattention to the meaning of terms, in words deny it. When the Bible speaks of the foundations, or of the pillars of the earth, or of the solid heavens,

10. Joseph Clark, "The Skepticism of Science," *Biblical Repertory and Princeton Review* 35 (Jan. 1863): 43–75.

11. [Unsigned editorial], "Scripture and Science," *New York Observer,* Mar. 12, 1863, p. 82.

or of the motion of the sun, do not you and every other sane man, interpret this language by the facts of science? For five thousand years the Church understood the Bible to teach that the earth stood still in space, and that the sun and stars revolved around it. Science has demonstrated that this is not true. Shall we go on to interpret the Bible so as to make it teach the falsehood that the sun moves around the earth, or shall we interpret it by science, and make the two harmonize? Of course, this rule works both ways. If the Bible cannot contradict science, neither can science contradict the Bible. . . . There is a two-fold evil on this subject against which it would be well for Christians to guard. There are some good men who are much too ready to adopt the opinions and theories of scientific men, and to adopt forced and unnatural interpretations of the Bible, to bring it to accord with those opinions. There are others, who not only refuse to admit the opinions of men, but science itself, to have any voice in the interpretation of Scripture. Both of these errors should be avoided.[12]

Hodge's overly simple belief in the hard-edged character of "facts," whether perceived in nature or in the Bible, was part of his own educational inheritance that ill served later evangelicals. But his advice on proper ways of letting science inform the study of Scripture spoke for a broad range of the period's evangelical leaders who together achieved remarkable results in thinking along Christian lines about science. It was a consensus that allowed for much intelligent work to be done at two levels, on individual issues of harmonizing texts of Scripture and specific claims of scientists, as well as on the more important level of understanding in principle how God's "two books" may be read together, without one replacing the other.

The path for which Hodge provided a theoretical guide was pursued practically by a number of consequential evangelical scientists in both Britain and North America, including James Dana, John Wil-

12. Charles Hodge, "The Bible in Science," *New York Observer*, Mar, 26, 1863, pp. 98–99. Hodge says much the same thing about the relationship between biblical theology and natural science in "The Unity of Mankind," *Biblical Repertory and Princeton Review* 31 (June 1859), and in his *Systematic Theology*, 3 vols. (New York: Charles Scribner's Sons, 1872–73), 1:59, 170–71, 573–74.

liam Dawson, Asa Gray, Arnold Guyot, Joseph Henry, Lord Kelvin, Hugh Miller, and Matthew Fontaine Maury. A host of theologians likewise followed this path, among others A. A. Hodge, James Iverach, James McCosh, George Macloskie, William G. T. Shedd, A. H. Strong, B. B. Warfield, and Alexander Winchell.[13] These intellectuals by no means agreed among themselves concerning specific details of contemporary scientific controversies, including various aspects of evolutionary theory. In fact, their disagreements were often severe. They were, however, united in believing that biblical interpretation needed a contribution from the day's best science, even as it exerted an influence on the application of scientific conclusions.

The Impact of Fundamentalism

Precisely this belief — that properly scrutinized results of the main culture's scientific enterprises should assist biblical interpretation — was the sacrifice offered by the evangelical mind on the altar of fundamentalist theology. The sacrifice was constrained partly by the world in which fundamentalism existed and partly by fundamentalist theology itself.[14]

Fundamentalist science arose in response to the rapid secularization of the modern academy, which continued in nineteenth-century fashion to use "science" as an authority of great weight, but while cutting out the doxological, or God-oriented, way of doing science that had prevailed widely in the nineteenth century. In a world where, as Mary Midgley put it, "evolution is the creation myth of our age,"[15] it

13. See Livingstone, *Darwin's Forgotten Defenders,* for the best general account.

14. Essential background for this subject are essays by George Marsden, including "The Evangelical Love Affair with Enlightenment Science" and "Why Creation Science?" both in Marsden, *Understanding Fundamentalism and Evangelicalism* (Grand Rapids: Eerdmans, 1991); "The Collapse of American Evangelical Academia," in *Faith and Rationality: Reason and Belief in God,* ed. Alvin Plantinga and Nicholas Wolterstorff (Notre Dame, IN: University of Notre Dame Press, 1983); and "Everyone One's Own Interpreter? The Bible, Science, and Authority in Mid-Nineteenth-Century America," in *The Bible in America,* ed. Nathan O. Hatch and Mark A. Noll (New York: Oxford University Press, 1982).

15. Mary Midgley, "The Evolution of Evolution," in *Darwinism and Divinity:*

is little wonder that folk who continued to believe that God had made the world became profoundly ill at ease. Modern-day "creationism" — or the effort to construct an alternative, fundamentalist science based directly on the Bible — was the result.

Promoters of fundamentalist creation-science have been justifiably upset with the way that the academy and, in recent decades, many governmental agencies have transformed scientific speculation about the origins of the universe into quasi-religious conclusions about how everything works. Creation scientists have performed an excellent service by denying that vast cosmological claims about the self-sustaining, closed character of the universe can ever arise from scientific research itself. They are just as insightful when claiming that such grand conclusions are as much an act of faith as any other large-scale religious claim. Furthermore, their resentments are justified at the idea of paying to buy textbooks or support teachers who champion a supposedly neutral and up-to-date science as a better path to ultimate truth than the traditional religions. In a word, fundamentalist and evangelical resentment at how capital-*s* Science is practiced, funded, preached, and prescribed in our culture could not be more appropriate. It is quite otherwise with the fundamentalist practice of science. Fundamentalist social resentment may be well grounded, but not fundamentalist science.[16]

Goaded on by the questionable use of science in the larger culture, fundamentalists and their evangelical successors dropped the nineteenth-century conviction that the best theology should understand and incorporate the best science. But even as that hereditary conviction was set aside, fundamentalists and their evangelical successors maintained the nineteenth-century convictions that it was important to harmonize the Bible and science (if only an untainted form of science could be found) and that Baconian method still afforded the best way of pursuing any subject. The effect of these developments has been well

Essays on Evolution and Religious Belief, ed. John Durant (Oxford: Blackwell, 1985), 154–80, quotation 154.

16. For a shrewd analysis of the social dimension of modern creation science, see James R. Moore, "Interpreting the New Creationism," *Michigan Quarterly Review* 22 (1983): 321–34.

stated by Edward Davis, a contemporary historian of science, at the end of a truly depressing article. The article concerns a story that has been widely circulated among evangelicals since the end of the nineteenth century that a British seaman lived for several days in the belly of a whale. The story has been passed on by many evangelical leaders, including some of the founders of creation science. As Davis's exhaustive research through an ocean of pseudo-Baconian "fact" ultimately showed, the story was a fiction. Davis's conclusion about the motives of two of the communicators of this fable aptly summarizes what was at stake for evangelicals when they gave up the nineteenth-century belief that it was important to make a positive adjustment to an era's best science:

> Rimmer and Gook wanted more than anything else to give people reasons to believe, to strengthen their faith in the gospel by strengthening their faith in the literal words of the Bible, to debunk the claims of atheistic scientists and apostate theologians. What better way to do this than to use scientific evidence itself as a weapon against the scoffers? . . . I want to emphasize that there was nothing unique about Rimmer's anxiety. The tendency to muster pseudo-scientific "facts" to defend the reliability of scripture against biblical critics was absolutely characteristic of much evangelical and fundamentalist literature of the period. This represents a significant change from the general state of affairs in the 19th century, when a number of highly respected Christian scholars had produced a substantial body of literature harmonizing solid, respectable science with the faith of the lay believer. . . . These works had the positive purpose of forging a creative synthesis between the best theology and the best science of their day; they were not intended merely to defend a particular view of the Bible or to "prove" the bible against skeptics. However, there is no comparable body of literature from the first half of the present century.[17]

Under the social pressures of the early twentieth century as well as the impetus of their own movement, fundamentalists gave in to the

---

17. Edward B. Davis, "A Whale of a Tale: Fundamentalist Fish Stories," *Perspectives on Science and Christian Faith* 43 (Dec. 1991): 234.

weaker elements of their theology, with harmful results for the practice of science. In particular, fundamentalism retreated to Manichaeism, under the assumption that science was a battlefield in which the forces of light must yield nary an inch to the forces of darkness.[18] It adopted a form of super supernaturalism, which had the effect of demonizing the ordinary study of nature. It also fastened on to notions of the "literal interpretation" for the Bible that made it very difficult to see how earlier believers had found the Scriptures a stimulus to full-scale investigation of the physical world. The rise and, from the perspective of the nineteenth century, surprising strength of scientific creationism among evangelicals is the best illustration of these inclinations.

The Rise of Creation Science

The word *creationism* by rights should define all who discern a divine mind at work in, with, or under the phenomena of the natural world. Yet by a most unfortunate set of events, the term has come to mean only the view that God created the world ten thousand or fewer years ago and that God used a worldwide flood in the days of Noah to form the geological conditions that most modern scientists think reveal an ancient earth with evolutionary changes over great expanses of time.

Despite widespread impressions to the contrary, creationism was not a traditional belief of nineteenth-century conservative Protestants or even of early twentieth-century fundamentalists.[19] The mentality of fun-

---

18. In fact, as excellent recent work has shown, the warfare image for the relation of science and religion was a bit of historical mythology manufactured by progressives who did not want to acknowledge the checkered, but very real, contribution of Christianity to the development of modern Western science. See Moore, *Post-Darwinian Controversies*, 17–122; David C. Lindberg and Ronald L. Numbers, "Beyond War and Peace: A Reappraisal of the Encounter between Christianity and Science," *Church History* 55 (1986): 338–54; and David N. Livingstone, "Farewell to Arms: Reflections on the Encounter between Science and Faith," in *Christian Faith and Practice in the Modern World,* ed. Mark A. Noll and David F. Wells (Grand Rapids: Eerdmans, 1988), 239–62.

19. The following paragraphs rely on Ronald L. Numbers's superb recent book, *The Creationists: The Evolution of Scientific Creationism* (New York: Knopf, 1992).

damentalism lives on in modern creation science, even if some of the early fundamentalists themselves were by no means as radical in their scientific conclusions as evangelicals have become in the last forty years. For instance, during the century before the 1930s, most conservative Protestants believed that the "days" of Genesis 1 stood for long ages of geological development or that a lengthy gap existed between the initial creation of the world (Gen. 1:1) and a series of more recent creative acts (Gen. 1:2ff.) during which the fossils were deposited. As we have seen, some conservative Protestants early in the century — like James Orr of Scotland and B. B. Warfield of Princeton Theological Seminary, both of whom wrote for *The Fundamentals* (1910–15) — allowed for large-scale evolution in order to explain God's way of creating plants, animals, and even the human body. (As it happens, their position closely resembled official Roman Catholic teachings on the subject.) Popular opponents of evolution in the 1920s, like William Jennings Bryan, had no difficulty accepting an ancient earth. Bryan, with an acuity that his patronizers rarely perceive, saw clearly that the greatest problem with evolution was not the practice of science but the metaphysical naturalism and consequent social Darwinism that scientific evolution was often called upon to justify.

Modern creationism arose, by contrast, from the efforts of earnest Seventh-day Adventists who wanted to show that the sacred writings of Adventist-founder Ellen G. White (who made much of a recent earth and the Noachian deluge) could provide a framework for studying the history of the earth. Especially important for this purpose was the Adventist theorist George McCready Price (1870–1963), who published a string of creationist works culminating in 1923 with *The New Geology.* That book argued that a "simple" or "literal" reading of early Genesis showed that God had created the world six to eight thousand years ago and had used the Flood to construct the planet's geological past. Price, an armchair geologist with little formal training and almost no field experience, demonstrated how a person with such a belief could reconstruct natural history in order to question traditional understandings of the geological column and apparent indications for an ancient earth. Price's ideas were never taken seriously by practicing geologists, and they also had little impact outside of Adventist circles. One exception was the Lutheran Church — Missouri Synod, where a few energized critics of the modern world found Price's biblical literalism convincing, despite the fact that on almost every other religious question the Missouri Synod was about as far removed from Seventh-day Adventism as it was possible to be. Although Price and various associates founded several creationist organizations (like the Deluge Geological Society), these groups were short-lived. Similarly, early creationist literature seemed to have little visible effect beyond a narrow circle. A few fundamentalists, like the Presbyterian minister Henry Rimmer (1890–1952), proposed somewhat similar views concerning the Flood, but Rimmer's influence had greatly lessened by the time of his death.

When a rising corps of university-trained conservative evangelical scientists founded the American Scientific Affiliation (ASA) in 1941, creationist flood geologists thought this society would provide a receptive forum for their conclusions. It did not. Although leaders of the ASA maintained strict views of biblical authority and defended the sovereignty of God over the natural world, almost all of them held to the older day-age or gap theories. Some even came to feel that divine revelation in Genesis and natural revelation from empirical investigation did not need to be harmonized in the ways that had been repeatedly tried, revised, and tried again since the early nineteenth century. Internal debates on these questions have been interminable in the ASA. Contention over such matters — that is, contention over the fundamentalist agenda — has been one of the reasons for the ASA's limited influence in the more general world of science, although the ASA has sustained a solid roster of capable scientists and published remarkably helpful material on controversial scientific issues.[20]

Undaunted by their failure to take over the ASA, creationists continued to prosecute their case. At last in the late 1950s, a breakthrough occurred. John C. Whitcomb, Jr. (b. 1924), a theologian at Grace Theological Seminary (Winona Lake, IN) of the Grace Brethren denomination, and Henry M. Morris (b. 1918), a hydraulic engineer

---

20. For an overview of ASA activities, see *Origins and Change: Selected Readings from the Journal of the American Scientific Affiliation,* ed. David L. Willis (Elgin, IL: American Scientific Affiliation, 1978); *Teaching Science in a Climate of Controversy: A View from the American Scientific Affiliation* (Ipswich, MA: American Scientific Affiliation, 1986); and essays on the history of the ASA in *Perspectives on Science and Christian Faith* 43 (Dec. 1991): 238–79 and 44 (Mar. 1992): 2–24.

of Southern Baptist background, had each been moving in a creationist direction for quite a while before finding confirmation in Price's work. Each was also disturbed by a book published in 1954 by the evangelical Baptist theologian Bernard Ramm, *The Christian View of Science and Scripture,* which had delighted most members of the ASA by proposing a much more flexible approach to reconciling evidence from nature and understanding from the Bible. Ramm, for example, chastised fundamentalists for failing to read the Bible in its proper cultural contexts instead as a nineteenth-century Baconian text: "The radical error of the hyperorthodox is his failure to see that there is a measure of accommodation. *We believe that the true position is that the revelation of God came in and through the Biblical languages and their accompanying culture.*"[21] Ramm also leveled stern attacks on the harmonizations provided by Price and Rimmer.[22] Soon after the appearance of Ramm's volume, Whitcomb and Morris met. Their cooperation was productive and led in 1961 to the publication of *The Genesis Flood,* an updating of Price's work, but one that, because of Whitcomb's theological contribution and Morris's scientific expertise, made Price's points more persuasively.

The reception of the book was overwhelming.[23] It was obviously a match thrown onto well-seasoned tinder. There was massive demand for the volume (twenty-nine printings and sales in excess of 200,000 by the mid-1980s). The creationist viewpoint was popularized (by Whitcomb, Morris, and others) in millions of other books, articles, pamphlets, and Sunday school lessons. Creationism soon exerted an influence in Britain, where conservative antievolutionists had almost never before promoted the idea of a young earth. Creationist materials were translated into many foreign languages, including Turkish, for use in Islamic education. Some creationists sponsored a drive to move from a Christian-oriented "biblical creationism" to a public-oriented demand for equal time in public education on behalf of "creation science." Several institutes were established to promote creationism. Spirited publicists defended creationism in highly publicized public debates with

21. Bernard Ramm, *The Christian View of Science and Scripture* (Grand Rapids: Eerdmans, 1954), 71.

22. Ibid., 180–88, 199–205.

23. Details are from Numbers, *The Creationists,* 200–208 and elsewhere.

evolutionists. Eventually, a few university-trained geologists came to advocate the creationist viewpoint. Legislators in Arkansas and Louisiana passed laws, later overturned by the courts, to teach creation science as an alternative to evolutionary theories. Presidential candidate Ronald Reagan called for the nation's schools to provide equal time for creation science. Wounded defenders of establishment science published books in rejoinder. And intense battles have taken place in many towns and cities over how evolution was or was not taught in the schools. In sum, since 1960 creationism has done more than any other issue except abortion to inflame the cultural warfare in American public life.

Why Did Creation Science Take Off?

Reasons for the success of creation science are, by the nature of the case, complex. Doubtless a combination of factors accounts for what is one of the great innovations of recent evangelical history — the establishment of an alternative form of science to the form taught by the intellectual establishments of the culture. Nothing like such an alternative has existed in Anglo-American religious history since, in response to the theories of Isaac Newton, the traditional Anglican John Hutchinson offered his alternative explanation of the physical world.[24] Hutchinson had been displeased both with the use made by Newton of England's theological moderates and with the mechanical character of Newton's science itself. Hutchinson held, by contrast, that the early chapters of Genesis as well as the Christian doctrine of the Trinity provided direct scientific teaching about the way fire, air, and light (in various combinations) could explain all physical phenomena. Hutchinsonianism lasted as a significant force among theological conservatives for nearly a century, but by the early 1800s it had been set aside even by the firmest defenders of the Bible's authoritative character.[25]

24. See C. B. Wilde, "Hutchinsonianism, Natural Philosophy, and Religious Controversy in Eighteenth-Century Britain," *History of Science* 18 (1980): 1–24; on the parallel with creation science, see Moore, "Interpreting the New Creationism," 324.
25. Archibald Alexander's inaugural contains a paragraph on why Hutchinson's

Creationism exploded as a public force among evangelicals, first, because of the intuitive belief of many evangelicals that it embodied the simple teachings of Scripture. In the words of David Watson, "Tens of thousands of Christians have been convinced by Morris and Whitcomb's books because *they made sense of the Bible.*"[26] So important is this matter that we will consider the biblical basis of creation science separately below.

Second, the growth of the national government since World War II almost certainly played a role in the public rise of creationism. The intrusion of the federal government into local educational concerns has politicized all topics on the borders between science and religion. After the USSR launched its *Sputnik* in 1957, the United States poured unprecedented amounts of money into a frenzied effort aimed at reinvigorating the teaching of science in American schools. One of the by-products of this effort was the production of influential biology textbooks that not only introduced major contemporary findings but also propounded grandly phrased metaphysical claims about the evolutionary character of the cosmos. Such hegemonic governmental intrusions have regularly produced intense localist reactions. Creationism has been one of the most intense.[27]

Similarly, creationists no doubt express the widespread resentment against America's self-appointed knowledge elites. As such, they are part of a natural reaction to the intellectual imperialism so regularly practiced by at least some of the scholars at the nation's best-known universities. A world in which a physicist like Cornell's Carl Sagan becomes a guru concerning "All Things," or a paleontologist like Harvard's Stephen Jay Gould presumes to define the theoretical limits of "science," is a world primed for an ancient languages expert like Whitcomb and an engineer like Morris to offer their own counterexplanations about How The World Is.

Beyond personal belief and the dynamics of recent social history

---

biblical science, though "calculated to prepossess the pious mind in its favour," was yet "too deeply enveloped in clouds and darkness to admit of its becoming generally prevalent" (*Inaugural Address,* 77).

26. Quoted in Numbers, *The Creationists,* 338.

27. This analysis echoes the conclusions of Robert Wuthnow, *The Restructuring of American Religion* (Princeton: Princeton University Press, 1988), who argues that the expansion of government has tended to politicize and polemicize religion in the United States.

the spread of creationism also reflects dynamics arising from fundamentalist theology, particularly the eschatological mentality and the
fascination for dispensations. A biblical literalism, gaining strength since
the 1870s, has fueled both the intense concern for human origins and
the end times. Literal readings of Genesis 1–3 find their counterpart
in literal readings of Revelation 20 (with its description of the thou-
sand-year reign of Christ). The observation by Ronald Numbers —
that, "for Christians expecting the end of the age, Whitcomb and Morris
offered a compelling view of earth history framed by symmetrical
catastrophic events and connected by a common hermeneutic"[28] —
only confirms a connection that both creationists and premillennial
dispensationalists had identified long ago. In 1923, George McCready
Price made the link explicit:

> The most timely truth for our day is a reform which will point this
> generation of evolutionists back to Creation, and to the worship of
> Him who made the heaven and the earth. Other reforms in other
> days have been based upon various parts of the Bible here and there.
> The reform most needed in our day is one based on the first part of
> the Bible — and upon the last part also. For he who is looking for
> the return of his Lord, and for the imminent ushering in of the new
> heaven and the new earth, must necessarily believe in the record of
> the first part of the Bible which tells of the Creation of the earth.
> Surely it is useless to expect people to believe in the predictions given
> in the last chapters of the Bible, if they do not believe in the record
> of the events described in its first chapters.[29]

The connection has continued to be drawn, as from dispensationalist John Walvoord in 1975:

> In the last quarter of the nineteenth century, Darwinian evolution
> began to penetrate the ranks of postmillenarians. Liberals hailed the
> theory of evolution, with its easygoing optimism, as the true divine
> method for bringing in the predicted golden age. Recognizing this

28. Numbers, *The Creationists*, 339.
29. George McCready Price, *Science and Religion in a Nutshell* (Washington,
D.C.: Review and Herald, 1923), 13.

as a departure from the faith, more conservative postmillenarians and amillenarians attempted to refute the new evolutionary concept. One of the means used was the calling of great prophetic conferences which were held in the last part of the nineteenth century and continued into the twentieth. As amillennialism and postmillennialism have little to offer by way of refutation of the concept of evolutionary progress, these prophecy conferences soon became dominated by premillennial interpreters.[30]

Eschatologies, in other words, implicate their holders in a wide range of stances, including views of human origins. Perhaps the statement would be just as true if it were reversed.

There may be even more to connect the earlier spread of dispensationalism with the later popularity of creation science. Creationism could, in fact, be called scientific dispensationalism, for creation scientists carry the same attitude toward catastrophe and the sharp break between eras into their science that dispensationalists see in the Scriptures.[31] For creationists, there are major structural disjunctions between the original created order and the postfall (or postflood) world as we live in it. In the same way that divine guidelines for human life have been altered in each dispensation, so too the original structures of nature have been dislocated by the Fall and the Flood. As in the history of redemption, so too the natural world has its own series of "dispensations" through which it must pass.

Whatever the exact relation of internal and external factors, creation science and attitudes cultivated by creation science have become a major presence in modern evangelicalism. However one accounts for the rise and popularity of creation science, and however much it is possible to see a valuable social purpose in much creationist activity, for the sake of evangelical thought, creationism has been anything but favorable.

---

30. John F. Walvoord, "Post-tribulationism Today," *Bibliotheca Sacra* 132 (1975): 19–20.
31. The notion of such a connection comes from Arie Leegwater and David Livingstone.

The Damage Done by Creation Science to the Evangelical Mind

Creation science has damaged evangelicalism by making it much more difficult to think clearly about human origins, the age of the earth, and mechanisms of geological or biological change. But it has done more profound damage by undermining the ability to look at the world God has made and to understand what we see when we do look. Fundamentalist habits of mind have been more destructive than individual creationist conclusions. Because those habits of mind are compounded of unreflective aspects of nineteenth-century procedure alongside tendentious aspects of fundamentalist ideology, they have done serious damage to Christian thinking.

A first problem is the indulgence of Manichaean attitudes toward knowledge about the natural world. If creationists are justified in attacking pretentious claims for science, their own strategies confuse the ongoing discussions at the intersection of Christianity (which has always made important claims about the reality of empirically observable events) and empirical science (which has always proceeded within the context of religious-like assumptions about the world). In Western history, negotiations between religion and science have always been convoluted, complicated, and sometimes ironic. But these negotiations have rarely led to outright intellectual warfare.[32] Creationists, however, push religious-science negotiations toward the brink of battle.

By so doing, creationists add their weight to the politicizing of science that has been going on with a vengeance at least since the age when "Darwin's bulldog," T. H. Huxley, used his master's scientific conclusions as a weapon to replace an old guard of clerical naturalists with a new wave of professional, academic scientists.[33] By their all-or-nothing attitudes, creationists make it harder, rather than easier, to isolate the critical issues at the intersection of religion and science. The roar of battle between "creationists" and their "scientific" opponents drowns out more patient, more careful voices. Both those who want actually to look at nature as a way of understanding nature and those

---

32. See the documentation cited in n. 18 above.
33. See Desmond and Moore, *Darwin,* for a full account of that strategy.

who want actually to look at themselves as a way of understanding how cosmological explanations are formed get shouted down. One great tragedy of modern creationism is that its noisy alarums have made it much more difficult to hear careful Christian thinkers — like many in the American Scientific Affiliation or like Phillip E. Johnson in his attacks on the philosophical pretensions of grand-scale Darwinistic theories[34] — whose work could carry evangelicals beyond the sterile impasse of earlier decades.

Even more damaging, an odd combination of creationist profession and creationist practice actually fosters a stunted ability to perceive the world of nature. The profession is to be Baconian in intellectual procedure; the practice is to misapply Baconianism with respect to Scripture and to abandon it with respect to nature. Creationists regularly reaffirm the principles of Baconian science: no speculation without direct empirical proof, no deductions from speculative principles, no science without extensive empirical evidence. The tragedy is that creationists preserve a misguided Baconianism for the Bible and abandon a healthy Baconianism for science.

Evangelicals make much of their ability to read the Bible in a "simple," "literal," or "natural" fashion — that is, in a Baconian way. In actual fact, evangelical hermeneutics, as illustrated in creationism, is dictated by very specific assumptions that dominated Western intellectual life from roughly 1650 to 1850 (and in North America for a few decades more). Before and after that time, many Christians and other thinkers have recognized that no observations are "simple" and no texts yield to uncritically "literal" readings.

The evangelical Old Testament scholar Bruce Waltke, for example, has argued that in order to interpret the early chapters of Genesis adequately, it is necessary to make use of thorough historical study of the ancient world, carefully nuanced exegesis, and wide familiarity with scientific procedures and results. His own conclusion, based on such study, is that Genesis 1:1–2:3 is in some sense "myth" (not in the sense of a fairy tale, but in the sense of a story explaining how God works among humans), that (by modern standards) it both is and is not

34. Phillip E. Johnson, *Darwin on Trial* (Washington, D.C.: Regnery Gateway; Downers Grove, IL: InterVarsity Press, 1991).

"history," that (again by modern definitions) it is not primarily "science," and that it is "theology" in substance but not in style.[35] Waltke may or may not be correct in his conclusions, but his painstaking chain of reasoning demonstrates that it is anything but a simple matter to move from the central meaning of early Genesis (that God is to be worshiped as the source of matter, life, and human civilization) to detailed explanations of how God brought about the creation.

When evangelicals rely on a naive Baconianism, they align themselves with the worst features of the naive positivism that lingers among some of those who worship at the shrine of modern science. Thus, under the illusion of fostering a Baconian approach to Scripture, creationists seek to convince their audience that they are merely contemplating simple conclusions from the Bible, when they are really contemplating conclusions from the Bible shaped by their preunderstandings of how the Bible should be read.

This misguided Baconianism toward the Bible has led to the practical abandonment of Baconianism toward nature. In an effort to avoid the godless conclusions to which some scientists put their results, creationists abandoned the practice of empirical openness to what their senses told them for the practice of deductive dogmatism. In these terms, creationism is the extrapolation of a particular preunderstanding of how the Bible should be read onto the natural world and into the metaphysical issues posed by modern theories of evolution. Actually looking at the earth or actually carrying out experiments has been relatively unimportant for creationists. Research does take place, and experiments occur, but usually because creationists are checking out something they discovered in scientific literature that seems to pose problems for large-scale evolutionary theories. Creationism, at root, is religion. It has become politics because of the overweening metaphysical pretensions of elitist pundits exploiting the prestige of "science."[36] But

35. Bruce K. Waltke, "The Literary Genre of Genesis, Chapter One," *Crux* 27 (Dec. 1991): 2–10.

36. To observe that creationism is primarily religion, and then secondarily politics, is not to disqualify it from a place in the public square, or from commenting on the workings of professional scientists or on the metaphysical assumptions of those who employ science for their own large-scale metaphysical claims. It means, rather, that creationism must be understood for what it is — a political, religious protest. To

it is only marginally a way of studying the world. In their enthusiasm for reading the world in light of Scripture, evangelicals forget the proposition that the Western world's early modern scientists had so successfully taken to heart as a product of their own deep Christian convictions — to understand something, one must look at that something.[37]

The result is a twofold tragedy. First, millions of evangelicals think they are defending the Bible by defending creation science, but in reality they are giving ultimate authority to the merely temporal, situated, and contextualized interpretations of the Bible that arose from the mania for science of the early nineteenth century. Second, with that predisposition, evangelicals lost the ability to look at nature as it was and so lost out on the opportunity to understand more about nature as it is. By holding on so determinedly to our beliefs concerning how we concluded God had made nature, we evangelicals forfeited the opportunity to glorify God for the way he had made nature. In a mirror reaction to the zealous secularists of the twentieth century, evangelicals have gone back to thinking that we must shut up one of God's books if we want to read the other one.

Stephen Toulmin, a modern historian of science, has commented on the peril of linking any religion to any scientific scheme as securely as evangelicals did to Baconianism:

> Twice already, Christian theologians have committed themselves enthusiastically to the detailed ideas of particular systems of scientific theory. This happened, firstly, when the medieval church naturalized Aristotle, and gave his views about nature an authority beyond their true strength: secondly, when, from the 1680s up to the late nineteenth century, Protestant thinkers (especially in Britain) based a new religious cosmology on mechanical ideas about nature borrowed from Descartes and Newton, as interpreted by an edifying

---

regard it simply as providing knowledge about the world is to risk overlooking its particular view of what "knowledge of the world" means as well as its more basic function as protest.

37. See Eugene Klaaren, *Religious Origins of Modern Science: Belief in Creation in Seventeenth-Century Thought* (Grand Rapids: Eerdmans, 1977); and R. Hooykaas, *Religion and the Rise of Modern Science* (Grand Rapids: Eerdmans, 1972).

reading of the argument from design. In both cases, the results were unfortunate. Having plunged too deep in their original scientific commitments, the theologians concerned failed to foresee the possibility that Aristotle's or Newton's principles might not forever be the last word; and, when radical changes took place in the natural sciences, they were unprepared to deal with them.[38]

An even more chilling commentary on evangelical practice comes from Benjamin Farrington, who summarizes the case that Francis Bacon made in the seventeenth century against the Christians in his age who proclaimed that they were doing science the way that the church had done it successfully for hundreds of years: "What, then, precisely was the nature of the sin which had rendered Aristotelianism and so much else of Greek philosophy fruitless for good? It was the sin of intellectual pride, manifested in the presumptuous endeavor to conjure the knowledge of the nature of things out of one's own head instead of seeking it patiently in the Book of Nature."[39]

The Special Question of the Bible

The appeal to Scripture remains the heart of creationism. Creation science does not merely contradict contemporary cosmologists who use science in defense of agnosticism, nor does it merely provide a way of preserving traditional harmonies between Scripture and science. Rather, it is persuasive for so many evangelicals because it seems to honor the Scriptures; it seems to lead to a form of science that proceeds as any Christian exploration of anything surely ought to proceed — namely, by trying to see first what the Bible says and then using those conclusions to shape our investigation of what we are concerned about.

The problem with this reasoning is not confidence in the Bible, but confidence in ourselves. That problem is compounded by the powerful

38. Stephen Toulmin, "The Historicization of Natural Science: Its Implications for Theology," in *Paradigm Change in Theology,* ed. Hans Küng and David Tracy (New York: Crossroad, 1989), 237.

39. Benjamin Farrington, *Francis Bacon: Philosopher of Industrial Science* (New York: Collier, 1961), 118. I owe this reference to Jonathan Peik.

(though usually unobserved) force that an appeal to "normal" or "plain" or "literal" interpretation gained in a Baconian, democratic America over the course of the nineteenth century. Was it not simply self-evident that, if the Bible was God's supreme revelation, the best way to understand the Bible was by using the methods of ordinary common sense open to all men, women, and children in all ages? The answer to that nineteenth-century way of framing the question is that, while such common-sense interpretations of Scripture may have seemed self-evident, they were in fact the product of particular circumstances in North American evangelical history. In chapter 9, we return to the question of what the Bible itself says about its own reason for existence and how the Bible itself suggests that its truth may most fruitfully shape the intellectual life. Here it may be enough to enlist a weighty cloud of witnesses who, in previous centuries, thought very carefully about how Christians should interpret the Scriptures. The point to be made in presenting this array of witnesses is that the habitual instincts of nineteenth-century evangelical America, which, filtered through fundamentalism, continue to be instinctive for many evangelicals today, are not in fact universal, self-evident, or the product of universal common sense.

It will first be useful to present a representative statement of the creationists' trust in Scripture in order to see how that trust grows quite naturally out of the emphases of the fundamentalist era and, at one remove further, of nineteenth-century evangelicalism. The statement, altogether laudable in its intent, is from the introduction to Whitcomb and Morris's *Genesis Flood:*

> Our present study . . . has a twofold purpose. In the first place, we desire to ascertain exactly what the Scriptures say concerning the Flood and related topics. We do this from the perspective of full belief in the divine inspiration and perspicuity of Scripture, believing that a true exegesis thereof yields determinate Truth in all matters with which it deals. [The authors then quote from a work published by B. B. Warfield in 1893 to define what they mean by the truth-telling character of Scripture.] The second purpose is to examine the anthropological, geological, hydrological and other scientific implications of the Biblical record of the Flood, seeking if possible to orient the data of these sciences within this Biblical framework. If this means substantial modification of the principles of uniformity

and evolution which currently control the interpretation of these data, then so be it.[40]

In other words, Whitcomb and Morris were "simply" moving from what the Bible says to an examination of the claims of scientists about the age of the earth and other geological questions. But this procedure is not as simple as it sounds. In the absence of self-criticism and an awareness of how circumstances shape the mind, "ascertain[ing] exactly what the Scriptures say" is not as self-evident as it seems.

One of the earliest full statements of the problem involved in carrying self-evident, literal, normal, simple, or common-sensical interpretations of the Bible into the arena of science is also one of the earliest. It was written by Augustine in the fifth century toward the end of his life, and after several decades of nearly constant toil at interpreting the Scripture. When Augustine wrote the work entitled *The Literal Meaning of Genesis,* it represented a substantial revision of his earlier attempts to understand the first book of the Bible. Now, sobered by his own earlier speculations and by repeated contact with learned individuals of his own age, Augustine, while defending the need to interpret Genesis "literally" (as he defined the term), nonetheless had no patience with those who used the early chapters of Genesis to promote views about the natural world that contradicted the best science of his day:

> Usually, even a non-Christian knows something about the earth, the heavens, and the other elements of the world, about the motion and orbit of the stars and even their size and relative positions, about the predictable eclipses of the sun and moon, the cycles of the years and the seasons, about the kinds of animals, shrubs, stones, and so forth, and this knowledge he holds to as being certain from reason and experience. Now, it is a disgraceful and dangerous thing for an infidel to hear a Christian, presumably giving the meaning of Holy Scripture, talking nonsense on these topics; and we should take all means to prevent such an embarrassing situation, in which people show up vast ignorance in a Christian and laugh it to scorn. The shame is

40. John C. Whitcomb, Jr., and Henry M. Morris, *The Genesis Flood: The Biblical Record and Its Scientific Implications* (Philadelphia: Presbyterian and Reformed, 1961), xx.

not so much that an ignorant individual is derided, but that people outside the household of the faith think our sacred writers held such opinions, and, to the great loss of those for whose salvation we toil, the writers of our Scripture are criticized and rejected as unlearned men. If they find a Christian mistaken in a field which they themselves know well and hear him maintaining his foolish opinions about our books, how are they going to believe those books in matters concerning the resurrection of the dead, the hope of eternal life, and the kingdom of heaven, when they think their pages are full of falsehoods on facts which they themselves have learnt from experience and the light of reason? Reckless and incompetent expounders of Holy Scripture bring untold trouble and sorrow on their wiser brethren when they are caught in one of their mischievous false opinions and are taken to task by those who are not bound by the authority of our sacred books. For then, to defend their utterly foolish and obviously untrue statements, they will try to call upon Holy Scripture for proof and even recite from memory many passages which they think support their position, although *they understand neither what they say nor the things about which they make assertion* [quoting 1 Tim. 1:7].[41]

Augustine's claim is nothing less than that a Christian who attempts to interpret passages of the Bible with cosmological implications will *misinterpret* the Bible if that believer does not take account of what can be learned "from reason and experience." To limit oneself only to the Scriptures in such instances, says Augustine, is to misread the Bible.

Strikingly similar testimony about the need to interpret the infallible Scriptures with the assistance of an appropriately criticized science is found in two of the founders of early modern science, Francis Bacon and Galileo Galilei. Bacon the Protestant and Galileo the Catholic both were content with traditional views of the Bible as the inspired word

41. Augustine, *The Literal Meaning of Genesis,* 2 vols., trans. John Hammond Taylor (New York: Newman, 1982), 1:42–43. For discussion of this and other passages from Augustine's *Literal Meaning of Genesis,* see two essays by Davis A. Young: "The Contemporary Relevance of Augustine's View of Creation," *Perspectives on Science and Christian Faith* 40 (Mar. 1988): 42–45; and "Theology and Natural Science," *Reformed Journal,* May 1988, pp. 10–16.

of God, although both felt that wooden interpretation of Scripture had retarded a God-honoring understanding of nature. Both were right.

In 1623, toward the end of his life, Bacon published a work entitled *The History of the Winds* in which he complained about how easy it was to fool ourselves into thinking that traditional scientific interpretations (from Scripture or elsewhere) represented the simple meaning of the Bible itself, especially if those interpretations were backed by time-honored traditional patterns of thought:

> Without doubt we are paying for the sin of our first parents and imitating it. They wanted to be like Gods; we, their posterity, still more so. We create worlds. We prescribe laws to nature and lord it over her. We want to have all things as suits our fatuity, not as fits the Divine Wisdom, not as they are found in nature. We impose the seal of our image on the creatures and works of God, we do not diligently seek to discover the seal of God on things. . . . Wherefore, if there be any humility towards the Creator; if there be any reverence and praise of his works; if there be any charity towards men, and zeal to lessen human wants and human sufferings; if there be any love of truth in natural things, any hatred of darkness, any desire to purify the understanding; men are to be entreated again and again that they should dismiss for a while or at least put aside those inconstant and preposterous philosophies, which prefer theses to hypotheses, have led experience captive, and triumphed over the works of God; that they should humbly and with a certain reverence draw near to the book of Creation; that there they should make a stay, that on it they should meditate, and that then washed and clean they should in chastity and integrity turn them from opinion. This is that speech and language which has gone out to all the ends of the earth [Ps. 19], and has not suffered the confusion of Babel; this must men learn, and, resuming their youth, they must become again as little children and deign to take its alphabet into their hands. . . . [Bacon closed this essay with a prayer:] May God the Creator, Preserver, and Restorer of the universe, in accordance with his mercy and his loving-kindness toward man, protect and guide this work both in its ascent to his glory and in its decent to the service of man, through his only Son, God with us.[42]

42. Quoted in Farrington, *Francis Bacon,* 118–19.

At just about the same time, Galileo was faced with those who claimed his account of a heliocentric universe could not be true because the Bible clearly taught that the sun moved around the earth (as in Eccl. 1:5). Galileo contended, in response, that a full confidence in Scripture as God's revelation meant that investigators should have more confidence, not less confidence, in what their senses told them about the physical world:

> It is most pious to say and most prudent to take for granted that Holy Scripture can never lie, as long as its true meaning has been grasped; but I do not think one can deny that this is frequently recondite and very different from what appears to be the literal meaning of the words. . . . I think that in disputes about natural phenomena one must begin not with the authority of scriptural passages but with sensory experience and necessary demonstrations. For the Holy Scripture and nature derive equally from the godhead, the former as the dictation of the Holy Spirit and the latter as the most obedient executrix of God's orders; moreover, to accommodate the understanding of the common people it is appropriate for Scripture to say many things that are different (in appearance and in regard to the literal meaning of the words) from the absolute truth; on the other hand, nature is inexorable and immutable, never violates the terms of the laws imposed upon her, and does not care whether or not her recondite reasons and ways of operating are disclosed to human understanding; but not every scriptural assertion is bound to obligations as severe as every natural phenomenon; finally, God reveals Himself to us no less excellently in the effects of nature than in the sacred words of Scripture . . . ; and so it seems that a natural phenomenon which is placed before our eyes by sensory experience or proved by necessary demonstrations should not be called into question, let alone condemned, on account of scriptural passages whose words appear to have a different meaning.
>
> However, by this I do not wish to imply that one should not have the highest regard for passages of Holy Scripture; indeed, after becoming certain of some physical conclusions, we should use these as very appropriate aids to the correct interpretation of Scripture and to the investigation of the truths they must contain, for they are most true and agree with demonstrated truths. . . . I do not think

one has to believe that the same God who has given us senses, language, and intellect would want to set aside the use of these and give us by other means the information we can acquire with them, so that we would deny our senses and reason even in the case of those physical conclusions which are placed before our eyes and intellect by our sensory experiences or by necessary demonstrations.[43]

For Galileo, as for Bacon and Augustine before him, to think that one could interpret the Bible on scientific questions without employing a dialogue between natural and biblical observations was to guarantee *misunderstanding* of Scripture.

The last witness testifying to the same understanding about the interpretation of the Bible with respect to science is the most relevant, for it is B. B. Warfield, the very theologian cited by Whitcomb and Morris as providing the doctrine of biblical inerrancy from which they thought they derived, in a simple and literal fashion, the principles of flood geology. If Warfield refined the meaning of biblical inerrancy, it is obvious that inerrancy was important for Warfield when he examined the natural world.

But when Warfield turned to the natural world, his conclusions were anything but anticipations of the flood geologists. On the question of the age of the earth, Warfield was blunt: "The question of the antiquity of man has of itself no theological significance. It is to theology, as such, a matter of entire indifference how long man has existed on earth. . . . The Bible does not assign a brief span to human history; this is done only by a particular mode of interpreting the Biblical data, which is found on examination to rest on no solid basis. Science does not demand an inordinate period for the life of human beings on earth."[44]

43. "Galileo's Letter to the Grand Duchess" (1615), in *The Galileo Affair: A Documentary History*, ed. Maurice A. Finocchiaro (Berkeley: University of California Press, 1989), 92–94.

44. B. B. Warfield, "On the Antiquity and the Unity of the Human Race," *Princeton Theological Review* 9 (1911): 1–25, as quoted from *The Works of Benjamin B. Warfield*, vol. 9: *Studies in Theology* (New York: Oxford University Press, 1932), 235–36.

On the possibility of evolution Warfield was equally straightforward. At the end of a long discussion of Calvin's view of creation, published in 1915, Warfield summarized what were clearly his own views as well: "Calvin's doctrine of creation is, if we have understood it aright, for all except the souls of men, an evolutionary one. . . . [Calvin's view, properly adjusted in the light of modern knowledge,] is not only evolutionism, but pure evolutionism. . . . All this, we say, is a very pure evolutionary scheme."[45]

The point to be made about Warfield's conclusions must be stated clearly. What Warfield concluded is not the primary concern; he may have been right or wrong on the age of the earth, on Calvin's view of the material creation, or on his own conclusions about the natural world. But that Warfield, the biblical inerrantist par excellence, came to conclusions opposite from Whitcomb and Morris on questions of science must mean that it is anything but a simple, common-sensical, or intuitive procedure to move from a belief in biblical inerrancy to conclusions about any specific areas of science — including the conclusions of creation science.

The testimony of Augustine, Bacon, Galileo, and Warfield can be summarized by focusing on a concrete example: if the consensus of modern scientists, who devote their lives to looking at the data of the physical world, is that humans have existed on the planet for a very long time, it is foolish for biblical interpreters to say that "the Bible teaches" the recent creation of human beings. This does not mean that at some future time, the procedures of science may shift in such a way as to alter the contemporary consensus. It means that, for people today to say they are being loyal to the Bible and to demand belief in a recent creation of humanity as a sign of obedience to Scripture is in fact being unfaithful to the Bible, which, in Psalm 19 and elsewhere, calls upon followers of God to listen to the speech that God has caused the natural world to speak. It is the same for the age of the earth and for all other questions involving the constitution of the human race. Charles Hodge's words from the middle of the nineteenth century are still pertinent: "Nature is as truly a

45. B. B. Warfield, "Calvin's Doctrine of the Creation," *Princeton Theological Review* 13 (1915): 190–255, as quoted from *The Works of Benjamin B. Warfield*, vol. 5: *Calvin and Calvinism* (New York: Oxford University Press, 1931), 304-5.

revelation of God as the Bible; and we only interpret the Word of God by the Word of God when we interpret the Bible by science."[46]

What B. B. Warfield concluded about evolution in 1895 — at a time when he was less certain than he would later become, that evolution adequately explained the divine creation of the world — states even more clearly "the better way" toward science that evangelicals, to their great loss, largely abandoned in the wake of fundamentalism. "The really pressing question with regard to the doctrine of evolution," wrote Warfield, "is not . . . whether the old faith can live with this new doctrine. . . . We may be sure that the old faith will be able not merely to live with, but to assimilate to itself all facts. . . . The only living question with regard to the doctrine of evolution still is whether it is true." By "true" Warfield did not have in mind a question of scriptural exegesis but a question of natural science: whether "(1) we may deduce from the terms of the theory all the known facts, and thus, as it were, prove its truth; and (2) deduce also new facts, not hitherto known, by which it becomes predictive and the instrument of the discovery of new facts, which are sought for and observed only on the expectation roused by the theory."[47] Warfield may have been too sanguine about the pristine character of "facts" in the natural realm, but he saw very clearly that the promotion of evangelical thinking required the observer to read the book of Scripture and the book of nature together.

The influence of a creationism that, while using Warfield's doctrine of Scripture, abandoned his approach to nature, has grown remarkably since World War II. That expanding influence is the firmest indication that the damaging intellectual habits of fundamentalism maintain a powerful grip in the evangelical world. Since World War II, however, there have also been indications that at least some evangelical scientists have been willing to pick up the theoretical question where Warfield and his generation, as the last representatives of the nineteenth-century synthesis of evangelicalism and science, left it. Whether those indications — and developments in other fields — constitute a decisive rebirth in evangelical thought is the question to which we now turn.

46. See n. 12 above.
47. Benjamin B. Warfield, "The Present Status of the Doctrine of Evolution," *Presbyterian Messenger* 3:10 (Dec. 5, 1895): 7-8.

PART 4

HOPE?

CHAPTER 8

Is an Evangelical Intellectual Renaissance Underway?

In the preceding chapters I have argued that contemporary "evangelical thought" is best understood as a set of intellectual assumptions arising from the nineteenth-century synthesis of American and Protestant values and then filtered through the trauma of fundamentalist-modernist strife. Given that history, prospects for evangelical thought in the later twentieth century were not good. The nineteenth-century assumptions, though intellectually fruitful during the period in which they arose, labored under limitations (especially beliefs concerning the impersonal, hyperobjective character of intellectual activity) that became increasingly more evident over the course of this century. The fundamentalist filter may have strained out enough atheism to preserve a kernel of supernatural Christianity, but for intellectual purposes, fundamentalism also strained out most of the ingredients required for a life of the mind.

From the perspective of 1930, the evangelical mind in America was nearly dead, or at least perceptive commentators, including H. Richard Niebuhr, thought it was.[1] Not only were the nation's universities alien territory for evangelicals, but fundamentalists, the most visible evangelicals, had made a virtue of their alienation from the world of learned culture. Appearances, however, as often before in the history

---

1. H. Richard Niebuhr, "Fundamentalism," in *Encyclopedia of the Social Sciences* (New York, 1937), 6:526-27.

of Christianity, proved deceptive. At the apparent nadir of American evangelical thought, new life was stirring that would soon contribute to a more positive use of the mind.

This chapter examines those positive stirrings through a general account of influences that, especially after World War II, reinforced each other to breathe life into evangelical intellectual efforts. To expand upon the general picture, the chapter then pauses to track in more detail budding efforts to renew evangelical political reflection and then comments briefly on evangelical science and philosophy. The reasons why evangelical philosophy has been remarkably successful, evangelical political reflection only moderately so, and evangelical thinking about science hardly so, raise a fundamental question about the nature of recent evangelical thought.

That question hinges on the distinction between evangelical thinking and Christian thinking done by evangelicals — that is, between thought guided by the distinctives of evangelicalism itself and thought inspired by other Christian traditions that take root among evangelicals. Once this distinction has been made, the question can be asked whether recent evangelicals, in order to pursue Christian thinking, have had to abandon what is distinct about the American evangelical heritage. The conclusion of this chapter suggests that, at least into the 1990s, the renewal of evangelical thought that has indeed taken place is mostly a matter of evangelicals' overcoming the encumbrances of the evangelical heritage and finding themselves in a position to exploit patterns of thought offered by other Christian traditions. The book's last chapter, however, pauses to meditate on the resources, as yet largely untapped, that may reside within American evangelicalism itself for loving the Lord God with the mind.

An Awakening Evangelical Mind

Four parallel developments in the 1930s and 1940s prepared the way for distinct improvement in evangelical thinking. Each development represented a modification of some prominent feature of earlier evangelicalism in order to make room for the mind. Against the heritage of intuition appeared somewhat more self-criticism, against simple biblicism a growing awareness of the complexities of Scripture, against populism an increased longing for advanced higher education, and alongside activism the beginnings of respect for study.[2]

Postfundamentalism

The first and most dramatic story was the emergence within American fundamentalism of younger leaders seeking an intellectually responsible expression of the Christian faith. Public reverses for fundamentalism in the 1920s seemed to signal the end of intellectual vitality among conservative evangelicals. Before too long, however, ambitious young preachers, scholars, and journalists who had been raised as fundamentalists frankly rejected the dispensationalism of their heritage.[3] They had had enough of second-degree separatism, apocalyptic biblicism, and social passivity. Harold John Ockenga (1905–85), at various times the president of Fuller and Gordon-Conwell seminaries, called for a "new evangelicalism" that would value scholarship and take an active interest in society while maintaining traditional Protestant orthodoxy. Edward John Carnell (1919–67) was a leader among those who sought training at the nation's best graduate schools. After attending evangelical institutions, he completed doctorates at both Harvard and Boston University before entering a career of writing, teaching, and administration at the new Fuller Theological Seminary in California.[4] Carl

2. An earlier version of this attempt to chart the recent intellectual history of evangelicals is found in "Introduction: Modern Evangelicalism," in *Christian Faith and Practice in the Modern World: Theology from an Evangelical Point of View,* ed. Mark A. Noll and David F. Wells (Grand Rapids: Eerdmans, 1988).

3. The best general coverage of this era is in Joel Carpenter's manuscript "Revive Us Again: The Recovery of American Fundamentalism, 1930–1950"; on the importance of antidispensationalism for the early years of "new-evangelicalism," see Donald W. Dayton, " 'The Search for the Historical Evangelicalism': George Marsden's History of Fuller Seminary as a Case Study," *Christian Scholar's Review* 23 (Sept. 1993): 12–33, with responses by Marsden and others on pp. 34–71.

4. For an account of why Carnell's transitional stance, as one moving out of fundamentalism, may have undercut his long-term influence, see John G. Stackhouse, " 'Pioneer': The Reputation of Edward John Carnell" (M.A. thesis, Wheaton College, 1982).

F. H. Henry (b. 1913), who expressed his concern for an intellectually responsible evangelicalism through teaching at Fuller and as the founding editor of *Christianity Today* (1956), called fundamentalists to a new engagement with American society and a new concern for theological reflection.[5] Together these and like-minded leaders sought better education, better theology, and better cultural analysis.

The evangelist Billy Graham (b. 1918) played a surprisingly large role in promoting the intellectual enlightenment of evangelicalism.[6] Graham has never pretended to be a scholar, but he did nursemaid *Christianity Today* into existence out of a desire to have a serious evangelical counterpart to mainline Protestant and Catholic journals of opinion. Graham also lent his name and influence to several of the seminaries and colleges that hoped to reestablish evangelical academic respectability. But his most important contributions to intellectual life have been intangibles, particularly a willingness to cooperate with other types of Christians in all parts of the world. Through his example, other American evangelicals began to overcome fundamentalist Manichaeism, and also began to realize that American cultural traditions were no more absolute for the intellectual life than they were for the gospel itself. Through his cooperation with Ockenga, Henry, and like-minded leaders, Graham provided the evangelical equivalent of an imprimatur for serious intellectual labor. More than any other public figure, Graham protected evangelical scholars from the anti-intellectualism endemic to the movement.

Help from the Protestant Mainline

The second development concerns theological conservatives who never became fundamentalists. The major American denominations always

---

5. Henry's autobiography, *Confessions of a Theologian* (Waco, TX: Word, 1986), provides a revealing account of the intellectual and theological aspirations he maintained for the evangelical movement.

6. John Pollock, *Billy Graham: Evangelist to the World* (San Francisco: Harper & Row, 1979), and William Martin, *A Prophet with Honor: The Billy Graham Story* (New York: Morrow, 1991), are good biographies, but no one yet has taken the measure of Graham's general influence on the evangelical movement.

contained individuals who valued the traditional confessions and who sought to exert a leavening restraint on the drift toward theological modernism that has characterized many older churches in the twentieth century. For these individuals the significant development was finding fundamentalists who, like themselves, possessed confidence in a traditional understanding of Scripture but who also valued well-considered theological argumentation. As tumult from the fundamentalist-modernist wars receded into the historical background, it became easier for these theological conservatives to reestablish lines of contact with evangelicals.

Exemplary figures came from many of the older denominations. The Baptist historian Kenneth Scott Latourette (1884–1968) built bridges from his teaching post at Yale to postfundamentalists by his histories of Christian missionary endeavor.[7] The Presbyterian historian E. Harris Harbison (1907–64) did the same from Princeton with works on the Reformation and on Christian approaches to historical study.[8] An interest in C. S. Lewis propelled the Episcopal minister Chad Walsh (1914–91) into the eager arms of the former fundamentalists, in whom Walsh seemed to take a genuine, if bemused, interest.[9]

Maturing Immigrant Communities

The third story was one of assimilation. By the early twentieth century, European Protestants with strong attachment to traditions from the Reformation era had established significant communities in America. The largest of these were Lutheran. Despite efforts by leaders like Carl

---

7. As tangible indications of larger networking trends, Latourette originally published his seven-volume *History of the Expansion of Christianity* from 1937 to 1945 with Harper and Brothers (New York) and Eyre and Spottiswoode (London). When it was reprinted, it appeared from evangelical publishing houses — Zondervan in Grand Rapids (1970, 1978) and Paternoster in Exeter, England (1971).

8. Harbison, *The Christian Scholar in the Age of the Reformation* (New York: Scribner, 1956; reprint, Grand Rapids: Eerdmans, 1983) and *Christianity and History* (Princeton: Princeton University Press, 1964).

9. Walsh, *C. S. Lewis: Apostle to the Skeptics* (New York: Macmillan, 1941) and *The Visionary Christian: 131 Readings from C. S. Lewis* (New York: Macmillan, 1981).

Henry, however, connections between America's "new evangelicals" and the Lutherans have always remained somewhat tenuous. The situation was different with various Mennonite bodies and with another group of European confessionalists, the Dutch Reformed. Especially after World War II, Mennonite contacts broadened to the point where they exercised a telling influence on the shape of evangelical social ethics, even as evangelical norms modified some aspects of historic Mennonite separatism.[10]

The influence of the Hollanders was even more profound. During the 1930s and 1940s, members of the Christian Reformed Church, the denomination representing the most recent immigration from the Netherlands, continued the process of Americanization that had started in earnest during World War I.[11] Evangelicals offered these Dutch Reformed an important reference point as they moved closer to American ways. The Dutch, like the American evangelicals, confessed reliance on the Scriptures and greatly valued practical spirituality. Although their standards of piety bore the impress of Europe (drinking and smoking, for example, were never forbidden as they were for most American evangelicals), they could appreciate the spirituality of American pietists. As they grew closer to evangelical networks, the Dutch Reformed offered their American counterparts a heritage of serious academic work and experienced philosophical reasoning. In their native Holland, these Dutch Reformed had founded a major center of higher education, the Free University of Amsterdam; they had made significant contributions to political theory and practice (their leader, Abraham Kuyper, was prime minister of the Netherlands from 1900 to 1905); and they took for granted a full Christian participation in artistic and cultural life.

The most obvious link between these Dutch Reformed and American evangelicals came through their publishers. By the late 1940s, several firms in Grand Rapids, Michigan, a center of Dutch settlement,

10. Perry Bush, "Anabaptism Born Again: Mennonites, New Evangelicals, and the Search for a Usable Past, 1950–1980" *Fides et Historia* 25 (Winter/Spring 1993): 26–47.

11. The key study is James D. Bratt, *Dutch Calvinism in Modern America: A History of a Conservative Subculture* (Grand Rapids: Eerdmans, 1984).

were publishing the books of Carl Henry, E. J. Carnell, and other American evangelicals. Especially the William B. Eerdmans Publishing Company was aggressively seeking new authors and markets from the world of American evangelicals.

Across the Atlantic

Eerdmans also played an important role in drawing a fourth strand of evangelical renewal into the American picture. Beginning in the 1930s, a number of British evangelicals — from the Church of England as well as from dissenting denominations — united in efforts to recover influence in the universities.[12] The cradle for this effort was the British Inter-Varsity Fellowship (IVF), the nursemaids were graduate students and young professors convinced of the intellectual integrity of evangelical faith. Led by preachers like Martyn Lloyd-Jones, scholars like F. F. Bruce and John Wenham, and organizers like Douglas Johnson, these British evangelicals made significant progress in a relatively short time. Forceful, yet dignified preaching missions to Oxford, Cambridge, and other universities established an evangelical presence and led to the conversion of undergraduates. By the end of the 1940s, the Theological Students Fellowship of IVF had established Tyndale House in Cambridge to encourage evangelical study of the Scriptures, and soon thereafter evangelicals began to gain research positions in biblical studies at major British universities. The British Inter-Varsity Press published many products of this renewed evangelicalism, often with Eerdmans as a cosponsor or the American distributor. The printed word thus served as a medium linking British evangelicals to Americans of several varieties — including postfundamentalists, mainline conservatives, and Americanizing confessionalists. In addition, by the 1950s, American evan-

12. On the importance of British developments for American evangelical thought more generally, see Ian S. Rennie, "Fundamentalism and the Varieties of North Atlantic Evangelicalism," in *Evangelicalism: Comparative Studies of Popular Protestantism in North America, the British Isles, and Beyond, 1700-1990,* ed. M. Noll, D. Bebbington, and G. Rawlyk (New York: Oxford University Press, 1994); and Mark A. Noll, *Between Faith and Criticism: Evangelicals, Scholarship, and the Bible,* expanded ed. (Grand Rapids: Baker, 1991), chap. 4, "An Alternative: Great Britain, 1860–1937."

gelicals were regularly going across the Atlantic to pursue graduate work with scholars either holding a similar faith or open to its emphases at the British universities.

Parenthetically, it is important to note the immense importance of another Briton for the life of the mind among twentieth-century American evangelicals. C. S. Lewis took care to repudiate distinctly evangelical traits of the Protestantism with which he grew up in Northern Ireland, and he did not understand the use of the word "evangelical" when its American distinctives were once explained to him.[13] Yet Lewis's writing has constituted the single most important body of Christian thinking for American evangelicals in the twentieth century. His defense of supernatural Christianity, his ability to exploit learned culture, his example as a writer of fiction, his demonstration that the truths of the faith could be expressed in lively prose — all contributed an unusual measure of intellectual stimulation to evangelicals on this side of the water.

Signs of Renewal

The glue uniting the different strands of evangelical intellectual renewal came in several forms. Besides educational exchange carried on by private parties, notable individuals, projects, and institutions also made a contribution. Billy Graham was a contact point of nearly universal recognition. What he did on a large-scale through popular evangelism to establish networks of evangelical interest, the work of British "missioners" to the universities, like Martyn Lloyd-Jones or John Stott, accomplished among more strictly academic groups. Cooperative publishing ventures such as the *New Bible Commentary* and the *New Bible Dictionary* from British Inter-Varsity, Carl Henry's work at *Christianity Today*, and several different projects at Eerdmans drew evangelical scholars from both sides of the Atlantic and from many ecclesiastical traditions into common labor. Eventually, other institutions, like the American InterVarsity Christian Fellowship, or the Lausanne Com-

---

13. Sheridan Gilley, "A Prophet neither in Ireland nor in England (The C. S. Lewis Lecture)," *Journal of the Irish Christian Study Centre* 3 (1986): 1–10.

mittee for World Evangelism, became arenas that strengthened cross-cultural evangelical ties.

The result has been the establishment of an evangelical intellectual network with certain well-fixed reference points in the United States, Great Britain, Canada, as well as other parts of the world. The extended connections of British Inter-Varsity, the insights of Dutch Reformed confessionalists, ethical prodding from the Mennonites, literary stimulation from Anglicans like C. S. Lewis and Dorothy L. Sayers, a common valuing of the classical Protestant heritage, and an ingrained respect for an even broader range of historic Christian expressions have all improved the quality of evangelical intellectual life over the last five decades.

The new leaders of a more intellectually aggressive evangelicalism also took in hand the revitalization of institutions. Already in the 1930s a few colleges with evangelical convictions were beginning to emerge from the trauma of fundamentalist separation. Even more significant was progress in advanced theological study. During the 1940s, Fuller Seminary joined Westminster as a professional school dedicated not only to the preparation of ministers but also to the prosecution of research.[14] Before another two decades had passed, other seminaries — including Asbury, Bethel, Gordon-Conwell, Trinity, and several of the Southern Baptist, Adventist, and Church of Christ schools — were also stressing academic thoroughness in a new way. The scholarly reinvigoration that resulted was most visible for work in biblical studies; broadly, these evangelicals testified to a much more serious engagement of the mind through dedicated academic preparation and a thorough approach to learning.

After World War II evangelicals also formed a series of academic associations, some focusing on biblical and theological subjects, but others also for the increased numbers of professionals in philosophy, history, literature, sociology, economics, and other academic disciplines. With the exception of the Society of Christian Philosophers, these associations have not exerted a compelling influence on their larger

---

14. For the intellectual strains of that effort, as well as for a delightful institutional account, see George M. Marsden, *Reforming Fundamentalism: Fuller Seminary and the New Evangelicalism* (Grand Rapids: Eerdmans, 1987).

disciplines. But they do testify to a rekindling of intellectual interest across a broad spectrum.

At least since the 1970s, evangelicals have also benefited from the cooperation of outstanding scholars at scattered research universities in the United States and Canada. These scholars — sometimes evangelicals themselves or merely sympathetic fellow travelers — receive little direct encouragement from their universities in probing Christian dimensions of their various fields. But with the paucity of serious research at the evangelical colleges and of serious research pushing theology out into other areas of thought at the evangelical seminaries, these scattered scholars constitute what is, in effect, *the* evangelical response to the first-level intellectual issues of the day. The presence of these scholars (as only a partial list) in the history of science at Harvard, history at Queen's University in Ontario, history and philosophy at UCLA, literature at the University of Ottawa and University of Illinois in Chicago, sociology at Princeton and Virginia, philosophy and economics at Wisconsin, philosophy at Syracuse and Yale, and even religion (at Yale, Duke, and Iowa) means that aspiring evangelical graduate students have at least a few places where their Christian concerns are not a hindrance to their progress.[15] At Notre Dame the desire to foster Catholic scholarship has come to be understood broadly enough to provide a supportive research environment for a solid handful of first-order evangelical scholars.[16]

In sum, the intellectual situation for evangelicals since the era of the fundamentalist-modernist controversy is much improved. Striking gains have been made. At least in some parts of the evangelical community, the need for Christian thinking has been recognized. And significant steps have been taken toward promoting a Christian mind, not only for theology but also for other aspects of existence. At the same time, it would be well for us evangelicals not to congratulate

15. The more general problem of graduate students' faith commitments in the largely secular universities is well explored in John Desjarlais, "Graduate Teaching Assistants," *InterVarsity,* Spring 1993, pp. 4–7.

16. That Notre Dame would provide a base for the new Pew Evangelical Scholars Program, which since 1991 has provided funding for research by a modest number of evangelicals, suggests the breadth of that institution's concern for Christian learning broadly defined.

ourselves too much, since a further examination of thinking in specific spheres reveals the provisional character of recent improvement as well as the extra-evangelical sources for much of the recent intellectual energy.

Political Reflection

Evangelicals may be simply too activistic ever to sustain absolutely first-rate thinking about politics. Yet despite (or maybe because of) the renewal of evangelical political activism over the last quarter century, a steady growth in worthy political reflection has been underway. That thought well illustrates the path that the more general intellectual renovation has taken, but also says something about the way that past evangelical habits have had to be overcome in order for progress to take place.

The most visible figure in reawakening a concern for social and political thought was Carl F. H. Henry, who not only roused the troops with his *Uneasy Conscience of Modern Fundamentalism* in 1947 but, as a theology professor and then founding editor of *Christianity Today,* urged evangelicals to a more reflective engagement with the modern world. His own works, like *Christian Personal Ethics* (Eerdmans, 1957) and *A Plea for Evangelical Demonstration* (Baker, 1971), provided a mandate for political engagement rooted in historic Protestant themes of regeneration and sanctification by the Holy Spirit. The reference works he edited, like *Baker's Dictionary of Christian Ethics* (Baker, 1973), contributed still more. For that volume, as an example, Henry assigned the article "International Order" to Charles Malik, the Orthodox Lebanese diplomat whose later challenge to evangelicals we have already reviewed. Malik told his evangelical readers what they already knew when he said that the visible political world was but a reflection of the truly substantial realm of Christ's eternal rule. Yet he went on immediately to show how important, and Christian, it was to study systematically "the visible international order."[17] Henry's own political thought may have been

17. Charles H. Malik, "International Order," in *Baker's Dictionary of Christian Ethics,* ed. Carl F. H. Henry (Grand Rapids: Baker, 1973), 332.

more straitjacketed by the social reflexes of fundamentalism than he realized,[18] but he nonetheless exerted an extraordinarily positive influence toward the recovery of an evangelical politics.

Changes in the geography of evangelicalism may have helped political reflection even more than the Herculean efforts of Carl Henry, as hitherto isolated bodies of conservative Protestants took their first steps toward greater involvement with evangelicalism at large. The new engagements, especially by Mennonites and the Dutch Reformed, yielded important political results. Mennonite association with evangelicals was spurred by the general turmoil of World War II, which brought these Anabaptist pacifists into much fuller contact with Americans in general, and also by growing networks of educational and pastoral relationships between Mennonites and evangelicals. For the Dutch Reformed, it was the publishing houses of Grand Rapids that led the integration. The result was productive cross-pollination. Mennonites and the Dutch Reformed began to sound a little bit more like American evangelicals. For their part, at least some American evangelicals were being confronted with new, and sometimes disconcerting, social theories. Evangelicals could recognize that these theories were rooted in the Bible, but it was also clear that they were neither conventionally intuitive nor traditionally American in anything like the forms to which evangelicals had been accustomed.

Through the labors of individuals like Henry and larger religious changes, like the partial integration of Dutch Reformed and Mennonites into the evangelical mosaic, evangelical political reflection began to blossom. While the alarums of the New Religious Right (and those of opponents frightened by the New Right) have dominated public attention, the recent past has also witnessed, at least on the margins of evangelicalism, a self-conscious attention to the principles of politics. Nothing quite like this kind of reflection had existed before in American evangelical history. Perhaps it was the shaking of confidence in America itself, caused by the cultural upheavals of the 1960s and the escalating politicization of daily life that has taken place in subsequent decades, that weaned some evangelicals away from their intuitive commitments

---

18. See the detailed study of the early *Christianity Today* by Dennis P. Hollinger, *Individualism and Social Ethics* (Lanham, MD: University Press of America, 1983).

to simple "American values." Whatever the cause, recent evangelical political thought has rested not simply on instinct but on serious theology and systematic social analysis.

In typically evangelical fashion, some of this prompting toward a less intuitive politics arose as a by-product of activism. Evangelicals who picketed abortion clinics alongside Roman Catholics were less prone to perpetuate the antipapal instincts indigenous to their tradition. Incongruous political phenomena — like the evangelical interest group JustLife, which campaigned against both abortion and nuclear arms, or a purebred evangelical Congressman like the late Paul Henry, Republican from Michigan, who did not subordinate all else to the pro-life cause[19] — have promoted thought, as well as simple reaction, from fellow evangelicals. The evangelist and popular apologist Francis Schaeffer also urged, in the midst of his own activism, more careful attention to the theological meaning of general cultural developments.[20] Something of his same burden has been carried on by Charles Colson, whose conversion transformed him from a power-hungry political adviser into an effective publicist for Christian political integrity.[21]

These first steps toward self-conscious evangelical reflection also received direct theoretical support.[22] From the early 1970s, at least some evangelicals worked hard at developing theologies for politics and politics informed by theology. On the more directly theological side, evangelicals harvested the fruits of their own broadening mosaic. John Howard Yoder's *Politics of Jesus* (1972) was a book by a Mennonite, but

19. For an illustration of his approach, written before he entered electoral politics, see Paul B. Henry, *Politics for Evangelicals* (Valley Forge, PA: Judson, 1974).

20. On Schaeffer's widespread influence, see the glowing assessments in Lane Dennis, ed., *Francis A. Schaeffer: Portraits of the Man and His Work* (Westchester, IL: Crossway, 1986); and the more critical treatments in Ronald Ruegsegger, ed., *Reflections on Francis Schaeffer* (Grand Rapids: Zondervan, 1986).

21. For example, Charles W. Colson, *Against the Night* (Ann Arbor, MI: Vine, 1989) and *The Body* (Waco, TX: Word, 1992).

22. For especially helpful analysis extending beyond evangelical groups, see James W. Skillen, *The Scattered Voice: Christians at Odds in the Public Square* (Grand Rapids: Zondervan, 1990). A useful earlier account is Robert Booth Fowler, *A New Engagement: Evangelical Political Thought, 1966–1976* (Grand Rapids: Eerdmans, 1982).

directed toward a non-Mennonite audience. Its advocacy of uncompromising Christian pacifism has not by any means carried the day among evangelicals, but it was a landmark effort that has led to much more serious consideration of Jesus' own life as the norm for political behavior. Much the same may be said for the work of Ron Sider in promoting an Anabaptist political economy.[23] Sider's books have not established a new evangelical paradigm, but their push toward a practical, instead of merely formal, allegiance to Old Testament practice and New Testament ideals has certainly enriched evangelical political discussion.

Similarly, Richard Mouw's *Political Evangelism* (1973), and *Politics and the Biblical Drama* (1976), and his meditations on Isaiah 60, *When the Kings Come Marching In: Isaiah and the New Jerusalem* (1983), are examples of a self-consciously Reformed literature that was speaking from the Dutch heritage of Abraham Kuyper, but out to the wider evangelical world. The message that it and similar Kuyperian works conveyed has not revolutionized evangelical politics any more than has the work of Yoder and Sider.[24] Yet its concern for transnational norms of justice rooted in the great acts of salvation history has added a thoughtful new element to evangelical political life.

Political theology of a vastly different sort has also been advanced by the network of Theonomists or Reconstructionists, who have tried to extrapolate the theological vision of Rousas Rushdoony, itself based on the philosophical theology of Cornelius Van Til, into practical proposals for public life.[25] Whatever its Dutch or Armenian roots,

23. For example, Ronald Sider, *Rich Christians in an Age of Hunger* (Downers Grove, IL: InterVarsity Press, 1977) and *Christ and Violence* (Scottdale, PA: Herald Press, 1979).

24. For other examples, see Nicholas Wolterstorff, *Until Justice and Peace Embrace: The Kuyper Lectures for 1981 Delivered at the Free University of Amsterdam* (Grand Rapids: Eerdmans, 1983); and the work of the Canadian Citizens for Public Justice.

25. For examples, Rousas Rushdoony, *The Institutes of Biblical Law* (Nutley, NJ: Craig, 1973); Greg Bahnsen, *Theonomy and Christian Ethics,* 2nd ed. (Phillipsburg, NJ: Presbyterian and Reformed, 1984); and Gary North, *The Dominion Covenant* (Tyler, TX: Institute for Christian Economics, 1985). The best critical commentaries on this movement are from William S. Barker and W. Robert Godfrey, eds., *Theonomy: A Reformed Critique* (Grand Rapids: Zondervan, 1990); and Richard John Neuhaus,

Theonomy sounds a good deal like populist libertarianism, yet by insisting on carefully formulated theological foundations for political action, it too pushes toward a more self-conscious political reflection than is customary in the evangelical tradition.

Alongside these theologies for politics has come also new attention to politics informed by theology. Since the early 1970s a growing number of thoughtful evangelicals have striven self-consciously for a more realistic assessment of contemporary political situations, a more thorough attention to the bearing of human nature on political possibilities, and a more systematic analysis of politics itself. The most thorough of such proposals, like advocacy of a principled pluralism from James Skillen, Rockne McCarthy, and the Center for Public Justice, still depend upon sources from outside the American evangelical tradition.[26] But other voices, which have been schooled more by American traditions of political realism, have also contributed significantly. Such scholars do not constitute a cohesive movement, but the careful conservative realism of individuals like Mark Amstutz, Doug Bandow, Alberto Coll, and Dean Curry is marked by a desire, not altogether universal among evangelicals, to think first before leaping into action.[27] In something of the same category is the political thought of Harold O. J. Brown, which, drawing upon warnings from Continental precedents, has also striven toward a self-consciously Christian political theory.[28]

Finally, notable progress has also occurred in the study of political

---

"Why Wait for the Kingdom? The Theonomist Temptation," *First Things,* May 1990, pp. 13–21.

26. For example, Rockne McCarthy, James W. Skillen, and William A. Harper, *Disestablishment a Second Time: Genuine Pluralism for American Schools* (Grand Rapids: Eerdmans, 1982), which draws on Dutch Calvinist insights.

27. As examples, Mark Amstutz, *Christian Ethics and United States Foreign Policy* (Grand Rapids: Zondervan, 1987); Doug Bandow, *Beyond Good Intentions: A Biblical View of Politics* (Westchester, IL: Crossway, 1988); Alberto R. Coll, *The Western Heritage and American Values: Law, Theology, and History* (Washington, D.C.: University Press of America, 1982); and Dean Curry, ed., *Evangelicals and the Bishops' Pastoral Letter* (Grand Rapids: Eerdmans, 1984).

28. For example, Harold O. J. Brown, *The Reconstruction of the Republic* (New Rochelle, NY: Arlington House, 1977).

behavior. Again, these efforts are carried out by political scientists who are evangelicals or sympathetic to the movement. Their recent efforts — to define "evangelicalism" carefully enough to make the term useful for public polling, to chart the salience of religious belief in comparison with other determinants of political action, and to find out the simple (but historically neglected) question of who evangelicals have actually voted for since World War II — make little pretense at defining norms of political conviction or action.[29] But by using sophisticated techniques from the academy, these scholars have been able to illuminate a subject — the actual political behavior of evangelicals and how it differs from those in other religious traditions — to which neither the academy nor the church has ever paid much attention.

These recent examples of evangelical political theology and theologically informed politics no more constitute cohesive political reflection than the various segments of the evangelical mosaic constitute a cohesive religious movement. At the same time, however, they may be important straws in the wind. The New Christian Right has represented a populist repristinization of the politics of William Jennings Bryan. But alongside this new burst of activism has also arisen a considerable body of evangelical political thought.

To a certain extent, this recent political reflection is clearly a product of historic evangelical concerns. Certainly it depends upon the new sense of political urgency that has been growing among evangelicals since the 1960s, an urgency that pulled evangelicals out of their untypical passivism of the World War II era and back toward the more typical activistic stances of earlier American history. But in other ways, evangelical political reflection represents a repudiation of historic evangelical norms, or at least a wariness toward traditional habits of mind.

29. As examples of much recent work, see James L. Guth and John C. Green, eds., *The Bible and the Ballot Box* (Boulder, CO: Westview, 1991); Lyman Kellstedt and Corwin Smidt, "Measuring Fundamentalism: An Analysis of Different Operational Strategies," *Journal of the Scientific Study of Religion* 30 (Sept. 1991): 259–78; James Guth, John Green, Lyman Kellstedt, and Corwin Smidt, "The Sources of Anti-Abortion Attitudes: The Case of Religious Political Activists," *American Politics Quarterly* 21 (Jan. 1993): 65–80; and David C. Leege and Lyman A. Kellstedt, eds., *Rediscovering the Religious Factor in American Politics* (Armonk, NY: M. E. Sharpe, 1993).

At least some evangelicals, for example, are not as intuitively convinced as they once were about the supposed triumphs of "the American Way"; some no longer act as if the application of Scripture to public life can be carried out with predictable or conventional results; and some have questioned traditional populism by calling upon fellow Christians to repudiate the practices of the democratic majority. To the extent that evangelicals make these moves, they are also questioning the historical character of evangelical political thought.

The rejuvenation of evangelical political reflection has also de-parted from recent evangelical tradition in the way theology is put to use. Many evangelical thinkers now routinely reject the sharp divide between right-minded Protestants and all others. Some of the most interesting evangelical politics, for example, comes in the self-conscious borrowing from Continental Reformed sources, from the Anabaptist heritage, from the mainline Protestantism of Reinhold Niebuhr, or from the neo-conservative Catholicism of Richard John Neuhaus, Michael Novak, and George Weigel. The separatism and pious anti-intellectu-alism fostered by both pentecostal and Holiness movements is also a thing of the past for most evangelical political theorists. So too is the dispensational approach to Scripture. Whatever one might conclude theologically about the relevance of Scripture to contemporary life, the practical effect of dispensationalism was to limit the relevance of much of the Bible for the present. While the question of Old Testament Israel's relationship to the New Testament church might be worth further debate in narrow theological terms, the evangelicals who have made progress in using the Christian faith as a guide to political thought have simply assumed that the whole of the Bible is relevant to the whole of human history and experience. The results of this assumption are by no means uniform. Anabaptist application of Jubilee and the Sabbath from the Old Testament or of the Sermon on the Mount from the New Testament, Kuyperian understanding of "the rule of Christ," Theono-mist renovation of the Deuteronomic law, neo-conservative reflection on Paul's comments concerning the state — these diverse approaches to the Bible leave evangelical political thought scattered all over the map. What these serious-minded efforts have in common, however, is the repudiation of dispensationalist squeamishness about the relevance of previous biblical epochs for today. Although some evangelical

thinkers remain intensely eschatological, they also share a repudiation
of the way that dispensational concern for the End overwhelmed attention to the present age.

In sum, evangelical political reflection is not now a torrent. But
it is more than a cloud the size of a man's hand. The waters that have
nourished the recent flourishing of political thought come only partly,
however, from the historical springs of evangelicalism.

The Situation in Science and Philosophy

Much more wisdom, time, and energy than I possess would be required
to chart the recent history of evangelical thinking in every area of
contemporary thought. But what has been said about political reflection
does provide an orientation to the general picture. Where evangelicals
leave behind the specific shape of fundamentalist theology or fundamentalist spirituality, thought advances. Where evangelicals sift fundamentalist theology and spirituality to retain traditional Christian orthodoxy, where they are able to benefit from other Christian traditions,
and where they make use of learning from the world more generally,
then thinking for the glory of God has taken place. To defend such
propositions fully would require a second book. But their plausibility
can be illustrated by brief accounts of recent evangelical thinking in
science and philosophy. These spheres suggest, respectively, the perils
and prospects of the current moment.[30]

30. Prospects for evangelical theology, which are critical as a necessary support
for all other forms of Christian thinking, have been well canvassed by several recent
scholars — pessimistically by David Wells, *No Place for Truth; or, Whatever Happened
to Evangelical Theology?* (Grand Rapids: Eerdmans, 1993); more optimistically by
Gabriel J. Fackre, *Ecumenical Faith in Evangelical Perspective* (Grand Rapids: Eerdmans, 1993). Other spheres of thought deserve their own special study. For indications
of recent Christian thinking in the various disciplines, see "Life of the Mind," in
Twentieth-Century Evangelicalism: A Guide to the Sources, ed. Edith L. Blumhofer and
Joel A. Carpenter (New York: Garland, 1990), 187–239; Keith E. Yandell, ed., *A New
Agenda for Evangelical Thought* (= *Christian Scholar's Review* 17 [June 1988]); and a
series of introductory textbooks in various disciplines from HarperCollins entitled
"Through the Eyes of Faith," sponsored by the Christian College Coalition.

Science

The fundamentalist influence remains particularly strong in science, probably because scientific issues seem to implicate the Bible most directly, and also because applied science touches so obviously on moral questions of deep concern to the evangelical constituency. Because of that influence, reflection on the Christian meaning of nature remains in a retarded state among evangelicals. To be sure, American evangelicals have made valuable attempts at such reflection and provided an eager reception for several such proposals from abroad.[31] The American Scientific Affiliation also regularly promotes far-reaching, serious-minded discussion at the juncture between science and evangelical theology. In addition, many of the Christian colleges employ scientists who are respected in their various fields, and first-order scientific work is conducted by individual evangelicals at research universities, in government agencies, and with business. But estimable as these achievements are, they lack sustained reflection on the larger meanings of the physical world and the particular strengths and weaknesses of scientific methods, carried out in self-conscious relation to the deepest principles of the Christian faith in such a way as to edify the evangelical public and shape discussions in the larger scientific community.

Furthermore, the reason that the latter kind of specifically Christian and scientifically responsible work does not fare well, despite the manifold talents of many evangelical scientists, is precisely the populism

31. Examples from Americans include Charles E. Hummel, *The Galileo Connection: Resolving Conflicts between Science and the Bible* (Downers Grove, IL: InterVarsity Press, 1986); Del Ratzsch, *Philosophy of Science: The Natural Sciences in Christian Perspective* (Downers Grove, IL: InterVarsity Press, 1986); Howard J. Van Till, Davis A. Young, and Clarence Menninga, *Science Held Hostage: What's Wrong with Creation Science and Evolutionism* (Downers Grove, IL: InterVarsity Press, 1988); and Howard J. Van Till, Robert E. Snow, John H. Stek, and Davis A. Young, *Portraits of Creation: Biblical and Scientific Perspective on the World's Formation* (Grand Rapids: Eerdmans, 1990). Examples from abroad include, from Britain, Donald Mackay, *The Clockwork Image* (Downers Grove, IL: InterVarsity Press, 1974); and Colin A. Russell, *Cross-Currents: Interactions between Science and Faith* (Grand Rapids: Eerdmans, 1985); and, from the Netherlands, R. Hooykaas, *Religion and the Rise of Modern Science* (Grand Rapids: Eerdmans, 1972).

and the biblicism of the evangelical movement. The postwar record of potentially fruitful explorations falling prey to populist opposition is dismal. In the 1950s when a few biologists in the ASA cautiously explored potential Christian use of evolutionary ideas, those who taught at evangelical colleges were, in effect, silenced through a combination of public discontent and administrative pressure.[32] In 1984, when InterVarsity Press published a book by an antiabortion New Zealander who nonetheless questioned the all-or-nothing mentality of some pro-life positions, a well-orchestrated campaign of demagoguery forced the publisher to withdraw the book.[33] Later in the 1980s, when the United States surgeon general, C. Everett Koop, heretofore an evangelical hero for his combination of forthright Christian witness and pioneering surgery on infants, directed an information campaign against AIDS that some evangelicals felt was morally compromised, some of Koop's former admirers turned on him with extraordinary bitterness. Also in the late 1980s, when Calvin College professors published cosmological speculations that advanced what were, in effect, variations on the themes of B. B. Warfield, they were vilified as heretics and made the occasion for threats of schism within the Christian Reformed Church.[34]

In each of these instances, the point at issue for a historian of the intellectual life is not whether the new ideas were right or wrong. The point is that a combination of self-confident biblicism and populist political mobilization greatly restricted, if it did not altogether shut down, promising lines of scientific debate. In such controversies, heat almost entirely replaced the light that might otherwise have been generated to correct, expand, refine, redirect, or otherwise build upon the commendable intelligence of the proposals.

32. See Ronald L. Numbers, *The Creationists: The Evolution of Scientific Creationism* (New York: Knopf, 1992), 158–83.

33. D. Gareth Jones, *Brave New People: Ethical Issues at the Commencement of Life* (Downers Grove, IL: InterVarsity Press, 1984). For a moving account of the public controversy, see Jones, "The View from a Censored Corner," *Journal of the American Scientific Affiliation* 37 (Sept. 1985): 169–77.

34. Howard J. Van Till, *The Fourth Day: What the Bible and the Heavens Are Telling Us about the Creation* (Grand Rapids: Eerdmans, 1986). For a refreshingly informative discussion of these basic issues, see Howard J. Van Till and Phillip E. Johnson, "God and Evolution: An Exchange," *First Things*, June/July 1993, pp. 32–41.

The social reality for evangelical thinking about science is starkly illustrated by contrasting the conclusions of an evangelical, well trained in geology, with the convictions of the larger evangelical world. Davis Young, a defender of biblical inspiration, is also an experienced geologist who, on the basis of his scientific study, has come to the following conclusions:

> The universe is far older than a few thousand years. . . . animals and plants died long before human beings ever appeared on the earth. . . . the human race has been on earth for tens of thousands of years, quite possibly hundreds of thousands of years. . . . Geology provides no evidence whatever for a universal flood. . . . Paleontology and biogeography render impossible the notion that animals from all over the world migrated to the ark and were redistributed therefrom. . . . The evidence of paleontology and biology strongly suggests that there has been progression in life forms throughout time. Call it biological evolution if you will, it is clear that evolutionary theory still lacks the fully convincing mechanisms. . . . [But] the lack of fully satisfying mechanisms does not render invalid the evidence for progression of life and the relatedness of organisms by descent.[35]

As an evangelical, however, Young must immediately follow the presentation of such conclusions with a statement that they do not violate the essence of Christianity, in a climate with very different notions about how to read both the Bible and the natural world. Gallup polling in 1990, for example, revealed that more Americans as a whole (31 percent) believe "the Bible is the actual word of God and is to be taken literally, word for word" than believe (24 percent) that "the Bible is the inspired word of God. It contains no errors, but some verses are to be taken symbolically rather than literally."[36] Among evangelicals, a recent survey of *Christianity Today* readers showed that 70 percent held

35. Davis A. Young, "Theology and Natural Science," *Reformed Journal,* May 1988, 14–16. Young's reasons for giving up on once-traditional methods of harmonizing conclusions of science and the exposition of early Genesis are ably presented in "Scripture in the Hands of Geologists," *Westminster Theological Journal* 49 (1987): 1–34, 257–304.

36. George Gallup, Jr., and Robert Bezilla, *The Role of the Bible in American Society* (Princeton: Princeton Religious Research Center, [1990]), 6.

that "if we believe in an innerant Scripture, we must take the creation stories of Genesis 1 and 2 as literal history," and 63 percent believed that "creation science is a legitimate scientific theory that ought to be taught in schools on an equal footing with standard approaches to biology and geology."[37]

Given such a disparity of conviction — between, on the one side, professionally trained scientists, who spend most of their working days looking at the physical world, and a vast evangelical populace, on the other side, with deeply settled convictions about what the Bible means — it is little wonder that thinking about God in relationship to the physical world can only creep along slowly (if at all) among evangelicals. Neither is it surprising that scientists like Young are discouraged about the apparent unwillingness of evangelicals at large (in contradistinction to many evangelical scientists) to take seriously the task of looking at the world. Young himself phrases the problem like this:

> The modern evangelical church is extremely sensitive about open discussion of scientific issues that bear on Genesis 1–11. Enough Christians are so afraid of what might turn up in such discussions that anyone who does try to explore the issues is in ecclesiastical jeopardy. The prevailing atmosphere of fear tends to squelch attempts to deal with these issues. The issue of the origin of humankind is especially sensitive. It seems that the church is afraid to look into paleoanthropology. Where is the curiosity about the physical history of human beings? Among the multitude of evangelical commentaries on Genesis, hardly any of them addresses the problems of anthropology. Geology is often discussed. Some of the commentators have admitted the possibility of a local flood; others are not yet sure of the legitimacy of geological findings. But virtually all of the commentators assume the anthropological universality of the flood without any engagement whatsoever with the archeological and anthropological data relevant to the question of the flood's impact on the human race. It's as if the hundreds, perhaps thousands of ancient human sites around the world didn't exist.[38]

---

37. Unpublished *Christianity Today* readership survey report, Sept. 14, 1992.
38. Young, "Theology and Natural Science," 13.

For deeply embedded historical reasons, evangelical thinking about science is still but a shadow of what God, nature, and the Christian faith deserve.

Philosophy

The lingering effects of fundamentalist thought that continue to cripple evangelical scientific reflection have been largely absent from the remarkable renewal of orthodox Protestant philosophy that has occurred in the United States over the last several decades. Evangelical philosophers enjoy the ambiguous luxury of carrying on their work largely out of sight of the population at large. Far fewer people in the churches care about the ontology argument, for instance, than take an interest in the cosmologies being taught at the local high school or in the debates carried on over pro- and anti-abortion legislation. Almost by definition, the study of philosophy is insulated from both the inspiration and the headaches arising from the populist, activistic character of American evangelicalism. In addition, specific questions of biblical interpretation do not appear to concern philosophers nearly as directly as they do politicians or scientists. Issues that philosophers do take up — like the existence of God or the nature of human evil — bear generally, rather than specifically, on what the Bible says.

If general conditions among evangelicals are better for philosophers than for those who think about science or politics, general conditions by themselves do not explain the recent renewal of Christian philosophy. What does explain that renewal is the same combination of factors, in miniature, that lay behind the general renovation of evangelical thinking after World War II.[39] First was the determination of a few postfundamentalists to find their vocation, in a distinctly Christian sense of the term, in philosophy, despite the lack of interest among fundamentalists and evangelicals for philosophical questions and despite the unease among some evangelicals about displacing trust in

39. An informative overview by a participant-observer of this recent history is Kenneth Konyndyk, "Christianity Reenters Philosophical Circles," *Perspectives*, Nov. 1992, pp. 17–20.

the Bible with trust in reason. Preeminent among these postfundamentalists was Arthur Holmes, who in 1954 began an annual philosophy
conference at Wheaton College that has continued to feature many of
the best evangelical philosophers as well as many nonevangelicals who
carry on work of interest to the Christian community.[40]

Second, evangelical philosophy also eventually came to benefit
from the Christian interests of mainline Protestants, like William Al-
ston, Robert Adams, Marilyn Adams, and Eleanor Stumpf, who, upon
becoming weary of religious contemporaneity, turned to traditional
expressions of Christian belief. As they did so, they were met by throngs
of evangelicals who, from a different point on the theological compass,
had set out for the same goal.

Third, evangelical philosophy received a huge boost from the
Dutch-American Reformed community. Diligent philosophy had
maintained a place among Dutch immigrants to the New World. Often
in relative isolation — because they were immigrants separated from
the Old Country and immigrants not fully assimilated to American
ways — Dutch Christian philosophy nonetheless soldiered on with
considerable sophistication in the decades before and after World
War II. The evangelical community as a whole hardly knew that individuals like O. K. Bouwsma, William Frankena, and Henry Jellema
existed, but their work kept alive a tradition of painstaking Christian
philosophy that would eventually spill out from the Dutch Reformed
tradition into much wider Christian circles. The next generation of
Dutch-American philosophers entered into their work at just the time
when more and more evangelicals had undertaken the search for more
intellectually satisfying ways of pursuing philosophical questions than
they had found in traditional American evangelicalism. Led by philosophers at Calvin College, especially Alvin Plantinga and Nicholas Wolterstorff (both of whom eventually left Calvin for university appoint-

---

40. Holmes's own books have done much to help other evangelicals recognize
the legitimacy of careful reasoning and also the importance of the created realm. See
his *Christian Philosophy in the Twentieth Century* (Nutley, NJ: Craig, 1969); *All Truth
Is God's Truth* (Grand Rapids: Eerdmans, 1977); *Contours of a World View* (Grand
Rapids: Eerdmans, 1983); ed., *The Making of a Christian Mind: A Christian World
View and the Academic Enterprise* (Downers Grove, IL: InterVarsity Press, 1984); and
The Idea of a Christian College, rev. ed. (Grand Rapids: Eerdmans, 1987).

ments), the Dutch Reformed thinkers galvanized entire squadrons of evangelical admirers, even as they made their mark in academic philosophy more generally. For evangelicals eager for a more responsible use of the mind, the Reformed philosophers were a tonic — bold in confessing historic Christian faith, expert in carrying on sophisticated philosophical argumentation, and far-reaching in proposing new theories. Especially in their attack on "foundationalism" — the notion that beliefs of the sort held by Christians had to be grounded in neutral, universal, and scientific-like axioms — these philosophers pushed historic Christianity back into the arena of modern philosophical debate.[41]

Finally, in the postwar era a small band of British philosophers, against odds almost as long as in North America, also maintained the compatibility of traditional Christianity and the best philosophical reasoning. Led by individuals like Basil Mitchell, these philosophers also labored in relative obscurity — scorned by the academia, of little interest to the church — until roughly the 1980s, when their voices again began to gain more respect in both church and university.

Along these different lines, therefore, momentum built in the postwar decades until by the 1980s it was clear that something remarkable was underway. Philosophical publications aimed at both scholarly and popular audiences forthrightly expounded classic Christian teaching as the basis for right thinking and right behavior.[42] Essays defending some aspect of classical Christian dogma became the centerpiece of

41. Two fine introductory articles are Merold Westphal, "A Reader's Guide to 'Reformed Epistemology,'" *Perspectives,* Nov. 1992, 10–13; and Nicholas Wolterstorff, "What Reformed Epistemology Is Not," ibid., 14–16. Wolterstorff's *Reason within the Bounds of Religion* (Grand Rapids: Eerdmans, 1976) was an early statement of several important themes of these Reformed philosophers. On Plantinga's influence, see Dewey A. Hoitenga, *Faith and Reason from Plato to Plantinga* (Albany: State University of New York Press, 1991).

42. Examples of that writing can be sampled in the journal *Faith and Philosophy* and in many symposia, among which those edited by Thomas V. Morris are unusually insightful: *The Concept of God* (New York: Oxford University Press, 1987); *Philosophy and the Christian Faith* (Notre Dame, IN: University of Notre Dame Press, 1988); and *Divine and Human Action: Essays in the Metaphysics of Theism* (Ithaca: Cornell University Press, 1988). Such writing appears also in a more popular series edited by C. Stephen Evans, "Contours of Christian Philosophy," from InterVarsity Press, and in numerous monographs by a host of philosophers.

concentrated discussion in at least some philosophical quarterlies. A Society of Christian Philosophers was organized in 1978. Soon thereafter it began a quarterly, *Faith and Philosophy*, which rapidly established itself as a leading journal in the philosophy of religion. And meetings of the society, both regionally and nationally, have been scenes of considerable intellectual stimulation. In sum, Christian philosophers had made their presence felt in the world of scholarship more substantially than intellectuals in any other discipline.

Evangelicals made up the majority of those who participated in this resurgence of Christian philosophy. From the first, Asbury College picked up part of the tab for *Faith and Philosophy;* the Wheaton College philosophy conference continued to expand as a showcase for much of the most interesting new work; increasing numbers of philosophy students from the evangelical colleges continued on for advanced study; and many evangelicals have published results of their philosophical investigations in solid journals and the best academic presses.

Despite the full-scale evangelical participation in the renewal of Christian philosophy, however, that renewal has owed relatively little to the distinctive features of American evangelicalism. An indication of that reality is the roster of those who attended the organizational luncheon in Chicago that led to the formation of the Society of Christian Philosophers. Ten individuals attended that meeting — one Roman Catholic, three Episcopalians, four members of the Christian Reformed Church, and two postfundamentalist evangelicals.[43] The proportion represents well the relative intellectual contributions to the resurgence of Christian philosophy. Evangelicals may have provided the troops, but the ideas came largely from outside the American evangelical tradition.

Philosophers clearly must bracket (as they say) the distinctive elements of the evangelical ethos if they are to make progress as philosophers. That is, philosophers might approve of Christian activism, but their job is contemplation. They cannot afford to be intuitive about their intellectual commitments, for the essence of philosophy is excruciating self-consciousness about presuppositions and assumptions. Neither have the Christian philosophers practiced the populist or bi-

---

43. Konyndyk, "Christianity Reenters Philosophical Circles," 18.

blicist styles that defined much of earlier evangelical thought. Their work, by its nature, has always been relatively esoteric, and so not amenable to the populist politicking that looms so large for evangelicals in other intellectual spheres. The concerns of American Christian philosophers with the Bible have been general and historical; the effort to refurbish Christian truth has focused on the main traditional dogmas; and it has often proceeded by selectively reviving the classical Christian arguments of Augustine, Anselm, Thomas Aquinas, Calvin, Pascal, or Jonathan Edwards.

The relatively minor role that American evangelical *ideas* has played in the rejuvenation of Christian philosophy for evangelicals is also evident when considering the more basic structure of the evangelical mind. The intellectual emphases of evangelicalism, as spelled out conveniently in David Bebbington's definition (see chap. 1 above), include conversion, the Bible, and the centrality of the cross. Yet the major intellectual stimulations for the renewal of Christian philosophy have not featured these intellectual elements, at least in an evangelical way. The Dutch Reformed tradition has been the single strongest intellectual resource for the renewal of Christian philosophy. But the Dutch Reformed are not strongly conversionist (they expect, rather, baptized children to grow gradually into maturity as Christians). They do emphasize the work of Christ, but often by balancing Christ's saving work with his rule over every aspect of life in the present.[44] To be sure, the Dutch Reformed manifest an intense loyalty to the Bible, but not in the terms favored by American evangelicals. Their hermeneutics are not literalistic, they are not disposed to a dispensational understanding of the unity of Scripture, they are not prone to moralism based on individual prooftexts, and they are almost never premillennialists. For the Roman Catholics and the mainline Protestants who have also contributed so substantially to the renewal of Christian philosophy, the same sort of differences with traditional evangelical emphases are present, only more so.

---

44. A great rallying cry from Abraham Kuyper has often been repeated by his American admirers in the postwar period: "There is not one square inch of the entire creation about which Jesus Christ does not cry out, 'This is mine! This belongs to me!'" (quoted in Richard J. Mouw, *Uncommon Decency: Christian Civility in an Uncivil World* [Downers Grove, IL: InterVarsity Press, 1992], 145).

In sum, evangelicals have made up a very important element in the emergence of philosophy as a sturdy, academically respectable, and faithfully Christian enterprise. But in order to become part of that renewal, evangelicals have either left behind, or largely ignored, the habits of mind that for nearly two centuries defined the evangelical experience in America.

Conclusion

Even a brief examination of recent evangelical thought in politics, science, and philosophy leads to inescapable conclusions: Evangelicals now are participating fully in the renewal of Christian thinking that has been underway for several decades in North America. That thinking in certain areas, like philosophy, probably merits the term "renaissance," and in other areas, like political reflection, certainly has registered notable advances. For the most part, however, the intellectual vitality of this renewed Christian thinking does not arise from the historic resources of American evangelicalism.[45]

The dismaying status of evangelical scientific reflection might lead to the conclusion that American evangelicalism must be abandoned before solid Christian thinking can occur. But experience in political reflection and philosophy is not as discouraging. In these arenas, evangelical tradition provides energy, interest, and enthusiasm, and it is possible to see a happy alliance of convenience between the recruits supplied by the evangelical tradition and the ideas offered from other Christian traditions.

Still, even in those areas where the evangelical past does not function as a deterrent to God-honoring thought, the question must remain whether evangelicalism as it has taken shape in North America

---

45. The field of literature might also illustrate this same conclusion. Where evangelicals have developed self-conscious literary criticism, it tends to be an imitation of British Anglicans (C. S. Lewis, Charles Williams, Dorothy L. Sayers) or Roman Catholics (J. R. R. Tolkien, G. K. Chesterton), even though none of these estimable individuals shared the conversionism, the biblicism, the sort of activism, or even (at least in the same terms) the crucicentrism of traditional American evangelicalism.

contributes anything intrinsic to the life of the mind. Historically considered, especially over the course of the twentieth century, it is difficult to find such a contribution. Apart from accidents of personal history that explain the evangelical commitments of some intellectuals, there seems little encouragement in the evangelical tradition itself for pursuing the life of the mind.

And here this book might end. The scandal of the evangelical mind seems to be that no mind arises from evangelicalism. Evangelicals who believe that God desires to be worshiped with thought as well as activity may well remain evangelicals, but they will find intellectual depth — a way of praising God through the mind — in ideas developed by confessional or mainline Protestants, Roman Catholics, or perhaps even the Eastern Orthodox. That conclusion may be the only responsible one to reach after considering the history sketched in this book. Even if it leaves evangelical intellectuals trapped in personal dissonance and the evangelical tradition doomed to intellectual superficiality (or worse), the recent past seems to point in no other direction.

But because North American evangelicalism is a form of Christianity, a religion notable for its paradoxes of faith, hope, and love, perhaps there is more to say. Perhaps in spite of its history, there is within evangelicalism itself at least hints of a better way. The hope that we American evangelicals might yet worship God with our minds rests ultimately not on our recent history but on the nature of the religion we profess.

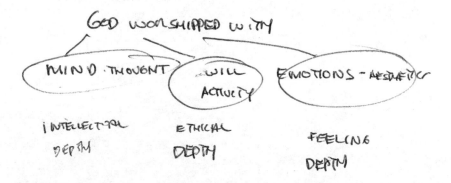

CHAPTER 9

Can the Scandal Be Scandalized?

Can a Christian mind develop out of American evangelicalism? Based solely on twentieth-century historical precedent, it does not seem likely.

Evangelicalism, however, is a form of Christianity in which the cross of Christ has figured prominently. That cross, the apostle Paul reported, was a *skandalon* to those who did not believe; for those whom God called, however, the cross became "the power of God and the wisdom of God" (1 Cor. 1:23–24). These phrases raise an intriguing possibility. Might evangelicalism and fundamentalism, which have been scandalous in abjuring responsibility for the mind, ever become intellectually scandalous in another sense of the term, in the distinctly religious sense that the Christian message of a crucified God is a scandal to those who cannot believe? The "scandal of the cross" speaks of the seriousness with which God himself treated the realm of human existence. That realm was the theater of redemption, the arena in which God chose to reveal himself most fully. If God devoted so much of himself to the created realm — in order to purchase the redemption of sinners — is it imaginable that sinners who enjoy the salvation won in that realm might seek more diligently to fathom the realities of that realm — in order to worship their Redeemer?

That possibility is more than just a play on words. Redemption, which evangelicals often consider a means for God to rescue us *from* this world, was carried out (and is being carried out) *in* this world.

241

That reality should not diminish the larger reality of heavenly or eternal existence. Neither should that reality lead to the mistake at the other end of the spectrum, where eagerness to understand the workings of the world becomes an end in itself. John Calvin put it well when he said that "the human mind is . . . a perpetual forge of idols."[1] The solution to idolatry, however, is not to destroy all the materials from which idols are made. The solution is to treat the material from which we construct idols appropriately to its reality. The wood and stone from which idols are made do not deserve to be worshiped; because God made them, however, they deserve to be studied as wood or stone.

Once again it is worth stating the central point. The life of the mind is not necessarily superior to any other legitimate human pursuit. But it is a legitimate human pursuit. Christians who pursue intellectual activity should never wander far from the words of the prophet Jeremiah:

> This is what the LORD says:
> "Let not the wise man boast of his wisdom
>   or the strong man boast of his strength
>   or the rich man boast of his riches,
> but let him who boasts boast about this:
>   that he understands and knows me,
> that I am the LORD, who exercises kindness,
>   justice and righteousness on earth,
>   for in these I delight,"
>   declares the LORD.[2]

With these words guiding the Christian pursuit of learning, a proper form of Christian scholarship is possible. The pursuit of learning might provide an opportunity to boast in the Lord.

If intellectual life deserves to be rescued among evangelicals, what should be done? The answer lies in the evangelical community, with evangelical scholars, and in the thing itself.

---

1. John Calvin, *Institutes of the Christian Religion*, 1.11.8.
2. For an excellent discussion of this passage, the quotation from Calvin above, and much else relevant to this book, see Alan Flavelle, "The Importance of the Christian Mind in Ireland Today," *Journal of the Irish Christian Study Centre* 1 (1983): 3–10.

Evangelicalism

The tendency of American evangelicals, when confronted with a problem, is to act. For the sake of Christian thinking, that tendency must be suppressed. The problem of Christian thinking among American evangelicals is only tangentially a practical problem. It is not primarily a problem of organizing, instituting, building constituency, recruiting, mobilizing, or fund-raising — that is, the sort of tasks that are the glory of the evangelical enterprise. Rather, the problem of Christian thinking is a problem of intention. More activity, by itself, will not overcome the intellectual weaknesses of our hereditary activism. Only patient, purposeful intention to use the mind for Christ will move toward the balance that is needed.

Programs or institutions that grow out of altered attitudes might have a chance. The attitudes that most need correction, if evangelicals are ever going to pursue the life of the mind, are attitudes concerning our own distinctives, our tendency toward false disjunctions, and our hereditary intellectual intuitionism.

Distinctive versus Essential

In the first instance, historical study or travel throughout North America and the rest of the world should help evangelicals realize that much of what is *distinctive* about American evangelicalism is not *essential* to Christianity. To the extent that the distinctives of evangelicalism are subordinated to the essentials of Christianity, to that extent the chances are greater for the development of Christian intellectual life.

Evangelicals have been distinctive for activism, but essential to Christianity is an attitude of profound gratitude to God. Gratitude to God may indeed issue in activism, but it may also issue in other manifestations, like study or contemplation, that are less well known in North America.

Evangelicals have also been distinctive for the shape of their belief in the Bible — that is, for a literal hermeneutic, for a "scientific" approach to the verses of Scripture that was molded by the eighteenth-century Enlightenment, for keen preoccupation with the doctrine of

THINGS WILL CAN DO ORGANIZING, INSTITUTING, BUILDING CONSTITUENCY, RECRUITING, MOBILIZING, FUND RAISING biblical inerrancy, and for fascination with details of the apocalypse. What is essential to Christianity, however, is a profound trust in the Bible as pointing us to the Savior and for orienting our entire existence to the service of God. The purpose of the Bible is spelled out quite clearly in the Bible itself, as in John 20:31: "These are written that you may believe that Jesus is the Christ, the Son of God, and that by believing you may have life in his name." Even the classic passage in 2 Timothy 3, which includes a description of Scripture as "God-breathed," emphasizes the saving and orienting purposes of the Bible much more than the Bible's potential to serve as an immediate source of detailed knowledge. "But as for you [Paul writes to Timothy], continue in what you have learned and have become convinced of, because you know those from whom you learned it, and how from infancy you have known the holy Scriptures, which are able to make you wise for salvation through faith in Christ Jesus. All Scripture is God-breathed and is useful for teaching, rebuking, correcting and training in righteousness, so that the man of God may be thoroughly equipped for every good work" (vv. 14–17). When evangelicals more consistently use the Scriptures to explain "salvation through faith in Christ Jesus" and to outline what it means to be "thoroughly equipped for every good work," then evangelicals will be concentrating on what is essential about Scripture. And then the life of the mind may have a chance.

Evangelicals have been distinctive in featuring the crisis conversion. But what is essential to Christianity is the whole life committed to God, from the beginning of faith until death. Some individuals may report being drawn to faith through a crisis conversion; other believers in Christ may have a different story to tell. From this latter group may come insights concerning godliness that provide more room for the intellect.

In sum, the distinctive may be a feature of the essential, but not necessarily so. To confuse the *distinctive* with the *essential* is to compromise the life-transforming character of Christian faith. It is also to compromise the renewal of the Christian mind.

SINGLE MINDED ENTHUSIASM of   ATIVISM - WILL
SINGLE MINDED   "   EMOTIVISM - FEELINGS
"   "   INTELLECTUALS ac THOUGHT

False Disjunctions

To make room for Christian thought, evangelicals must also abandon the false disjunctions that their distinctives have historically encouraged. The cultivation of the mind for Christian reasons does not deny the appropriateness of activism, for example, but it does require activism to make room for study. Similarly, it is conversionism along with a consideration of lifelong spiritual development and trust in the Bible along with a critical use of wisdom from other sources (especially from the world that God made) that will lead to a better day. Modifying the evangelical tendency to Manichaeism may cost some of the single-minded enthusiasm of activism, but it would be worth it in order to be able to worship God with the mind. The prize-winning Irish poet Evangeline Paterson was brought up as a strict dispensationalist of the old school. Her later reflection on what it took to be able to throw herself into poetry for the glory of God speaks volumes about the false antinomies that bedevil evangelicalism: "I was brought up in a Christian environment where, because God had to be given pre-eminence, nothing else was allowed to be important. I have broken through to the position that because God exists, everything has significance."[3]

Beyond Intuition

Finally, if evangelicals are ever to cultivate the mind, habits of intuitionism — or the rapid movement from first impressions to final conclusions — must be changed. Many modern evangelicals do show a commendable willingness to listen to other Christians who, only a few decades ago, would have been considered beyond the pale, and this willingness reveals a desire to think through differences. If evangelicals will listen carefully to each other (Southern Baptists respecting a word from the Christian Reformed, Mennonites heeding the counsel of the charismatics, evangelical Left and evangelical Right talking to rather than past each other), then it is possible to imagine that a way will be

3. Joy Alexander, "In Conversation with Evangeline Paterson," *Journal of the Irish Christian Study Centre* 4 (1989): 42.

cleared to benefit from even broader Christian discussions, drawing in Roman Catholics, other Protestants, and the Orthodox, and still more expansive conversations including "persons of good will" at large. Prerequisite to the ability to learn from others is at least a partial suspension of the intuitionism that for two centuries has been an evangelical stock in trade. It would no longer be evangelicalism without the direct apprehension of spiritual realities and a dynamic populist expression of those realities. But unless such an intuition can be modified by a better theological way, evangelical reflection will never make a contribution living up to the dynamism of evangelical faith.

Other Christian traditions have developed principles of thought out of the depths of theological insight. Evangelicals are in a position to learn about, and learn from, those principles. For example, Lutherans, with Luther's belief that a Christian was *simul justus et peccator* (at the same time a justified saint and a sinner), could show evangelicals the virtue of looking at problems from several different points of view. The same sort of instruction might come from Calvinistic notions of *concursus,* expressed by Abraham Kuyper as a balance between "antithesis" and "common grace," or from Catholic notions of natural law, which Leo XIII put to use so effectively in *Rerum Novarum.* Once intuition has been expanded by study, it would even be possible to resuscitate for general purposes an idea from the evangelical heritage, that is, the notion of "the spirituality of the church" (or the idea that churches as formal organizations should encourage the Christian lives of their members but not themselves deal directly with politics, social issues, and the like). Shorn of the passivity that the defense of slavery forced upon it, this doctrine offers intriguing possibilities for a way of proclaiming the particular truths of the gospel within the congregation while yet acting outside the congregation according to norms acceptable in the world at large.[4]

Each of these instances, however, requires reflection alongside action. Each requires a measure of distance from pressing issues in order to bring the riches of the gospel to bear. The absence of some kind of

---

4. The possibility is explored briefly in John H. Leith, "The Spirituality of the Church," in *Encyclopedia of Religion in the South,* ed. Samuel S. Hill (Macon, GA: Mercer University Press, 1984), 731.

dual vision, the inability to speak at the same time with a common vocabulary both inside and outside the community of faith, has been a besetting weakness of evangelicalism and a particular problem of fundamentalism. The Lutherans, the Reformed, and the Catholics show what can be done in moving beyond religious intuition to theological reflection. They offer hope that evangelicals may one day do so as well.

Evangelical Intellectuals

For their part, evangelical intellectuals must simply set about the task. The virtues that Robert M. Hutchins, the dynamic president of the University of Chicago in an earlier era, commended for all scholars are worth commending to evangelicalism's would-be scholars: "high academic standards, development of habits of work, and research."[5] If the evangelical tradition has neglected the life of the mind, it does little good simply to bemoan the fact. Books with titles like *The Scandal of the Evangelical Mind* should not preoccupy the time of evangelical authors or readers, except on rare occasions when it might be helpful momentarily to step back and survey the landscape. But the survey having been taken, it is not "the evangelical mind," "Christian thinking," or such categories that are important. It is rather the specific task needing research, the nagging problem requiring further thought, and the current field to which one has been called.

Evangelicals are just as prone to the tendency that Bishop John Wright described for Roman Catholic scholars more than a generation ago:

Intellectually gifted Catholics suffer all too often from a "whining" tendency in their attitude toward the Church. They lament that they are not sufficiently appreciated or encouraged. They berate the indifference of their fellow Catholics to their vocation. In a curious paradox on the lips of Christians, particularly Christians with keener powers of

5. Robert M. Hutchins, "The Integrating Principle of Catholic Higher Education" (1937), as quoted in John Tracy Ellis, *Americans Catholics and the Intellectual Life* (Chicago: Heritage Foundation, 1956), 43.

insight and understanding than the rest, they protest against being made martyrs. Where in the New Testament, the Church of the Fathers, or the history of the saints from Paul to Thomas More were the genuinely thoughtful promised any other lot, whether at the hands of the world or at the hands of their uncomprehending brethren, than contradiction and constant testing?[6]

Evangelical scholars who expect their lot to be difficult — who assume that the larger evangelical world will pay little attention to what they do, or pay attention only to taunt, berate, or decry — are only being realists. The consolation that this neglect has happened before may not bring much comfort, but perhaps enough to keep working. If that kind of consolation is not enough, other reasons, intrinsic to the gospel itself, are at hand to encourage the scholars who receive no recognition and who doubt themselves. With modest resources, largely untapped potential, and the absence of recognition, evangelical scholars are well situated to understand the weakness and foolishness of the gospel itself. William E. Hull of Samford expresses clearly the advantage of such disadvantages: "A remnant strategy means that the Christian understanding of truth will have to commend itself by persuasion rather than by being accepted because of the sheer force of numbers as a totalist strategy would permit. As the New Testament so vividly il-lustrates, Christianity seems to work best from a modest position. That posture keeps its advocates humble, which is the paradoxically powerful servant stance; furthermore, informed dissent keeps the dialogue honest and delivers the Christian apologist from the twin perils of complacency or authoritarianism."[7]

The point of Christian scholarship is not recognition by standards established in the wider culture. The point is to praise God with the mind. Such efforts will lead to the kind of intellectual integrity that sometimes receives recognition. But for the Christian that recognition is only a fairly inconsequential by-product. The real point is valuing what God has made, believing that the creation is as "good" as he said

6. John J. Wright, Bishop of Worcester, "Prefatory Note," in John Tracy Ellis, *American Catholics and the Intellectual Life* (Chicago: Heritage Foundation, 1956), 9–10.
7. William E. Hull, "Toward Samford as a Christian University — Occasional Papers of the Provost," Samford University, Birmingham, AL, July 15, 1990, pp. 5–6.

it was, and exploring the fullest dimensions of what it meant for the Son of God to "become flesh and dwell among us." Ultimately, intellectual work of this sort is its own reward, because it is focused on the only One whose recognition is important, the One before whom all hearts are open.

For evangelicalism as a whole, not new graduate schools, but an alteration of attitudes is the key to promoting a Christian life of the mind. It is the same for evangelical scholars. The key thing is to work at it. The superstructures — appropriate institutions, lively periodicals, adequate funding, academic respect, meaningful influence — are not insignificant. Some attention is justified to such matters. But if evangelicals are ever to have a mind, they must begin with the heart.

Evangelicalism and the Intellectual Life

Many individual volumes would be necessary to explore the ways that learning could be nurtured by the inner resources of evangelicalism itself. The following paragraphs offer a sketch only. But perhaps they can suggest that there is hope for an evangelical life of the mind, not necessarily when considering the history of evangelical intellect directly, but by looking more generally at the characteristics of evangelicalism.

The most important sign of hope lies in the evangel itself. Christian thinking presupposes Christians. Evangelistic zeal, though it may often seem to impede thought, in fact turns out to be essential for a Christian life of the mind. In these terms, the movements that seemed to do such damage to evangelical thought — Holiness, Pentecostalism, dispensationalism — hid the most important thing behind a veil of secondary concerns. Whatever damage an excessive supernaturalism exerted upon evangelical thinking, that same supernaturalism did keep alive an awareness of transcendence and so passed on to succeeding generations the critical starting point for meaningful Christian thought. If the Spirit of God continues to dwell among evangelicals, then it is always possible for the life implanted by the Spirit to quicken reflection along with all other worthy human endeavors. If dispensationalism and its lingering effects eviscerated thinking, by the same token dispensationalist devotion to Scripture kept alive the hope of a new day.

At this stage in our existence, evangelicals do not have a lot to offer in intellectual terms as such. We have frittered away a century or more, and we have much catching up to do. We need a lot of help, which may come from other Christian traditions (Anabaptist, Eastern Orthodox, Lutheran, Reformed, Roman Catholic) where continuous intellectual activity has been undertaken as a spiritual discipline. Can evangelicals offer anything in return?

Perhaps we do not come entirely empty handed. For we evangelicals are people who know how desperately we need to be saved. We know something of the joy of salvation, however much we compromise that joy by clothing it unthinkingly in the fashions of our age. We have a little life, a little spiritual pizzazz, and, however ill equipped, a lot of recruits. In these terms, we can think of evangelicals as the lowly deuce. To be sure, in most card games one does not want a whole hand of deuces. But if one is playing poker with deuces wild, a deuce can make a pretty good hand much stronger. So it may be for the life of the mind. If we could use the evangelical deuce of spiritual urgency to fill the straight of Catholic natural law, or add it to the two pairs of Lutheran Two Kingdom theory, or to the three aces of Reformed confessionalism, we might contribute as evangelicals to thought as well as to action.

Personal faith in Christ is a necessary condition for Christian intellectual life, for only a living thing may develop. So long as evangelicalism keeps Christian faith alive, it contributes in no small way, often despite itself, to the possibility of Christian thinking.

Similarly, evangelical attachment to Scripture may often be more totemic than intellectual, but attachment to Scripture is the place to begin. For intellectual activities, evangelical use of the Bible has tended to be broad, in the attempt to let its pages answer *directly* the questions of learning posed by our day. But a broad use of the Bible is like a flooding river pouring out of its banks — the result is to spread a nourishing silt but also to wreak much havoc and to bring ordinary activities to a halt. But those who put to use the Bible broadly surely make up the best group of candidates for putting it to use deeply. To realize that the Bible is narrow ("these are written that you may believe that Jesus is the Christ") is to make it deep — like a well dug down and down until it refreshes all those who draw from it for every task of life. To pursue the Bible, as it reveals God-in-human-flesh, is to find not just Christ but the world that Christ created, the humanity that he joined, and the beauty that he embodied in himself. To move from a broad to a deep reading of the Bible might be a hard thing, but picking up the book was even harder.

Evangelical activism also has a fuller potential for sustaining the life of the mind than the evangelical history of North America might at first suggest. Here the evangelical contribution is quite specific, for it was evangelical activism that provided the drive for Protestant missions. In return, one of the great lessons that the "new Christians" are beginning to teach the missionary-sending regions concerns the culturally embedded character of the gospel. A Gambian, Lamin Sanneh, for example, has shown how translating the Bible into local languages produces a number of unexpected results. Such translations often stabilize shaky local cultures, they often encourage local revitalization, but they often also stimulate a form of Christianity that surprises the missionary translators.[8] Local varieties of Christianity inevitably take up and adapt various features of the local culture, sometimes to the consternation of the missionaries, but often to the long-term strength of the church. When missiologists — often trained by evangelicals and sponsored by evangelicals — study what happens when evangelicals communicate the gospel cross-culturally, the result is a stunning series of theologically grounded insights. Evangelical missiologists, for example, are able to see clearly that "Protestantism is essentially Northern vernacular Christianity"; their study of comparative societies shows that the gospel is invariably "the prisoner and the liberator of culture."[9] Their work, in short, produces exactly the vantage point for differentiating between distinctive cultural expressions of Christianity and essential Christian expressions in a given culture that evangelicalism

8. Lamin Sanneh, "Gospel and Culture: Ramifying Effects of Scriptural Translation," in *Bible Translation and the Spread of the Church: The Last 200 Years,* ed. Philip C. Stine (Leiden: E. J. Brill, 1990), 1–23; and *Translating the Message: The Missionary Impact on Culture* (Maryknoll, NY: Orbis, 1989).

9. Andrew F. Walls, "The Translation Principle in Christian History," in *Bible Translation and the Spread of the Church,* ed. Philip C. Stine (Leiden: E. J. Brill, 1990); and Walls, "The Gospel as the Prisoner and Liberator of Culture," *Missionalia* 10 (1982): 93–107.

has long required. It is more fitting than ironic that one of the most important products of evangelical missionary efforts may be to teach missionary-sending evangelicals how to use the gospel they proclaim as a means of thought.

Ultimately, however, the greatest hope for evangelical thought lies with the heart of the evangelical message concerning the cross of Christ. If evangelicals have systematically disregarded the implications of the work of Christ for the life of the mind, they nonetheless continue to talk about Jesus. In that talk is potential beyond estimation.

The great truth of the Incarnation is that the Son of God became flesh and dwelt among us. In this foundational truth we may emphasize the nature of the Son of Man himself, or we may emphasize his taking on flesh and dwelling among us. The condemning scandal for evangelicals is that they have neglected this second emphasis and all that it implies about the possibility of thinking about this realm of flesh. Their redeeming scandal is that they have not yet forgotten the first.

The questions with greatest intellectual moment for those of us who are fundamentalists and evangelicals are the questions with greatest moment — period. Does the cross show forth the death of an incarnate savior? Was the Son of God truly born of a virgin, truly incarnate in human nature? Did Jesus Christ, the incarnate Son of God, really live on this earth? Did Jesus die a real death? Did he really rise bodily from the grave? And does the Holy Spirit really extend to repentant sinners the benefits of the incarnate Christ in this life?

If evangelicals believe such realities, the life of our minds may yet awaken as well. The Christian doctrine of the Incarnation tells us that God himself chose this world — a world defined by materiality as well as spirituality, a world of human institutions as well as divine realities — as the arena in which to accomplish the salvation of the elect. The Christian doctrine of the Atonement tells us that God redeemed a people for life in this world, as well as for life in the world to come. The knowledge that the physical bodies of believers "are members of Christ" (1 Cor. 6:15), that believers are "to offer your bodies as living sacrifices, holy and pleasing to God" (Rom. 12:1), tells us something of how God values the material realm. And the fact that the gospel goes out as a universal offer to all humanity suggests something about the dignity *in this world* of all human beings and the potential value *in this world* of all that they do. The rudiments of an evangelical life of the mind may have been there all along. The scandal of the evangelical mind may be addressed by the scandal of the Cross. In Virginia Owens's graphic phrase, there is literally a world of meaning surrounded by the symmetry of Christ's life: "The bloody public death was foreshadowed by a bloody stable birth."[10]

In the end, the question of Christian thinking is a deeply spiritual question. What sort of God will we worship? With this question we return to the most important matter concerning the life of the mind. The Gospel of John tells us that the Word who was made flesh and dwelt among us, full of a glorious grace and truth, was also the Word through whom all things — all phenomena in nature, all capacities for fruitful human interaction, all the kinds of beauty — were made. To honor that Word as he deserves to be honored, evangelicals must know both Christ and what he has made.

The search for a Christian perspective on life — on our families, our economies, our leisure activities, our sports, our attitudes to the body and to health care, our reactions to novels and paintings, as well as our churches and our specifically Christian activities — is not just an academic exercise. The effort to think like a Christian is rather an effort to take seriously the sovereignty of God over the world he created, the lordship of Christ over the world he died to redeem, and the power of the Holy Spirit over the world he sustains each and every moment. From this perspective the search for a mind that truly thinks like a Christian takes on ultimate significance, because the search for a Christian mind is not, in the end, a search for mind but a search for God.

SPIRITUALLY — DIVINE REALITIES
MATERIALLY — HUMAN INSTITUTIONS

10. Virginia Stem Owens, "A Hand in the Wound," *Reformed Journal*, Apr. 1981, p. 15.

LIFE FOR THE WORLD TO COME
LIFE IN THIS WORLD

Acknowledgments

I thank Ann Heider and His Majestie's Clerkes for the words to Jacob Handl's motet "Mirabile mysterium."

It is difficult to ply one's trade as an observer of modern evangelicalism without occasional repetition, and thus I have used in this book occasional paragraphs and sentences that were originally written for other purposes. Where that use is substantial, grateful reference is found in the notes.

Time to work on this project was made available through the generous support of the Pew Charitable Trusts. To David Wells and Neil Plantinga I owe a great deal as coworkers in the project. The three meetings that were part of the Pew Trusts' support involved nearly forty different intellectuals in the sort of dialogue that challenges the all-encompassing indictment of this book's title.

I am grateful for the patience and the encouragement of Jon Pott at the William B. Eerdmans Publishing Company, and to Eerdmans more generally for doing so much over the years for Christian thinking in North America.

Different versions of various parts in this book were presented in public forums. For the hospitality and intellectual stimulation of such occasions, I would like to thank audiences at Bethel Seminary (MN), the Ethics and Public Policy Center (Washington, D.C.), an annual meeting of the Evangelical Christian Publishers Association, Gordon-Conwell Theological Seminary, the University of Iowa, Messiah College, Moody Bible Institute, Northwestern College (IA), and several groups at Wheaton College. At Wheaton I have been the beneficiary for several years of the McManis Professorship of Christian Thought, an arrangement that allowed free time to work on this book. For this appointment, I am deeply grateful to Richard Chase, David Johnston, Ward Kriegbaum, and Patricia Ward.

A number of individuals made helpful comments in response to earlier efforts at expressing some of the book's ideas. For stimulation to think more clearly and more like a Christian, I would like to thank Hudson Armerding, Thomas S. Baurain, David Benner, T. D. Bozeman, Gary Burge, Dorothy Chappell, Kenneth Cmiel, Mark Fackler, D. G. Hart, Gerald Hawthorne, Alan Jacobs, Walter Kaiser, Roger Lundin, Richard Neuhaus, George Rawlyk, Bob Roberts, John Stackhouse, George Weigel, Jay Wood, and a few others whose names I have now forgotten.

Several members of my family — George Noll, Craig Noll, Mary Noll, and especially Maggie Noll — also helped bring this book into existence. For their patient assistance on similar projects for now more than a generation, I am deeply grateful.

My "university" is the network of historians who for several years have participated in the work of the Institute for the Study of American Evangelicals. Thanking that group — including Randall Balmer, Daniel Bays, Edith Blumhofer, Jim Bratt, Larry Eskridge, Darryl Hart, George Rawlyk, Harry Stout, Grant Wacker, and the individuals mentioned in the next paragraph — is a poor return to the group of scholars who most thoroughly exemplify for me the ideals of Christian thinking.

Four intellectuals — Joel Carpenter, Nathan Hatch, David Livingstone, and George Marsden — made special contributions to the writing of this book. If they have time to read it, they will realize that its pages owe almost as much to their insights as my life does to their friendship.

Index of Names and Subjects

Index of Scripture References